Motorcy
in I

Roger W. Hicks

Collins
Glasgow and London

For Tiger

Illustrations: Barry Rowe

Maps: Mike Shand

Set in 9 on 10 pt Souvenir Light

Every effort has been made to give you an up-to-date text
but changes are constantly occurring
and we will be grateful for any information about changes
you may notice while you are travelling.

First published 1985
Copyright © Roger W. Hicks 1985
Published by William Collins Sons and Company Limited
Printed in Great Britain
ISBN 0 00 447468 6

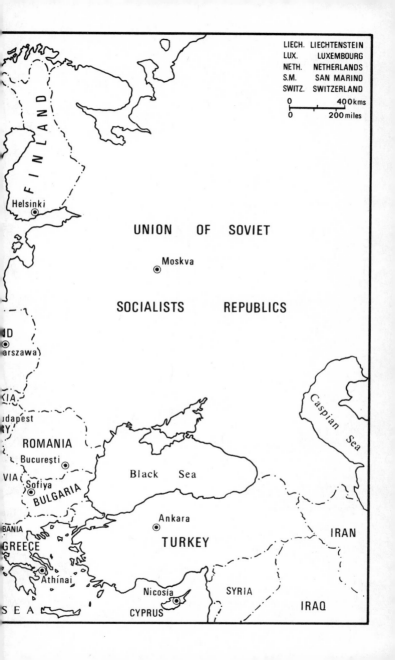

LIECH. LIECHTENSTEIN
LUX. LUXEMBOURG
NETH. NETHERLANDS
S.M. SAN MARINO
SWITZ. SWITZERLAND

0   400 kms
0   200 miles

FINLAND

Helsinki

UNION   OF   SOVIET

Moskva

SOCIALISTS   REPUBLICS

ND

arszawa)

KIA

udapest

RY

ROMANIA

Bucureşti

Caspian Sea

VIA

Sofiya

Black   Sea

BULGARIA

BANIA

Ankara

IRAN

GREECE

TURKEY

Athínai

Nicosia

SYRIA

SEA

CYPRUS

IRAQ

1   Articles of Faith

Motorcycle touring is like religion: if you have to ask why people do it, you will never understand the answers that you get. The only reason for doing it is because you want to; that is also the only qualification which you need to do it.

Almost the only qualification, anyway. Provided you hold a full licence, and complete a few fairly simple legal formalities, there is nothing to stop you going out of your door, starting your motorcycle, and heading for Paris or Istanbul. You'll probably survive. But you'll probably survive better and more comfortably if you have made some plans first, so that you know what you are doing. Besides, planning can be fun in its own right – not the dull and detailed bit, but the broad sweep and the anticipation of where you want to go.

Some people try to tell you that everything is more difficult that it is. They tell you about all the Terrible Things that will happen to you if you do not do everything by the book – their book. But this book was written because when I first started touring, there were no books which gave the information I wanted. What I have tried to do is to put in as much useful information as I could, whilst still making the book entertaining and readable. I have spent a fair amount of time touring in Europe, and (like anyone else) I like life to be as easy as possible. The advice and information in this book is aimed at just that, making life easy; if you find that doing things another way makes life easier for you, then do it your way. I don't hold the only key.

Motorcycle touring is many things to many people. Perhaps the greatest division is between those for whom the destination is the thing, and those for whom the ride is reason enough, but for most people it is something in-between. I prefer to ride comparatively short distances, say 150–250 miles in a day, so that I do not get too tired in the saddle, and spend a fair amount of time exploring. Sometimes, though, I will stay in one place for days; at other times, I will cover 400 miles in a single day. I like being in control; I like being free.

This is what motorcycle touring is about: freedom. Most motorcyclists ride for just that feeling of freedom, freedom from schedules and timetables and traffic jams, freedom to taste the air, to stop or to travel, to do what you please. When you combine that with a holiday – what more could you ask? Europe is a big place. You can ride to the mountains or the sea, explore little tracks that lead nowhere, enjoy stunning food and drink in an open-air picnic or a little restaurant, talk to people in a mixture of English and French and German and sign language and smiles: the number of people who want to talk about motorcycles alone is amazing.

The strangeness of a new place makes you all the more alive. All motorcyclists know the feeling of sun on their faces, the almost liquid cold of shadow in the early morning; if you are in an unfamiliar place, all these sensations are doubled. You live almost completely in the here and now; it really does begin to sound like religion.

Motorcycle touring also allows you to cut your coat according to your cloth. If your budget runs to it, you can stay at the finest hotels and eat at the best restaurants, or you can camp for next-to-nothing and live on bread and cheese. You can even mix the two. In most of Europe, motorcyclists are not merely tolerated: they are respected. Instead of being seen as a potential vandal, hooligan, and rapist, the motorcyclist is seen as someone with enough freedom of spirit to go out and enjoy himself.

At this point, social class begins to raise its sneering head. In England, motorcyclists are often looked down upon as people who cannot afford a car. In America, it is worse. But in most of continental Europe, it is accepted that motorcyclists can be highly-paid business executives as well as unemployed or day-labourers; the motorcycle is seen in its correct light as an instrument of freedom. I am not saying that you would be refused admission to an English restaurant – my opinion of expensive English restaurants is so low that I would rather not waste my money – but you will not receive the same service that you would in most other European countries. You are not judged by what you ride; you are judged by how you behave. This does not mean upper-class accents, because accents mean little in a foreign language (could you recognize an upper-class Bavarian accent?): it simply means behaving politely. An example may make it clear.

After a 300-mile ride in Portugal, on a most unpleasant day, my girlfriend and I arrived at the Pousada de Santa Barbara, near the border. It was 9:25pm, and *pousadas* stop serving dinner at 9:30. After we had ascertained that we would be in time for dinner, we threw our dripping waterproofs into the bathtub in our room and rushed into the dining room. We had already ordered dinner – with no sign that anything was amiss – when I wiped the corner of my eye with my napkin. It came away black. I checked in the back of the menu-holder, and my face was filthy with diesel smuts; I had a cleaner space where my goggles had been, just like a Hollywood version of a racing driver. I rushed upstairs to wash it before the soup arrived; the water in the washbasin looked the same way as it does if you wash your hands after working on the bike. Yet *no one* even commented, despite the fact that it was an expensive place (by Portuguese standards) and we had walked in wearing old jeans and sweaters. Honest dirt was not a cause for complaint.

This is not unusual. On another occasion, we were riding from Köln (Cologne) to München (Munich – it is worth getting used to foreign spellings, because that is the way they appear on signposts). Once again, it was a really vile day, raining hard, and we were wearing about five layers clothes under our waterproofs. We were on the *Romantische Strasse* (Romantic Road), which passes through many beautiful mediaeval towns, but the weather made us miserable. We stopped for petrol, and as I was paying, the lady in the filling station invited Frances (by now my wife) and me in for coffee: '*Das is keine Romantische,*' she said (This is hardly romantic). She spoke no English; we spoke about ten words of German between us. But the sentiment was clear.

From those two stories, it may sound as if everything is rain and gloom, but it is not so; you just remember those things better when they cheer you up. I could equally well tell of the magnificent restaurant between Paris and Calais, where we stopped after a beautiful morning's ride and had an unforgettable meal – *filet d'agneau* (fillet of lamb) for me, and *langoustines* (crayfish) for my wife, with a superb *vin de la maison* to accompany it. Or the perfect day in the Austrian Tyrol, where the scenery was so beautiful that we could not bear to stop for lunch. Or the deserted cobbled road in the

Algarve, where I rode at a totally illegal 95 mph and realized that this was what it must have been like for Lawrence of Arabia, astride his Brough Superior. Or the cop in Switzerland, who was just admiring the bike as it was parked on the sidewalk; he said ruefully that he had been in London two weeks before, and he had got a ticket for parking on the pavement. . . .

Yes, there are times when you will wish that you had never set out. It may be bitterly cold, and you have missed the last place that sells food and wine; or you have arrived too late at a popular time of year, and it takes you three hours to find somewhere to stay. But these times are not often, and you can console yourself with Chögyam's Law: the worse it is at the time, the better story it makes when you get back.

One thing that does help a great deal is trying to speak the local language. Some people are better than others at this, and it does tend to be something of a natural gift, but anyone can try. Contrary to popular belief, 'they' don't always speak English, and unless you are prepared to meet people half-way, you may find life difficult at times. At the very least, there are about ten words in any language that are worth learning (or writing on a piece of paper). They are *please, thank you, yes, no, where, room, toilet, more, how much?*, and *food* (or *eat*).

You can forget about the fancy grammar. You can make yourself clear enough without it, and most of it is so old-fashioned that even the natives do not use it: can you imagine saying (slowly and distinctly), 'Thank you kindly, good sir (or madam)'? Rely on a smile, a bit of arm-waving, and good will on both sides – except perhaps in the case of the French or (worse) the Spanish, who will look blankly at you unless you speak their languages perfectly. Do not forget ancient rivalries, either; most Portuguese will pretend to understand English better than Spanish, and as one Portuguese put it, 'I cannot stand the Spanish and their attitude to their language. They are even more proud than the French, with less to be proud about!' On a really good day, you may find yourself talking to someone in a language that neither of you speaks: I once had great fun directing a Spanish taxi driver in German, which neither of us spoke but which provided more common ground than my Spanish or his English.

If you can't think of the word, try the English – with a few alternatives, if there is more than one word. For example, *chop* (as in pork chop) is unlikely to get you anywhere – but *cutlet* is close enough to German, French, Spanish, Portuguese, Italian, and (for all I know) half the other languages in Europe to make yourself understood. Remember too that even someone who speaks no English is likely to understand a few words; television, the cinema, and pop music have seen to that.

A small phrase book is really useful, especially if your postilion is struck by lightning. Collins and Berlitz publish excellent ones, which are not expensive and which (if you get bored) are an entertainment in themselves. I find it hard enough to imagine chatting up a girl at a dance in a language I could not speak, but how do things get far enough for, 'If you do not stop immediately, I shall scream'? Are you still in a fit state to read the Berlitz phrase book at that point? It is also a good idea to carry a small pocket dictionary, (such as a Collins Gem) especially for menus, where it stops you ordering (as the famous joke has it), oral sex and chips.

A dictionary can also help sort out life's little mysteries. The first time we went to Luxembourg, we were puzzled by signs all over the place saying BOFFERDING. We thought it might mean 'Bed and Breakfast', but it didn't; the dictionary told us that much. We later found out that it is the most popular beer in the country, and so we adopted it to mean 'to go out on the beer' or 'to acquire a hangover' as in 'We were out bofferding all night' or 'I feel a bit boffered this morning.' Incidentally, Luxembourg is a lovely place if you are into drinking, but not if you want to sleep. Too much bofferding....

Amazingly, language turns out to be a minor difficulty; and so do all the other difficulties you anticipate. The French have a saying that life is like a Spanish inn; you only get from it what you bring. Although this is certainly true as far as personal qualities go, it is very far from true when you are counting the financial cost.

Motorcycle touring can be astonishingly economical. You have all the advantages that you do at home – low fuel consumption, free parking, the ability to stop almost anywhere without blocking the traffic, and a 'go anywhere' ability equalled only by a four-wheel-drive – plus low ferry fares, lower bridge, tunnel, and motorway tolls, and the ability (if you want) to carry your house on your back in the form of a tent and sleeping bag. The ferry fares reflect the fact that there is always room to tuck a motorcycle onto a ferry, which also means no waiting in queues: you win every way that there is to win.

Finally, the most important thing to remember is that there is next to nothing stopping you. Motorcycle touring is not difficult – if it were, I'd find a better way to spend my holidays – and you can enjoy the best holiday in the world.

2 A Sense of Proportion

Unless you have unlimited supplies of both time and money, you are going to have to make some compromises on your trip. To a certain extent, time and money are interchangeable, but most of us find that when we have time to spare, we have no money; and when we have money, we are too busy earning it to spare much time. For most people, the annual vacation is all that is available, supplemented perhaps by the occasional long weekend or brief break.

One way to spin the holiday out for as long as possible, though, is to plan it in advance and look back on it afterwards. Most people enjoy the planning stage, and that is what we are concerned with here.

First of all, where do you want to go? Have you any very clear ideas about this at all? You may have a general desire to go to Germany, or Portugal, or France – but they are all big countries, with many variations in climate and terrain. Taking Portugal as an example – an example which may seem to appear disproportionately often, because I find it such an incredibly attractive country – I was amazed the first time I went there, because the beautiful and mountainous northern part of the country was so completely unlike the southern beaches of the Algarve that I had in mind. I spent a fair amount of my holiday there, riding on roads with a thousand-foot peak on one side and a five-hundred-foot drop to the river on the other. Now, I would far rather go back to the north than to the better-known south.

You must be prepared, too, for a country to fail to live up to your expectations. Taking another personal example, I had always wanted to visit Switzerland. When I got there, I was frankly disappointed. The mountains were nothing like as impressive as I had expected, and the whole country had a certain blandness which amounted almost to boredom. On subsequent visits I have come to appreciate Berne, which is much closer to my idea of what Switzerland should be, but I should not be too concerned if I never saw Zurich again. Switzerland also furnishes another lesson, that of expense. We found that Swiss prices were almost identical, franc for franc, with French ones. But a Swiss franc will buy you approximately three French francs. . . .

If you do not have any very clear ideas, a good start is to go to the public library and look for the section labelled OVERSIZE: that is where most of the picture-books are to be found. When it comes to travelogues, the old saying that a picture is worth a thousand words is, if anything, an understatement. It takes a very good writer indeed to convey even a fraction of what a picture shows at a glance. After the pictures, you can look at the words; they fill in the details. You can also talk to people who have visited the countries you have in mind, but remember that everything they say is filtered through their own perception and experience: what you want, what you experience, and how you react to it, may be very different.

To be honest, luck plays a large part. A few good experiences, and a country seems wonderful; a few bad ones, and it can seem the worst place in the world. This is why I like to be as flexible as possible when it comes to arranging a holiday, organising things so that I can spend a lot of time in a place if I like it, or get out and go somewhere else if I don't. If I am returning to a place that I know I like, that is one thing; on another vacation, I may decide to cover a lot of ground just to see the maximum number of places, and (with luck) find somewhere else that I want to go back to.

This question of luck is one that many people – especially travel writers – are unwilling to face up to. For example, many people like Spain. I have not spent much time there, perhaps three weeks in all, but I have yet to have enough good experiences to outweigh the bad ones. I find it hard not to let this prejudice show, and I cannot be bothered to go back to Spain in an attempt to overcome it; there are simply other places I would rather be, like the Austrian Tyrol, or Portugal. With limited time available, this is inevitable.

There is also the matter of what sort of places you like. My own tastes run to the mountains and the sea; to mountain lakes; and to high desert and rocks. I love the California coastline, the Himalayas, the Tyrol, northern Portugal, the Mojave Desert, and the terrain between Mysore and Bangalore in southern India. Among cities, I have a great weakness for Paris – but I do not care for Lisbon, even if it is in Portugal, and I find the urban decay (and urban discontent) in Amsterdam profoundly depressing. You may

be completely different; the hippie/freak culture in
Amsterdam has many adherents (but watch out for the
police), and you may like beaches, or forests, or good
hunting country. This is why I have tried in this book to
provide information which is as objective as possible,
especially in the second half (the country-by-country guide).
Even if we like different things, the underlying principles are
the same.

Wherever you choose, you will have to be realistic about
four things: time, distance, money, and yourself. To a certain
extent, the first three are interchangeable. It is quite possible,
for example, to ride to Istanbul in two and a half weeks, and
then to return on the train with the motorcycle, leaving
Istanbul Sirkeci station late on Thursday night and arriving in
London in time for tea on Sunday (though schedules may,
of course, change from year to year). It will cost you a
frightening amount of money to come back on the train, but
it will take you close on 2000 miles through seven countries
while you rest, eat, and sleep. You would be rash to attempt
riding it in less than five days, and you would be worn out by
the time you got back, but if you did ride, and camped at
night, it would cost you less than a quarter of the train fare if
you ride solo; with a pillion, the savings would be even
greater.

The time available is already decided for most people,
so it is the simplest variable. You must remember, though,
that things do not always go smoothly. Allow a little extra
time for difficult border crossings, adverse weather, and
possible mechanical difficulties; don't press your schedule to
its limits. This is particularly important if you are tied to a
fixed return time, and it is one of the reasons why I prefer to
buy my ferry tickets at the dockside rather than trying to hit a
fixed hour. On one occasion, when I was committed to a
fixed ferry time, I decided to play safe and allow nine hours
for the last 120 miles to the boat. At mid-day, I was thinking
that I had been over-cautious; by two, caught in an
unseasonable blizzard in mountains I had crossed two weeks
earlier in shirt-sleeves, I was not so sure. At that point, I had
only to average 10 mph; which was just as well, because at
the worst point, visibility and a snowy road kept me down to
15 mph, and I was afraid that things might get worse.
Fortunately, they didn't, and I made the ferry.

Distance is obviously closely related to time. The basic

question is how far you *want* to ride in a day – not how far you *can* ride. As John Craig put it, 'The first time I rode 500 miles in a day, just to prove I could do it, I found that any fool could – and only a fool would!' It is actually possible to cover a thousand miles in a day, but it means sixteen hours in the saddle at an average speed of over 60 mph, which allowing for petrol and food stops is obviously pushing matters a little.

A lot will depend on your motorcycle, and on the roads that you choose. A Honda Goldwing is ideally suited to thundering down the motorway, *autostrada, autoroute, autobahn,* etc., at high speed for hours on end – indeed, there are those who would say that this sort of riding is all that it is good for. Under these conditions, 500 miles in a day is quite easy, if deadly boring. On the other hand, a Honda 90 is rather better suited for pottering along the back lanes; 150 or even 100 miles in a day might be all that you could face. We shall return to this in the next chapter.

No matter what roads you choose, the real thief of time is stopping. This includes not only the obvious stops, for petrol, food, drink, and toilets; it also includes the stops that you want to make in order to explore, to look around. In Bavaria, for example, there seems to be another mediaeval town every few miles; even if you choose to ride around the narrow streets, rather than getting off and exploring on foot, you will dramatically cut down the distance you cover in a day. There is nothing wrong with this: you are, after all, on holiday, so you can do what you like. but there is always a temptation to establish some sort of record, so that you can boast about it when you get home: 'Oh, yeah, covered 450 miles one day, could have made it 500, I wasn't tired at all, and the bike went like a dream.' If that means more to you than pottering around, fine; just ask yourself if it really does.

As a general guide, with fast roads and a fast motorcycle, I do not care to exceed 300 miles in a day, and prefer to cover something nearer 200. There have been days that I have ridden 400 miles, usually in order to get from A to B as fast as possible or (more often) because B turns out to be such a let-down that I go straight on to C without stopping. There have also been days when I covered no distance at all: staying in one place for a couple of days, and leaving the bike parked, also has its place in my holidays. I like to ride; I like to stop and explore. Depending on your own preferences, you can increase or decrease the total distance you plan to cover accordingly.

Actually estimating the distance you can cover requires three things. The first is an idea of the sort of speed you can average; the second is the number of hours you want to spend in the saddle; and the third is the distance between the places you want to visit. You can estimate the first fairly accurately, from past experience: my own figures would be 60–70 mph on motorways, 40–50 mph on mixed roads, and 30 mph or less on twisty mountain roads, all in fair weather. I knock off 5–10 mph for rain. The length of time you want to spend in the saddle is another matter: I reckon to average 5–6 hours, and I know that 3 hours is no time all whilst 8 hours is altogether too much. As a rough guide, I also allow an hour for lunch, and half an hour for petrol and other stops. If I am planning on riding after dinner, I allow $1\frac{1}{2}$ hours for that. The third figure, the distance between places, is the most difficult to estimate.

The big problem is that it is easy to look at an inch or two on the map and reckon that you can cover that easily. If the map is 16 miles to the inch, however, you are talking about anything up to an hour's riding; and on a very small-scale map like this, the actual twistiness of the road may not be too obvious. Add to this a natural desire to minimize difficulties, and a tendency (especially in my case) to make a rough guess at the distance and underestimate it, and you can end up riding for a lot longer than you think – even if you don't get lost.

This is where a good map and a miniature trundle wheel is invaluable – one of those little pocket-watch things that you roll along the road, and which gives you a direct read-out of the distance in miles or kilometres. Try to follow the course of the road on the map as accurately as possible, and add on 10% to be on the safe side. Then look at the other features on the map. Are there mountains there? If so, the road is likely to be twistier and slower that you think. Does it link two big commercial centres? It may be crowded. If it is a toll road, on the other hand, it may be surprisingly uncrowded. In most countries, motorway tolls can be very steep for cars, but you have to be travelling on a fairly tight budget before they matter all that much for motorcylces. Some idea of motorway tolls is given in the country-by-country guide in the second half of this book.

Given these three sets of figures, you can make a good guess at how long it will take to get from A to B, and whether you have time to add C to your itinerary as well. Even then, there is one additional factor to consider: whether you will be riding at night. Unless you are one of those people who likes to get up at dawn and ride a hundred miles before breakfast, you are unlikely to get away before 8:15 at the earliest, and possibly 9:00. In the early spring or late autumn, when the nights are long, it may begin to get dark at around 5:00 in the evening. Take out an hour for lunch and half an hour for other stops, and your maximum riding time before dark is about seven hours. Allowing for the odd diversion, and a little getting lost, and perhaps a few road works, you might say that you could cover 250 miles on mixed roads, or 350 miles on motorways, before it gets dark.

What is wrong with riding after dark? To begin with, it is slower and less enjoyable: a road which would be fun in the daytime can be a nightmare at night, because you cannot see the bends in the distance. It is more dangerous, for obvious reasons. It makes navigation more difficult: you need a street lamp to read your map, or else you have to get off and use the headlamp – or use a torch. It makes spotting and reading road signs more difficult, and increases your chance of getting lost. It makes pitching camp vastly more difficult, and if you are relying on hotels and guest-houses, the later you leave it, the more difficulty you may have in finding somewhere to stay. As a result of all this it is very much more tiring than riding in the daytime, quite apart from the fact that you cannot enjoy the scenery. If you can possibly avoid it, night riding is to be avoided. If it is raining as well, it is very foolish indeed to ride at night. We all do it from time to time; it is just worth planning ahead so that we do not do it any more than is strictly necessary.

Moving on to the third variable – money – it is very important not to underestimate. You can work out with a fair degree of accuracy what petrol will cost, and what you can afford for accommodation and food, but do not forget the odd souvenir; the admission charge to some attraction; the occasional drink; motorway, bridge, and tunnel tolls; and such things as laundromats. Laundromats are invaluable when you are touring on a motorcycle, but it is worth knowing that Swiss laundromats can be two or three times as expensive as French ones, and that they are fairly rare and expensive throughout most of Europe except Britain.

Take the money as travellers' cheques and in cash, but try to make sure that you have some means of getting more money if you need it. Best of all is a Euro-Cheque card, which allows you to write cheques on a national account against foreign funds in a foreign bank. Do not change more money than you need in any country, though, because you will lose on the reconversion – typically 5–10% – if you have any left over when you leave. Plastic money is very useful, with Visa probably the leader and Mastercard/Access, American Express, and Diner's Club following in no particular order. For some reason, the usefulness of credit cards appears to depend as much on what you want as on where you are: in Germany, about the only places that are willing to accept them are restaurants, whereas in France just about every filling station takes them. The country most aware of credit cards is probably the United Kingdom, though even some of the Communist countries are beginning to accept them. For obvious reasons, it tends to be the more up-market and expensive places that take credit cards; this is worth remembering if you are really in a jam. Finally, remember that if you run out of money your Embassy may (or may not) repatriate you, but they will leave your bike where it is.

The fourth variable, yourself, is not one that I can advise you about. As I have said before, I have my way of doing things; yours may be completely different. Even if it is, though, you should be able to see where our differences lie clearly enough to make the appropriate changes yourself. One thing that is worth considering carefully is just who you are trying to please. Is it yourself, or is it someone else? Trying to fit in with someone else's preconceptions can ruin a good holiday. At every turn, ask yourself if this is what *you* want to do. After all, it's your holiday and your money.

Once you have the broad principles sorted out – where you are going to go, how you are going to go about it, and what you are going to spend – you can begin to get down to the details. Once again, there are books in the library that can come to your aid; you may also want to buy the more useful ones. For general route planning, a big fold-out map of the whole of Europe is ideal; we shall return to more detailed maps later.

Of all the guide books, the best known are probably the Michelin guides, the Guides Bleus (also available in English), the *Europe on $X per day* (they started out as $5 and have been yielding to inflation ever since), Baedecker, and Fodor. Each of these has its own advantages and disadvantages. Both Michelin and the Guides Bleus are comprehensive, but expensive and not particularly helpful to the low-budget traveller. Michelin tends to be stronger on accommodation and garages, the Guides Bleus on background information. The '$X a day' guides are quite good if you are going to visit the specific cities they cover, but they are little use outside those big cities; the style is also somewhat gushing, not to say nauseating, and it is fair to say that they have in many cases been overtaken by imitators who update their information a bit more often. For example, Miles Turner's *Pauper's Paris* is vastly superior to anything Frommer (the author of the '$X a day' series) has done. Baedecker is more straightforward and rather more comprehensive than Frommer, but tends to concentrate on more expensive accommodation. Fodor is rather like Baedecker, but I find the style less sympathetic.

There are, of course, many others, and this is a case when visiting the bookshop is probably a good idea. The AA seems a bit ahead of the RAC on annual guides; their Travellers' Guide to Europe is pretty good, and revised annually. It is not always necessary to have the latest edition, however: the background information changes little, and the most useful thing about the hotel guides is that they tell you where to look. Most cities have their hotel quarters, and some areas are more expensive than others; once you know where to look, it is mostly a question of knocking on doors. In the country, guides are rarely any use anyway: just stop and ask. As a general rule, the UK is one of the most expensive places to stay (and eat) in Europe; after this come Switzerland and Scandinavia. Interestingly, Germany is only expensive in the big cities, and even Paris need not be particularly frightening: I reckon that a comfortable double room, with bathroom, in Paris costs less than in most English provincial cities, if you know where to look.

Returning to the subject of maps, there are two distinct schools of thought. One works everything out in great detail beforehand, and the other trusts to the fates. I have tried both approaches, and I now prefer the second. Plans never go exactly right, and I prefer an element of surprise.

Either way, there is a lot to be said for looking at a good map before you go. For the really determined planner, a good map is exciting in itself: he can imagine each place, plan the ride on the big red roads, the blue *autoroutes*, and the little winding dotted roads, and so on. For the more casual planner, looking at the map stops you making any really stupid mistakes – usually, anyway. I must confess that my best mistake to date was not in Europe, but in California. My wife and I drove up the Pacific Coast Highway, intending to turn inland a few tens of miles after Hearst Castle, going north. What we both ignored was the fact that any road which goes inland at that point has to cross some fairly high mountains; the El Cabrillo Highway turned out to be little short of terrifying, the more so because we were driving an old Plymouth Fury with an intermittent fault on the headlights. Admittedly, the map we were using should have made Rand McNally hang their corporate head in shame, but it was still our own stupidity that caught us out.

While large-scale maps, at 1"/mile (1:63360) or more are a delight, and give lots of information, they are really only suitable if you are concentrating on a very small area; they are more use to hikers and cyclists than to motorcyclists. Otherwise, expense and bulk rule them out. The largest scale that is normally practicable is $\frac{1}{4}$"/mile or so (1:250,000), which is the typical scale for a European atlas. Motoring atlases vary greatly in quality; beware of the ones that show only main roads, and no features such as mountains, rivers, or railway tracks, all of which are extremely useful for navigating and which also give you some idea of the terrain. If you are content to travel in general directions, rather than by specific routes, then much smaller-scale maps can be fine: 8 miles/inch (1:500,000) is ideal, and even 16 miles/inch (1:1,000,000) can be adequate. If you go for anything smaller, such as 32 miles/inch or 40 miles/inch (1:2,000,000 or 1:2,500,000), you will usually only have a vague idea of where you are. This is not necessarily as bad as it sounds: if you are in a hurry, you can follow the signposts to the main towns, and if you are not, you can afford to get lost and enjoy yourself in the process.

A useful alternative to actually buying maps is to beg one from the National Tourist Office of the country concerned: most are more that willing to give them away. Some are superb; others are not worth the paper they are

printed on. Two which stick in my mind as good are the
Germans' (who else?) and the Greeks', who produced a
superb mini-atlas of their country at 16 miles/inch general
scale and 5 miles/inch for Athens. The bad ones usually
come from the eastern bloc, who share the Russian mania
for secrecy.

One thing that is definitely not a good idea, unless your
knowledge of European geography is nothing less than
encyclopaedic, is to travel without any maps at all. Even the
roughest maps give you an idea of the relationships between
major cities and countries, and an idea of the direction in
which you want to travel. It is all too easy to go in a direction
180° from where you want to be; some people carry a small
compass for this very reason. Use it far enough from the bike
to escape the influence of the bike's iron and steel.

If you use a tank-top bag (considered at greater length
in Chapter 5), there will usually be a map pocket on top. In
addition to, or sometimes instead of, the map, you may wish
to write out an itinerary of the places you pass through: this
can be as detailed or as sketchy as you like. Two added
refinements are to list the approximate distances between the
various places, and to list the *undesirable* alternatives to left
and right, either in red or crossed out. For example, if you
are going south from Stockholm, you want Södertalje and
not Enköping or Uppsala. This may seem obvious to the
geographically minded, who have a good idea of the general
layout of Sweden, but I was thrown out of Geography when
I was fifteen. You will still need the map for those occasions
when totally different places from the ones you expected are
marked, and you have to hunt around in the small print.

When you are actually on the road, there is a golden
rule: if in doubt, check the map. If you don't quite manage
to read what is on a signpost, go back and read it: you can
save some pretty horrendous detours that way.

Armed with this much planning and foresight, you
should be able to get where you want to without getting too
lost, wearing yourself out, or running out of time or money
while you are over there. The next thing to consider is the
bike. The odds are that you already have it; but in case you
are considering changing it, and anyway because it throws a
fair amount of light on how to get the best out of whatever
you have, the next chapter deals with the ideal qualities of a
touring motorcycle.

3   Touring Motorcycles

You can go touring on any motorcycle that is reliable
enough to get you where you want to go, and back again.
You can even do it on an unreliable motorcycle, if you are a
mechanical genius, or very rich, or prepared to abandon the
motorcycle, but that is doing it the hard way.

There has to be a close relationship between the kind of
machine that you ride and your choice of roads, however. If
you have a lightweight, you have the same advantages that
you did at home: supreme economy and the ability to potter
along day in, day out, with the minimum of maintenance.
You would do best to confine yourself to back roads, where
the pace of life is easier and there is more to see; it may be
tempting to spend an hour on the motorway at full throttle,
just to cover the ground, but even an hour will be tiring,
boring, and possibly dangerous. My father once rode a
Honda 90 from Glasgow to Kent and back, just for the hell
of it, rarely travelling a hundred miles a day and stopping the
night at pubs and inns that caught his eye. That is a round
trip of a thousand miles or so; he took a couple of weeks to
do it.

Suppose, on the other hand, that you have a sports
machine. You bought if for speed and handling. Provided
you do not overload it with luggage, that speed and handling
will be just as attractive on a tour as on the roads near home
– more so, because they are something new. The seat may
be a bit hard for prolonged riding, but two or three hours in
the morning and two or three hours in the afternoon can
cover an awful lot of ground.

Again, you might have a Honda Goldwing, a mile-eater
on the autobahns but of limited appeal on the kind of fast
twisty road that is paradise on a sports machine. On lesser
roads, you might have to cut the Wing's speed a bit, but you
can still cream along all day. In complete contrast, you might
even decide to tour on a trail bike; to return to Portugal
once more, there is no end of inviting and very bumpy tracks
and paths leading off into the unknown.

Some machines are obviously better all-rounders than others, and here it is time to declare an interest. Although I have ridden many motorcycles, from 50cc upwards, my current machine seems to me to be just about the perfect tourer. It is the BMW R100RS, the last and biggest of all the classic flat twins. It may seem strange that I have chosen the 'sports' version of the big BMW rather than the tourer; but I think that the reasons will become evident in what follows.

The first requirement of a good touring bike is obviously reliability. It should not break down, and if it does, it should be readily repairable. In order to make a machine reliable, it must first of all be strongly made. The easiest way to do this is to understress the components. This may make the machine look heavy and relatively low-powered on paper, but on the road it pays endless dividends. The ultimate exponents of this kind of engineering are probably Harley-Davidson, with massive engines delivering power that is downright laughable in Japanese terms, mounted in frames that are huge and heavy in any terms; but unless you thrash then mercilessly, they will not wear out. At the other extreme are the racer-replica 'buzz-box' lightweights. Extreme power and light weight are at a premium on a race track, where long-term reliability is scarcely an issue, but less stressed engines and frames score higher in touring. Most machines fall between the two extremes, but the majority of experienced tourers would prefer something nearer the Harley-Davidson end of the spectrum. BMWs are one example; the odd-looking East German MZ (descended from the pre-war DKW) is another.

Simple machines are obviously easier to repair than complicated ones; once again, the relatively crude engineering of a Harley-Davidson, or better still a Triumph, is accessible to any mechanic. High-powered engines, especially those requiring special tools, are inclined to be more difficult. For me, a BMW strikes a reasonable compromise between power output and simplicity. This criterion of simplicity applies to every aspect of the motorcycle: for example, wire wheels are a better bet than cast, because you can always get someone to lace some sort of rim onto your hub, but a broken alloy wheel is a write-off.

Parts should also be widely available, and this is where BMW really scores: both Triumph and H-D have a good parts availability record, but they simply do not have the same size dealer network in Europe as BMW. The Japanese makers tend to come out badly here, because their policy of frequent model changes and virtually no interchangeable parts between models makes for vast numbers of spares, which no one can afford to stock in full.

Finally, under this heading, the machine should require a minimum of maintenance, and that maintenance should be as simple as possible. In one way, Japanese machines score very heavily on this count, in that they need only to be serviced regularly in order to be incredibly reliable. On the other hand, servicing may be difficult, and out-of-the-ordinary maintenance may be very difficult indeed. British, Italian, and German motorcycles require slightly more frequent attention, but almost anyone can do it.

Of course, not all systems on the machine are equally reliable. The Japanese and Germans make far more reliable electrics than the Italians and British, as a general rule. Not for nothing was Joe Lucas known as the Prince of Darkness! Again, a chain drive may be marginally more efficient than a shaft drive when both are new; but a chain is made up of a large number of plain bearings working in a very hostile environment (both wet and gritty), and it requires frequent adjustment or even replacement, whereas the shaft drive requires only the occasional oil change. If you must have a chain, a fully-enclosed chain case or an automatic chain oiler or both are well worth considering. Even such details as air filtration are worth watching; the Italians are notoriously cavalier about this, and if you replace the ram stacks and stone guards with proper filters the engine will last much longer.

Once you have satisfied yourself about the mechanics, the next thing to consider is comfort. I think that this is the right way round; most people would rather have an uncomfortable bike which works than a comfortable one which doesn't. Obviously, comfort is a distinctly personal matter, and in any case it can be extremely difficult to judge without going on a really long ride – at least a hundred miles, and preferably

two or three hundred. There is also the matter of getting
used to the bike. For the first few weeks that I had my
R100RS, I used to get an acute pain near my right shoulder-
blade after a couple of days' long rides. Then the problem
went away, for reasons I never discovered, and all that
happens now is an ache in the right buttock which comes on
after two or three hundred miles in one day (three or four
hundred towards the end of a long trip) and takes a night's
sleep to make it go away.

So, sit on the saddle. Is it immediately reasonably
comfortable? Can it be made more so by adjusting the
handlebars or the footrests, or both? Are they in fact
adjustable? The Laverda, for example, has bars which can be
adjusted from West Coast sit-up-and-beg to racing drops,
and the footrests are almost equally variable. Remember that
sit-up-and-beg bars are fine for short trips and low speeds,
but beyond about 50 mph they become increasingly
uncomfortable, and at 100 mph you may have difficulty in
staying on, let alone in getting comfortable. Incidentally,
many experienced touring riders prefer foot boards, like the
California Highway Patrol; but as the only machine I ever
rode for long distances with footboards was an LE Velocette,
I do not feel qualified to comment. I pass the tip on for what
it is worth.

Bounce up and down a bit. Is the seat well enough
padded? Some sports bikes have board-like seats, whilst
some highway cruisers go to the other extreme and have so
much squashy foam that you can move about dangerously
when accelerating, braking, or cornering. If the seat is too
high, it may be possible to remove some padding – check.
Few people ever find a seat too low.

If the seat is sculpted, or of the 'King and Queen' type,
it must (to put it delicately) be arse-shaped. Some saddles
are sculpted in all the wrong places, especially with a pillion.
If you intend doing much pillion riding, you had better have
your intended pillion with you – or at least a representative
sample! Check the shape of any seat carefully: hard edges,
even stiff foam, can block circulation and make you cold and
uncomfortable over a few hundred miles.

Can you work all the controls properly? Most machines
have their problems: the heavy clutch on old Laverdas, the
clunky gearshift on old BMWs, the Harley indicators which
have to be held down. Decide if you can learn to live with

them, but watch out for downright dangerous controls, such as kill switches that you can accidentally hit when dipping the headlights (it has been known!).

Take any machine that you are thinking of buying on a test ride; the idea that anyone should buy a motorcycle on the strength of paper specifications and showroom appearance, without riding it, is ridiculous. If your dealer has no test bikes, go to a proper dealer who has – and buy from him, even if it means spending a bit extra, because he probably cares more about both motorcycling and his reputation than the dealer who sells on price alone.

Make the ride as long as possible, across a wide variety of roads: winding, fast, bumpy, etc. How is the ride? A soft ride is a blessing on a tourer. How is the vibration? This is a matter of personal tolerance. You should be able to get away with ten or twenty miles; after that, you just have to trust to luck, and hope that those little foibles which appear after a hundred, or two hundred, or four hundred miles are not too nasty.

I have deliberately avoided the question of fairings until now. I used to be pretty solidly against them, and it is still true that most of the fairings on the market leave a lot to be desired, but I am now prepared to make exceptions for the BMW R100RS fairing and a very few others.

Any fairing will probably keep you warmer, cleaner, and (in wet weather) drier than no fairing, and in this way they are a Good Thing. On the other hand, they can keep you too warm in hot weather, and the vast majority affect handling for the worse. Too large a fairing also removes some of the immediacy of motorcycling: even the BMW R100RT fairing, which (like the R100RS version) was wind-tunnel designed for the BMW, and which does not therefore completely wreck the handling, is a bit like riding behind a barn door. The very best fairings, like the R100RS, remove nothing from the pleasure of motorcycling and actually improve high-speed handling, keeping the front wheel pressed to the ground (front-wheel lift is apparently neutralized instead of being increased) and reducing the effect of side-winds.

If you do choose an aftermarket fairing, then remember that the screen should be low enough to see *over*, rather than *through*. This is not just for obvious safety reasons, especially at night, when an optically dubious bit of plastic will do nothing to improve your vision: it is also a legal requirement in many countries that any screen which you look through must be fitted with a windscreen wiper. Short riders of Goldwing Aspencades beware!

The third requirement, after reliability and comfort, is a simple one: weight. A big heavy bike is more comfortable on the highway, but a small light one is far easier to manoeuvre, especially in the rough or in narrow winding streets, or if you have to manhandle it. I am 5' 10" and no weakling, but I find that my R100RS is about the limit of what I can manhandle, especially when fully loaded (the bike, not me!). It weighs about 500 lb, perhaps 60 or 80 lb more loaded, and I would be happier with 400–500 lb, but you can't have everything.

The fourth requirement is range. Some motorcycles have ridiculously small gas tanks; there was one 750cc model with a 1.1 gallon tank, the same as a Honda 90. Obviously range is dependent on both fuel consumption and tank size, but any motorcycle which cannot cover at least 200 miles between fill-ups is something of a liability; those which cannot cover a hundred miles are a joke. Of course, aftermarket tanks are available – but they are expensive. Once again, the R100RS seems just about perfect: I go onto reserve at between 180 and 220 miles, depending on how I have been riding, and I then have 40–60 miles in reserve (maybe more – I've never pushed my luck that far). There is apparently an aftermarket alloy tank holding over seven gallons, which would give me 280–360 miles, but I've never felt the need of it.

The fifth and final requirement is the least quantifiable: handling and performance. I have left this until last because it covers such a wide variety of questions. Handling is a personal matter, because it depends on what you are used to, on where you ride, on how you ride, and on how fast you go. I have ridden bikes which have terrified me – especially

Japanese two-strokes from the 1960s – and I have ridden
bikes which handled so well that they would recover,
seemingly without help from me, from situations (usually
slippery surfaces) which would have decked a lesser
machine. Unless you have experienced the response of a fair
number of motorcycles, you cannot really judge what is
going on: only the real death-traps will really frighten you.
Fortunately, most road-testers are fairly honest nowadays,
and Japanese bikes are vastly better than they were fifteen
years ago, so bad machines rapidly acquire a well-deserved
notoriety. Of course, a fast machine has its handling tested
more thoroughly than a slow one: my old LE Velocette
handled like a dream, but it required a steep downhill and
strong following wind to exceed 55 mph.

When it comes to performance, motorcyclists are both
spoiled and inconsistent. Even a modest 250 has the same
acceleration as a fast sports car, and by the time you get
much over 50 bhp there are very few riders who can even
begin to use the power to the limit – but you still get such
imbecilic complaints as the one that the MK100 BMW is
'only' 90 bhp. Sure, there are Japanese machines which
advertise 100 bhp and more – but how do you get it onto
the road? Not only that, but I am sure that some horses are
much bigger than others. The old Vincent Black Shadow was
'only' 55 bhp, but it was good for well over 120 mph and the
performance (as long as the clutch was dry) is still legendary:
the 150 mph Black Lightning had 70 bhp, the same as the
R100RS that is now decried as 'tame'. Even standing-start
acceleration figures can be overrated: who can put his hand
on his heart and say that he has ever taken a big machine
(70 bhp or more) to the limit in the first two or three gears?

Flexibility, which means a wide spread of torque, is
much more important in day-to-day motorcycling, especially
over long distances. This is where the huge Harley-Davidson
engine comes into its own, or where the relatively 'soft'
European engines score over Japanese engines with
nominally higher power output. I do not say that I would not
like more than my BMW's 70 bhp; but I do say that I have
never really felt the need of it.

There is little point in analysing the different types and
sizes of motorcycles, as it is by now obvious where my
sympathies lie. But I have not always ridden BMWs, and
indeed one of my favourite alternatives comes from the

other end of the price scale. The old MZ 250 Supa 5, with all its weird looks, even weirder noises, and resounding 19 bhp, was an excellent tourer. It was adequately nippy, surprisingly sweet-handling, and frugal: I used to get 75–85 mpg as a matter of course, even allowing for 70–80 mph cruising on the motorway. The all-enclosed chain was long-lived (the British replacement for the East German original was even longer-lived), the long soft suspension was reminiscent of a BMW, and the simple low-stressed engine was easy to work on – which was just as well, because the East German main bearing only lasted about 20,000 miles. The tool kit was comprehensive (if a little agricultural) – another plus point on any tourer – and as a solo machine it was fine. With a pillion, it would have been rather less fun.

As I said at the beginning of the chapter, you can tour on just about anything. I have never tried a Honda 90, but I have tried a Honda 185, two-up; I'd rather have the BMW, but I'd rather have the Honda 185 than nothing. And that is what it is all about.

4   **Rude Mechanicals**

'Six days shalt thou labour, and the seventh ride.' This used to be a common expression when the common bikes were BSA, Matchless, AJS, Norton, Panther, Triumph, and so forth; but I never found out whether it referred to the six-day working week and the freedom of Sunday, or to the amount of time that most people spent working on their bikes rather than on riding them.

Nowadays, motorcycles require far less maintenance. The oil does not have to be topped up regularly just to counteract the leaks; very rarely do bits vibrate loose and fall off; and electrics are no longer unpredictable mazes requiring spells and incantations to make them work. Even tuning for speed does not hold the appeal it did; in the days when 40 bhp was pretty good for a 500, there was more incentive to try 'go-faster' modifications than now, when all the power you want is available off the shelf.

This is not just a matter of engineering progress. To a large extent, it is a result of the Japanese attitude to marketing motorcycles. Instead of selling them to dyed-in-the-fingernails 'enthusiasts', they wanted to sell motorcycles to everyone. In order to do so, they had to make them more reliable and easier to run.

Regardless of the reasons behind the vastly improved reliability of motorcycles, there has been the inevitable result that fewer and fewer motorcyclists actually know much about the workings of their motorcycles. Fewer still are ready to do their own maintenance – and in this they are encouraged by the manufacturers, who prefer them to use Authorized Workshops for many reasons. It gets rid of the bunglers and bodgers (unless, as is depressingly often the case, they work for the Authorized Workshop); it keeps the dealers rich and happy, and allows them to discount their motorcycles more when they know that they can clean up on servicing and maintenance; it keeps knowledge of some truly awful engineering from the public, such as hardened-steel camshafts running directly in alloy heads without any bearings; it preserves the mystique of the manufacturer (just

think of 'Five-Star Service'!); it allows the machine to be
designed in a way that is very cheap to build, but almost
impossible to service without batteries of expensive
specialized tools; and it encourages people who have not the
wit to work on a machine themselves, by telling them that
they can leave all that sort of thing to someone else.

In *Zen and the Art of Motorcycle Maintenance*, Robert
Pirsig makes a strong case for doing all your maintenance
yourself. As he points out, that way you can be sure that it is
done properly; you can be sure that the machine is running
as the manufacturer intended it to run; and there is a good
deal of personal satisfaction to be had. Most people have
had the experience of having to finish the job that a so-called
professional mechanic had started, or of having to rectify
some new fault that the mechanic introduced when he cured
the old one. If you are your own mechanic, you make these
corrections and adjustments naturally and when they are
needed. I must confess that I do not follow the Pure
Doctrine of the *Roshi* Pirsig, but I do believe that it is worth
knowing something about the mechanics of the bike for at
least five reasons.

First, you need not be stranded by some minor fault
which can be fixed by the roadside. An example which
comes to mind was a loose HT lead on my MZ 250. It took
me about five minutes to diagnose, and thirty seconds to fix.
Compare that with the time you could spend waiting for
assistance.

Second, even if you cannot fix the fault yourself, you
will be better able to explain what is wrong when you talk to
the mechanic. You will also be able to guess whether you are
being ripped off when you see the bill.

Third, you can decide whether a fault should be fixed
immediately, or whether it is safe to press on and get it fixed
later. To take another example, a slightly slipping clutch on a
BMW is not particularly expensive to fix; but if you let it go, it
becomes steadily more expensive. On the other hand, you
may decide that it is better to take it easy and wait until you
see your regular dealer, rather than trusting some foreign
unknown, or paying Swiss labour rates.

Fourth, 'mechanical sympathy' will enable you to get the
best out of your machine: the best performance, the best
braking, the best safety. Mechanical sympathy is not
something which can easily be taught, but it is impossible to

learn without at least some appreciation of mechanics.

Fifth, you can understand what caused a particular fault: your driving, bad servicing, a stroke of bad luck, or a design fault on the machine. This is not merely for the satisfaction of knowing: if it is your fault you can probably rectify it, and if it is clearly the fault of the manufacturer or the garage then someone else will be paying to have it fixed.

There would be little point in explaining here how to strip and clean a particular carburettor, or how to adjust the points, because these features vary from machine to machine; and besides, there are already plenty of workshop manuals available for almost all makes of motorcycle. If you are a complete novice, a good introduction is something like Collins *Motorcycle Workshop*, which is illustrated with a lot of 'how-to' photographs of all kinds of motorcycles. For now, it is worth running through the main components and considering briefly what can go wrong with them.

It is usual to divide the mechanics into 'mechanical parts' and 'cycle parts', which is a slightly misleading way to do things because it implies that (say) wheel-bearings or shock absorbers are less 'mechanical' than carburettors and gearboxes. Nevertheless, it is a fairly useful division.

Cycle Parts

The cycle parts may be further divided into six: frame; suspension; wheels; brakes; controls; and seat.

The frame should require no maintenance unless it is bent (in which case straightening it is hardly a matter for the home mechanic) or the motor is rubber-mounted, which cuts down vibration dramatically but makes it advisable to examine the rubber mounts from time to time to make sure that they are not perishing. 'From time to time' is a flexible term; one good reason for washing the motorcycle occasionally is that it gives you an excellent opportunity to check this sort of thing

The front suspension (the front forks) should be checked from time to time to make sure that they are not weeping oil, and the oil level itself should be checked; this should be part of a 3,000 – or 5,000 – mile service. Unless you are a well-equipped enthusiast, you might as well leave renewing fork seals to the workshop. Slight weeping is no great problem; it is easier to live with it than to have it fixed.

The rear suspension (the swinging arm) should be checked to make sure that there is no play at the swinging arm pivot. With the machine on its centre stand, try to move the swinging arm from side to side. Any play is dangerous, but it is another thing for a workshop to fix.

The shock absorbers (dampers) both front and rear should do their job properly, so that the machine does not just bounce up and down at every irregularity in the road. Test them by bouncing both the front and rear of the motorcycle. Rear shocks are comparatively easy to fit yourself, but front fork rebuilds are a workshop matter again. It may seem that I am listing a lot of things which only the workshop can fix, but these are not common faults; they are, however, worth checking every month or two if you want to get the best from your bike.

Modern cast wheels should be examined for cracks every month or two. Cast wheels are something of a con job: they are certainly lighter, which makes them better for racing, and they are also cheaper to make than laced wheels, at least after the expensive die-casting machinery has been paid for. On the other hand, they can develop cracks under long-term use (which is not important in racing), and they are not repairable. A broken wheel means a complete replacement, and frequently a spares problem, whereas a spoked wheel can almost always have some sort of light-alloy or steel rim laced on in an emergency. Check a spoked wheel by running a pencil or screwdriver handle around the spokes: they should all 'plink' at the same note. A spoke that 'plonks' needs tightening. It is perfectly possible to do this yourself, though there is a danger of distorting the rim: it is usually safer, easier, and quicker to take it to a specialist wheelbuilder. If you do decide to do it yourself, be very careful that you file off any protrusions inside the wheel well, which could cause a puncture.

On a fast motorcycle, it is worth having the wheels balanced whenever a tyre is removed and replaced, or a new tyre fitted, but finding someone to do this may not be easy. You can try doing it yourself with stick-on weights and the wheel spinning freely on the spindle.

Check the wheel bearings by simply trying to rock the wheel on its spindle; also, make sure that the wheel bearings are regularly lubricated.

Check tyre pressures frequently; at least once a week,

and every day (in the morning, before you start) if you are going far. Examine the tyre tread for wear and for anything sticking into the rubber; remove stones, etc, with a penknife. Again, do this daily if you are going far. Whenever a tyre is replaced, replace the inner tube; keep an old inner tube for punctures. Patching inner tubes should be a get-you-home expedient only. Although repairing punctures yourself is possible, it is also messy, time-consuming, and frequently difficult. I do it when I have to, but if possible I have it done for me. If you are riding on a road where you know that horses are also ridden, stay well towards the crown of the road; this considerably reduces the likelihood of picking up thrown horseshoe nails. If you do remove and replace a tyre yourself, make sure that you put it on the right way round: almost all modern tyres have an arrow indicating the direction of rotation.

On the subject of tyres, a great deal of nonsense is talked about matching tyres to motorcycles, and the terrible gripping quality of some tyres as opposed to others. Japanese tyres used to attract the most horror stories, but now they have been eclipsed by the East German Pneumants. There is no doubt that some tyres are very much better than others, or that some motorcycles seem to handle better on some brands than on others, but (with few exceptions, mainly ultra-cheap tyres from exotic countries) the differences are nothing like as great as some people say. I run my BMW on Metzelers, because BMWs are notorious for running best on these or Continentals, but even when my old MZ had Pneumants I was only frightened once. By all means replace your Japanese or other non-European tyres with Avons, Pirellis, Metzelers, or Contis, but do not imagine that other brands are sudden death.

Brakes are obviously extremely important, and worth checking periodically. Most disc pads have grooves or some other indicator which allows their condition to be judged on the motorcycle, and some drum brakes have plugs in the drums which you can remove to examine their linings; otherwise, disassembly at the regular service periods is best. On hydraulic brakes, check fluid levels weekly, and make sure that the fluid is changed at the recommended intervals. If fluid levels are falling, find out why: don't just top up. Cable-operated brakes require regular cable lubrication; both cable and rod-operated brakes (most rear drums are of this type) usually have adjusters to take up excessive movement. The usual rule is to tighten the brakes until the shoes are just kissing the drum, and then slack off half a turn of the adjuster, but there may be alternative instructions for your particular bike. Check that the brake light works, too. On hydraulic brakes, it is usually operated by both front and rear brakes; with drums, it is quite usual for only the rear brake to operate the lamp.

While you are checking the brakes, you can check the other controls. The clutch is the obvious one; again, there is a small adjuster by the lever. The clutch should begin to disengage after a reasonable movement of the lever – this is best tested by riding along and pulling the lever in slightly – but on the other hand it should not begin to bite until the lever is a fair way from the handlebar. Check the lights and indicators; usually, failures are due to bulbs rather than to switchgear. In some countries, carrying a set of spare bulbs is compulsory; in all countries, it is a good idea. Check the throttle: like the clutch and brake cables, lubricate the cable as necessary. Interestingly, people no longer adjust throttles the way that they used to. The traditional approach was to adjust the throttle return so that it would stay where it was set, requiring very weak return pressure. Nowadays, the little braking screw is not even fitted to most motorcycles, and the throttle snaps shut against a spring as soon as it is released. Too strong a spring is obviously tiring; even if you like a self-closing throttle, which I do, it is still nice to be able to set it so that the brake takes up most of the closing spring's force.

Finally, there may not seem to be much to check on the seat, but it is well worth making sure that the seat bolts are secure. If the seat has been taken off in the workshop, during a routine service for example, it may not be refitted properly. Unless all the bolts are tight, it may come off, usually at the most embarrassing and dangerous time

Mechanical Parts

The mechanical parts of the motorcycle can be divided into the petrol tank; the carburettor and air filters; the electrics; the engine; the clutch; the gearbox; the final drive; and the exhaust.

It may seem odd to include the petrol tank, but it is after all the beginning of the whole process. Apart from checking it for corrosion, there are three other things to look at. The first is the filler cap. Unless the tank has some other form of breather (in which case you may need to check that), there must be an air hole in the cap in order to allow air to replace the petrol as it is used up. More than one mysterious case of fuel starvation has been traced to this – but it is really only worth checking if you do have fuel starvation problems. The second thing to check is the fuel tap, to make sure that it is not leaking – old ones sometimes weep – and the third thing is the fuel hoses themselves. Fuel line material is surprisingly expensive for what it is, but it will still not cost you a fortune to replace it if it is looking frayed and nasty.

The carburettors mix fuel and air in the correct proportions for combustion. Two typical designs, both by Mikuni, are on pp. 38–9. The only common faults are leaking float bowls (usually easily cured with a new gasket) and a sticking float, which causes the carburettor to overflow with petrol and can usually be cured with a sharp tap or by removing the float bowl and trying to spot the hang-up. Carburettor tuning, especially of multiple carburettors which have to be balanced, is too delicate an art to be discussed here. It is, however, easy to spot the need for a carburettor tune. Excessive fuel consumption is one giveaway, but for an accurate check, look at each plug in turn (out of the cylinder). If the mixture supplied to that cylinder is correct, the plug tip will be a light chocolate colour – like milky coffee. If it is very pale, or white, the mixture is too lean; if it is dark brown, or worse still black, it is too rich. Check the plugs after a run; if you have only been a short distance, with the choke on, they may well look dark anyway.

If the air filters are dirty, so that not enough air is getting to the carburettor, this will also have the same effect as running rich – though usually with more loss of power. Air filters are not expensive and are easily replaced on most bikes. Leaving the filters out – a favourite 'go-faster' trick – will allow the engine to breathe more freely, but it will also cause greatly increased wear. If the filters on your bike are really restrictive, it is usually possible to replace them with something better.

Considering the electrics before the engine itself is a little unusual, but a lot of irritating faults which are easily cured can be traced to the electrics. So can a lot of faults which are not easily cured!

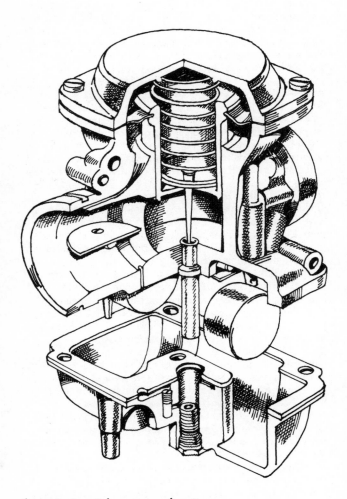

A constant partial vacuum carburettor

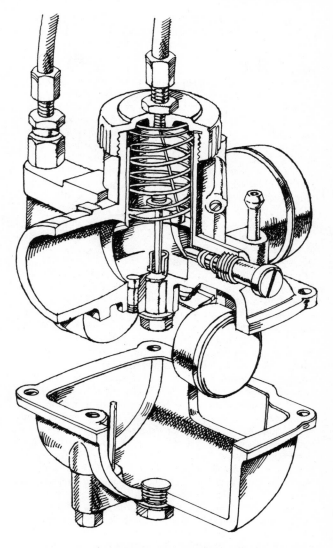

A variable-venturi, needle jet type carburettor

The most usual problems arise in the sparking plugs and leads. Make sure that the plugs are clean, and set to the correct gap; if you don't have a feeler gauge handy, an old trick is to use your thumb nail. Tap the bent (outer) electrode gently to bend it in; you should never have to use a screwdriver to lever it outwards, but sometimes you do have to. Never try to bend the central (inner) terminal, because you will probably break the insulator and ruin the plug. Two-stroke owners, and owners of four-strokes that foul up in traffic, usually carry a spare plug or set of plugs. They don't take up much room, are not expensive, and easy to fit.

Make sure that the plug-cap is tight on the plug, and that the high tension lead between the ignition coil and the plug or plugs is tight at both ends. Don't do this with the engine running – if you've never had a shock from a high tension coil, I can assure you that you don't want one.

There is not usually much you can do if the generator (whether dynamo or alternator) stops charging, but it is a good idea not to ride the bike too far if the little red charging light comes on: this can damage some generators. You can, however, check the battery (make sure that the plates are covered with electrolyte, and top up with distilled water if necessary) and the battery connections: bad connections are a frequent reason for starter motors not working.

The engine itself is not something that the rank beginner can set about repairing, but it is useful to know what is going on in there. This depends on whether it is a two-stroke or a four-stroke. The easiest way to distinguish between these two is with a pair of diagrams. (See pp. 41–2.)

The four strokes are properly known as induction, compression, explosion, and exhaust; or more familiarly, as suck, squeeze, bang, blow. The four-stroke engine is good at getting the most work out of a given amount of fuel, so it is described as having a high *thermal efficiency*. On the other hand, it is not usually so powerful for a given engine size (swept volume) as a two-stroke, so its *volumetric efficiency* is lower.

The two-stroke motor is more *volumetrically efficient* largely because it produces a power stroke once on every revolution, as opposed to the one stroke every other revolution for a four-stroke. The two-stroke really scores when you want to get the maximum amount of power out of

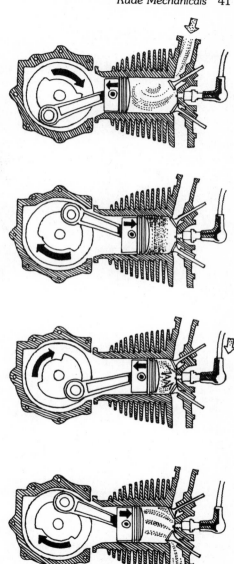

The four-stroke cycle

The two-stroke cycle

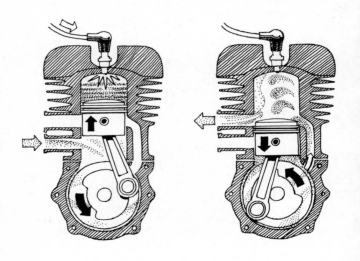

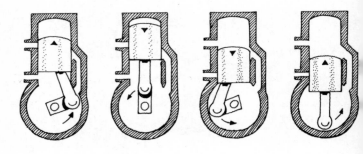

an engine of given capacity, whilst retaining reliability and a reasonably low price. Otherwise, a bigger four-stroke will be more suitable for general use, or a 'high-tech' four-stroke if cost is no object – as in racing.

Unfortunately, the days of the big, simple, low-powered engine are almost completely over; only the Enfield India (350cc, 18 bhp) and a few Communist machines continue in this tradition. This is a pity, because such motorcycles can be very pleasant to ride. It is interesting, however, to compare the power outputs of a typical British machine of the 1950s and a modern Japanese machine of the same capacity. An old British 500 might deliver 30 bhp; a typical Japanese machine of thirty years later would offer at least 50% more.

Whichever type of engine you have – and most riders would agree that a four-stroke is more agreeable for touring – it needs to be maintained. With a four-stroke, this usually means adjusting the valve clearances periodically and changing the oil. A two-stroke has no valves and burns its oil, either mixed with the petrol in the petrol tank (the 'petroil' system) or supplied from a separate oil tank, so it does not need valve adjustment and oil changes; but the petrol/oil mixture burns dirtier than the petrol of a four-stroke, so the cylinder head must be periodically removed and decarbonized or 'decoked'. A four-stroke should only need a decoke after some tens of thousands of miles; a two-stroke may need decoking after as little as two thousand, though five thousand would be more usual, and some can go to a lot more. Either type of motor shows the need for a decoke by loss of power, and in addition a four-stroke will suffer from 'pinking' or pre-ignition and a two-stroke will tend to smoke more.

The clutch transmits the power from the engine to the gearbox. Basically, it consists of friction plates which can be held apart (thus cutting off the drive from the engine to the box) or forced together (thereby passing the drive from the engine to the drive chain). If the plates cannot be separated properly, then the clutch will *drag* – the bike will tend to creep forward when the clutch is pulled but the gears are still engaged, and gear changing may be rather crunchy. If they cannot be forced together properly, the clutch will *slip*; the full power of the engine will not reach the gearbox. This is most obvious when you try to accelerate, and the engine speed increases but the bike's speed does not.

Replacing worn clutch parts is a lengthy and expensive business, but making sure that the clutch lasts as long as possible is easy. Clutch adjustment has already been covered on page 38, and apart from this, you should not slip the clutch when pulling away or riding slowly; keeping rapid acceleration through the gears to a minimum will also help. On most bikes, clutchless changes are quite possible in the higher gears, but they may be a bit jerky in the lower gears.

Gearboxes are another part which rarely give trouble, but which are difficult to fix if they do go wrong. As an aside, it is interesting to note that the number of gears provided is as much a matter of fashion as of necessity in many cases. On many bikes, four speeds are plenty; the main advantage of having five is that it reduces the gaps between gears. This makes matching engine speed and road speed less critical, and reduces twitches resulting from mis-matching. A 'soft' touring engine, with a wide spread of power from (say) 1000 rpm to 6000 rpm, really only needs four speeds: it is racing engines that need the extra gears to keep the engine 'on the cam'. If the engine's power band is from (say) 7000 to 9000 rpm, as it is on some racers, you may need six or more gears; but six gears on a road bike is either a complete waste, or an indication that the bike is not really suitable for road use at all, because you will be forever changing gears.

The final drive, which takes the drive from the gearbox to the rear wheel, may be of three kinds: chain, shaft, or belt. As already mentioned, chains start off very efficient but need constant adjustment and lubrication to keep them that way. Chain adjustment is not difficult, however. All you need to do is to slack off the wheel spindle; undo the locking nuts on the chain adjusting screws; turn the chain adjusters *by the same number of turns* in order to tighten the chain; and then tighten everything up again. The chain itself should not be bar-tight: you should be able to flex it by about $\pm\frac{1}{2}$" (10–15 mm) up and down with one finger. I have deliberately not gone into much detail here, because it is best to have someone show you how to do it.

Chain lubrication traditionally involved taking the chain off; washing it in petrol or paraffin; and then soaking it in chain grease melted in a tin on the stove. This made the chain last for much longer than we regard as normal these days, but it was dirty, unpleasant, and time-consuming, so hardly anyone does it any more. Even so, spray-on chain lubricants are much better than nothing. Remember that the chain drive sprockets also wear, especially the one on the rear wheel, so check them when a chain is replaced.

Shaft drives are somewhat less efficient than chains, but maintenance is confined to the occasional oil-change in the hub. This is obviously much easier than chain maintenance, and it is why so many touring motorcyclists prefer shafts.

Belt drives were common seventy years ago, and they have only just begun to come back. Modern toothed belts have many of the advantages of both shaft and chain: they are quiet like a shaft, they are efficient and cheap to manufacture like a chain, and they require far less frequent adjustment than a chain and no lubrication at all. They do, however, have to be changed. This is usually done at fixed intervals – say 20,000 miles – because no-one wants the belt to snap when they least expect it. People who forget or neglect to change belts may yet lead to their having a bad name, despite all their advantages.

Exhausts require little maintenance in the case of four-strokes, but two-stroke exhausts may clog up with carbon and unburnt oil and require 'decoking' in much the same way as two-stroke engines. This is another dirty and unpleasant job, but it pays dividends in the form of better performance and reduced fuel consumption.

Servicing

Much of what I have said in this chapter comes under the heading of 'routine servicing', or more correctly, 'preventive maintenance'. There are, after all, two ways of maintaining any machine. You can look after it, so that it does not go wrong, or you can wait until it does go wrong, and then fix it. Although the second approach is superficially attractive, it suffers from several serious drawbacks. First, it means that you never know what sort of state the bike is in: it may be fine, or it may be on the point of falling to bits. Second, for obvious reasons, it can be dangerous: how does a seized engine or a disintegrating wheel at 100 mph sound? Third, a well-maintained bike is more economical. Fourth, it is more powerful. Fifth, preventive maintenance can be done at a (fairly) convenient time and place: if you have to fix it when it breaks, you may be in Czechoslovakia at the time. You can think of other reasons for yourself, if you try.

Most manufacturers lay down a servicing schedule for their motorcycles, and it is a good idea to stick to it. The real question is who should do it. The best thing to do is to find a mechanic that you trust, and then always check what you can of his work afterwards – or, of course, do it all yourself. Usually, it will not matter if you exceed the recommended service interval by ten or twenty per cent, but it is best to have a service early if you know that you are going to be on a long trip and that you will exceed the service interval by any more than this.

Preparing For a Long Ride

Before going on any long ride – even a hundred miles or so – check the machine over: lights, brakes, tyres, and all the controls. For really long rides – over a thousand miles, say – either have a full service or check the bike carefully yourself, using this chapter and the manufacturer's servicing checklist as a guide.

Check your tool kit. Even if you cannot use it, it may include tools which a mechanic or a fellow motor-cyclist who stops to help you may not have. The quality of tool-kits supplied with the machine varies enormously: both the BMW and the MZ, for example, have tool-kits which allow a skilled mechanic to perform any reasonable maintenance or roadside repair. If you have an inferior tool-kit, or no tool-kit at all, the following is a good start:

A set of spanners of the appropriate sizes (metric, AF, or whatever). Plug spanner, large and small screwdrivers (including cross-head), pliers, feeler gauge, tyre levers, hand pump, puncture repair outfit, tyre pressure gauge. A *really good* adjustable spanner may also be a good investment, though you should only use it when you have to. If you spot a need for more tools, then this chapter is not really for you anyway.

It is also a good idea to carry a few spares. At the very least, carry spare bulbs, spare fuses, and some insulating tape; spare plug or plugs; spare points. Spare throttle and brake cables, a spare chain link, and a spare inner tube may also come in very useful. Some people like to carry some soft heavy wire (surprisingly useful stuff), and if you have room for it, some chain lubricant. You should also carry a workshop manual; a small torch; and some way of cleaning your hands, such as those small scented pads sold for removing make-up, or *Wet Ones*, or the like.

Trouble-Shooting

The aim of this chapter has not been to give a comprehensive guide to motorcycle mechanics, but to give the non-mechanical reader a rough idea of what goes on inside those aluminium cases. It has inevitably been somewhat basic, but I hope that no-one has felt insulted by it. To end with, a quick guide to trouble-shooting may be of use even to the most non-mechanical.

The algorithm on page 48 sums up the trouble-shooting guide very well, but there are a few comments that are worth making on the bare statements:

1   If the engine will not turn over, it is unlikely to be easily repairable. Some simple two-strokes will, however, free themselves if you let them cool down, but the fact that they have seized is an indication that the engine has overheated either as a result of your riding too fast or as a result of something else – usually too lean a mixture. Examine the plug.

2   Lack of fuel is still one of the most frequent causes of involuntary stops. You may be able to get the last few ounces of fuel into the right place by leaning the bike on its side or sloshing it around, or both.

3   Check for a blocked air vent (pages 38–9) or a dirty fuel filter. If the fuel line is inaccessible, the only way you can find out if the fuel is getting through is by seeing if the plugs get wet (see 6, below).

4   Some bikes do not rely on the battery for ignition – especially trail bikes. In this case, just check the plug, plug cap, and all connections (including the ignition switch!).

5   If you hold the plug (attached to the lead) about $\frac{1}{4}$"/6 mm from a metallic part of the engine – not the carburettor, or near spilled fuel – and turn the engine over, a clearly visible spark should jump the gap. If you

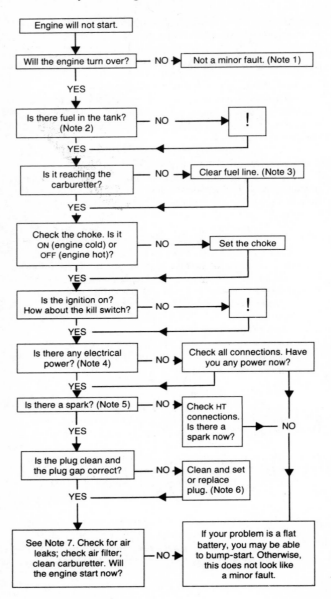

cannot see the spark or if it cannot manage the full distance, it may not be strong enough to fire the mixture. While the plug is out, check the gap; clean the inside (a matchstick with the end split is useful); and clean the *outside* so that dirt and water do not earth the spark before it reaches the plug gap. Ideally, carry spare plugs. Old ones can be cleaned with a blowtorch or a proprietary cleaner – but they are not that expensive!

6   If you have been churning the engine over for some time, it may be flooded with petrol. If so, take the plug and dry it, wait ten minutes, and put it back in. This will only help, of course, if you have cured the original fault – of if the original fault was flooding caused by trying to start a hot engine with the choke on!

7   If you have both fuel and a spark, the usual next step is to check that there are no air-leaks between the carburettor and the engine; to make sure that the air filter is not blocked; and to strip, clean, and reassemble the carburettor. Beyond this, you do begin to need real mechanical knowledge. It is very rare, though, that a simple spark-and-fuel check will not solve roadside problems.

5   Worldly Goods

The question, 'What should I take with me?' is about as meaningful as 'How long is a piece of string?' In fact, the parallel is exact: just as a piece of string is always half an inch shorter than you need, so will you find that you neglected to bring the one thing that could have made life much easier. The answer is not, however, to pack everything that you can think of.

A lot depends on who you are, where you are going, and what sort of machine you ride. For example, consider two would-be tourers. One is a 30-year-old BMW rider, with a year-old bike in excellent condition, who is touring Germany on his own for a couple of weeks. Money is no problem: he is planning to stay in hotels and guest houses. The other is a man of 65 who has just retired; he and his wife, who is two years younger, are going to fulfil the ambition of a lifetime by riding their 1957 Matchless to Athens and back. They have plenty of time, but have to be careful with their money.

The two situations are obviously wildly different. Perhaps the easiest way to decide what (and who!) to take is to divide the question into four parts: **companions** (whether pillion or on their own machines); **clothing** (for on and off the motorcycle); **equipment** (cameras, razors, make-up, you name it); and **camping kit**, if you are planning on camping. Tools and spares have already been dealt with, and documents are covered in Chapter 7.

Once you have decided who and what is going to accompany you, you will also have to decide how to carry them and it. To some extent, the two questions are inseparable, but the second part of this chapter is devoted to how to carry things and how to distribute the load.

Before we go on to look at the details, though, there is one golden rule. If you are not *absolutely certain* that something is necessary, leave it behind.

Companions

It may seem like an obvious question, but it is one that has to be faced. Are you going on your own, or with one or more companions? And do you intend to carry a pillion passenger, or will each person have his or her own bike?

If you travel alone, you have no ties, no restrictions, and no chance of arguments. You can go where you please and do what you want; if you make new friends, you can fall in with their plans if you wish. You have only your own needs to consider – food, drink, toilet stops – and you are totally free.

If you decide to travel with someone else, there are two completely different choices. One is to travel with a lover, and the other is to travel with less intimate friends.

Travelling with a lover has many obvious advantages. You share the good times, and you can console one another if things go wrong. The nights are obviously more enjoyable, and the feeling of being away from it all together can do wonders for your relationship. On the other hand, you will be very close to one another for a long time, and unless the relationship is sound to start with, you can soon run into trouble: there is no need to enlarge upon this, but it is worth pointing out that unless both of you are sure that the trip is a good idea, you may be better off either going on your own or not going at all. The real problem comes when the lover doesn't want to go, but doesn't want to be apart from you, and so agrees to go anyway. This is a recipe for disaster.

I used to prefer travelling on my own, but then I met a girl and did a lot of touring with her; and then I married her, and now she has a motorcycle of her own. So far, we have always toured two-up on the BMW, because it is much cheaper than taking two bikes; we also worry about each other more when we are on separate bikes. Also, most men like having a girl on the pillion, and there are plenty of girls who like it that way, too. From now on, incidentally, I shall assume that my readers are male. This is not just because most motorcyclists are male; it is also because I am, and the assumption comes easily, and because it gets around some horrible grammatical constructions and endlessly having to write 'he or she'. I wish my women readers (of whom I hope there are lots) the very best of luck, and I don't think I'm being patronizing.

Travelling with a lover is one thing: travelling with other people is quite another. Travelling with a son or daughter on the pillion is an odd sort of in-between state, in that most of the bugs in the relationship have been worked out or at least plastered over; it often works very well.

Usually, other companions will have their own machines. This has the advantage that you can share the load, which is especially useful when you are carrying camping gear, but it also makes communication difficult. If one of you wants (or needs) to stop, he has to convey it to the other. This is difficult at the best of times, unless you want to run a CB rig, but if it is merely a matter of idle curiosity – spotting something interesting that you would like to turn off and look at – the whole thing can be too much trouble, so that you just do not bother.

Furthermore, unless you all have the same interests and similar machines, some people are going to get very bored. If one person is into good meals and attractive architecture, when another is content with caff food but likes sunbathing, you have problems. The same goes for a party in which one person likes drinking and discos until four in the morning, while another likes to be up and riding at dawn. If you are on your own, you can make the choice; if you are with someone else, you will almost certainly have to make compromises. Again, if one person is riding a BMW with 100 mph cruising capability and a 200-mile range or more, he may be rather irritated if someone else is slower or has to stop more often for fuel.

As a result of this, travelling with one or more other people on separate bikes usually works best if you all have an agreed destination: the obvious example is if several of you are going to a particular race. Otherwise, you run the risks of losing one another; of delays while you try to find each other; of friction and arguments; and, ultimately, of losing precisely that freedom which is the greatest attraction of a motorcycling holiday. Riding with someone you meet on the road for a day can be great; riding with a friend for a couple of days can be marvellous; but riding with someone for a week or two weeks is another matter. More than one expedition has broken up after a thousand miles or so because no one could stand anyone else's company after a few days.

I have never been on one of those organized rides,

where a tour leader is in charge, so I suppose that I should not comment on them. I have heard favourable reports of the BMW tours in North America, where all baggage is carried in a van (which also picks up broken-down machines, Gott forbid!) and where hotels are pre-booked; but I have also read several long, boring, and ill-written articles by a leading tour organizer in Europe, and if he is as bad in real life as he comes across in his articles, I'd hate to go on a tour and be ordered about by someone like that. Even the best of these tours seem to me to involve a sacrifice of the kind of freedom that I want; on the worst of them, you might as well be on a coach tour. Rules and regulations I need like a hole in the head; like most motorcyclists, I am something of an anarchist, and have difficulty in remembering rules, let alone in following them.

Clothing

Although clothing is a less vexed subject than companions, it can still arouse strong feelings. There is a strong camp that says you should always wear leathers, full-face helmet, gloves, stout boots, and for all I know, a full suit of plate armour and chain-mail as well, rather than risk road-rash. It has been many years since I last rode barefoot, but I see nothing wrong with shirt-sleeves; if it's good enough for the California Highway Patrol, it's good enough for me.

Motorcycle clothing has three functions. It keeps you warm; it keeps off the rain; and it protects you, both from flying bugs and stones and in the event of flying down the road. You can judge it by how well it does these three things.

Unless you are riding in Southern California or somewhere similar, keeping warm is going to be a problem at least some of the time. Looking at wind-chill factors makes you realize just how much heat you can lose on a motorcycle. The figures given opposite show the actual temperature, and the temperatures which would produce the same heat-loss if you were sitting still instead of riding a motorcycle at 40 mph. They are only a rough guide, but still pretty telling.

If you were going out for a walk at 26°F, you would dress warmly. But you are not going to be walking: you are going to be sitting still in the middle of a gale. If you have never ridden a motorcycle for a long distance at low temperatures before, it is hard to imagine what it is like. A short ride of ten or even twenty miles with inadequate protection is uncomfortable, but you will survive: a hundred or two hundred miles can be genuinely dangerous. It is not just the immediate physical problem of hypothermia: you also slow down, make decisions less quickly and accurately, and run the risk of not controlling the bike adequately. Experienced riders, if they recognize these symptoms, may get off the bike and push it for a hundred yards (that always warms you up!), or do press ups. It is obviously better, however, not to get in this state in the first place.

Actual temperature		Effective temperature when riding at 40 mph	
F'Heit	C'grade	F'heit	C'grade
50	9	26	3
40	4	10	−12
30	−1	−6	−21

To begin with, you need clothes which trap air next to your body, and which will not allow any draughts in. Down waist-coats and string vests are classic examples of air-trapping clothes. As a general rule, several layers of material are better than fewer layers of thicker stuff, but this is not always the case; thick sweaters, for example, are very good if you have an outer layer which keeps the wind out. You must also be careful not to put on so many layers that you cannot move comfortably! Keeping out the draughts requires a thick and relatively impervious outer shell – leather is traditional and best – and careful attention to all joins. Ideally, the front of the jacket should overlap to a considerable extent, so that the wind cannot whistle in through the zip or button-holes, and you should pay particular attention to wrists, ankles, neck, and waist. Gauntlets which overlap the coat take care of the wrists; high boots take care of the ankles; a scarf, or a baby's nappy, takes care of the neck; and high-waisted jeans (such as *Levi*'s 501s) and a long jacket seal the middle. German riders are great believers in kidney-belts to wrap around the middle, and they may well have a point. For the inner layers, natural fibres are better than artificial for two reasons. First, they are more efficient at trapping air, and second, they have a 'wicking' effect which draws sweat away from the skin and makes you feel more comfortable.

Everyone has their own favourite warm clothes, but two of mine are *Thermolactyl* (the stuff Damart make) for 'long johns' and outer socks (thin cotton inners and wooly outers are equally good) and Tibetan shirts which button to one side like fencing shirts and have a large overlap – it gets pretty cold in Tibet! Under the helmet, a silk balaclava (try a ski store) can be useful, and for outer jackets, try government surplus stores. I have a superb $\frac{3}{4}$ length leather coat with a sheepskin collar, originally made for the Swedish police, which cost me about a fifth of what a comparable jacket would cost new.

There are also other ways of keeping warm. One is to use aluminized reflective material, like the 'space blankets' introduced for climbers and campers a few years ago. About the only practical application of these from our point of view, however, is in the form of thermal insoles. These really can be effective! Another approach is to use some external form of heat input. Some sports shops sell little hand-warmers which run for ages on lighter fuel or charcoal, and an even better way to get heat where you need it is to use electric gloves and (if you can afford it) electric underwear. These take surprisingly little current, and do not feel particularly warm at all: they just stop you from getting cold in a rather magical way! BMW supply optional electrically heated handlebar grips at a surprisingly modest price, which saves you from having to have umbilical cords connecting you to the machine; I keep meaning to get a set of these, but never get around to it. One danger with any electrically-heated clothing, though, is that if the power goes off and you have no other means of keeping warm, you have problems.

Another way to keep warm is, of course, the fairing. I have already dealt with these in Chapter 3, and all that I will do here is to repeat that only the very best are worth having, and that some types are altogether too warm on a warm day.

So much for warmth; what about keeping off the rain? Once again, strong feelings are aroused. Some people swear by the old black waxed-cotton suits, and there is no doubt that they are very effective. They are also ugly, unpleasant to handle, have to be reproofed periodically, and can leave black smears on things. If you can put up with the drawbacks, they are excellent; I can't.

Others sing the praises of lightweight one-piece plastic suits. A few – a very few – are genuinely rainproof at all seams (especially the crotch), and even fewer stay that way for long. The heavier waterproofs, usually two-piece, are much better: my wife uses Bruce's gear, and she swears by it.

Arguably the best of all, though, is yachting clothing. I use Henri Lloyd, which is horrifyingly expensive but seems to last forever; I think that my jacket is ten years or more old, and it has covered many tens of thousands of miles. After 120 miles in the rain on an unfaired bike at 60-70 mph, one lapel of my jacket was slightly damp – not enough to notice. On that occasion, I was wearing a three-piece business suit under the rain gear; it was surprisingly warm. Of course, now that I use the fairing, I have no problems at all with rain penetration.

Coming to our last heading, protection, the obvious place to start is the helmet. Although I probably owe my life to wearing a helmet, I still do not think that they should be compulsory; but they are, in almost every single Western European country that I have been able to find out about. Of course, the degree of enforcement varies, and so do the fines imposed (in Britain, they are surprisingly low, and they cannot arrest you for it). I like the old 'piss-pot' style of my youth, though I usually wear a jet-style Bell; I never could stand full-face helmets. The big advantage of open-style hats is that most of them allow you to wear goggles, which do not scratch and graze like plastic visors. The glasses and the straps are both replaceable on the Mk IV fighter-pilot style goggles my wife and I wear; they should last half way to forever. I like the image, too.

For the rest of the body, leather is best except when it rains; then, after it has soaked through, no amount of protection in the event of a spill could compensate for the discomfort. *Thick* quilted nylon is just as good: you can slide down the road quite freely, and it won't burn your skin when it melts from the friction like thin nylon does. Beware of cheap, skimpily-cut leathers; only the more expensive ones are really worth the money.

As it gets warmer, you can discard more and more layers. Ideally, thin leathers and a silk undersuit would suit warm weather, but for the less well-heeled, wear whatever suits you. It is fashionable to bang on about dressing in armour, as I said at the beginning of this section, but I'd rather be free and take a few risks sometimes.

What you take apart from your riding gear will depend very much on what you intend to do and how you intend to live. Many writers recommend drip-dry clothing which you can wash in your hotel room, but I loathe most man-made fibres (especially nylon) and anyway, most hotels and guest houses object if you wash clothes in your room. If you are staying in hotels, some will do your laundry for you for a very reasonable fee; otherwise, use laundromats, with the tumbledryers set at LOW unless you want to shrink all your clothes. I do, however, wash my silk Tibetan shirts in the room; they dry overnight, and what the hotel doesn't see won't hurt them.

Those who are given to snappy dressing (which, when compared with me, includes most people) should follow the golden rule given at the beginning of this chapter: if in doubt, leave it out. There is no need for a great wardrobe: most people are not going to see you two days running, let alone the same clothes. Ladies would be well advised to carry a skirt, however; in some Catholic countries, women in trousers are still frowned upon. My wife finds that silk, which can be rolled neatly, takes up very little space and looks good (as well as feeling good) when needed.

Equipment

Wallet, chequebook and cheque cards, credit cards, travellers' cheques or cash; these come at the top of the list because you can use them to replace anything that you forget or damage. It is worth remembering that a spare pair of jeans, for example, will cost you very little more in most European countries than they would at home – so why pack a spare pair 'just in case'?

Toothbrush *and container*. Soap and shampoo (or use a liquid soap like Badedas; it's easier to carry, and doubles as shampoo). Lavatory paper (apart from its obvious use, it is also a good mopper-up and source of handkerchiefs). A small first-aid kit, at least sticking plasters, aspirin or codeine, and some sort of soothing ointment. Add a bandage for those countries that insist you carry a first-aid kit. Any cosmetics and beauty aids you believe in (sun lotion, deodorants, lip salve, antihistamine, etc) Insect repellent if you can find one that works. Contraceptives (especially in Catholic countries: easy to forget, hard to replace). Rubber contraceptives apparently make useful emergency water carriers: this is said to be the reason why military survival kits carry them. Razor (or grow a beard). Spare spectacles or contact lenses if you wear them. Dental floss and toothpicks if you use them.

Swiss Army Knife (the sort with lots of blades, toothpick, tweezers, etc). Comb, pen, notebook. Spare set of keys: I didn't lose my last set of BMW keys, because I know where they are: on top of a petrol pump just outside Lisbon (though I suspect they've been moved by now).

After this lot, you are down to non-essentials and personal choice. Some people carry a towel; I prefer to rip off a few paper ones from convenient rest-rooms at intervals, but if you're camping you'll need one. I always carry at least one camera, which has to be well protected against vibration if screws are not to work loose. Something simple and mechanical, like the Leicas and Nikons I use, is often more reliable and always easier to repair than an electronic wonder. Film must be protected from excessive heat, or the colours go funny.

Whatever you decide to take, make a check-list – and keep it, so that you can add to it anything that you find you cannot live without. This may seem a rather sketchy section, but it is intended to provoke you into making your own checklists. Ours are given on pp. 60–61.

Camping

The 'kitchen sink' school of camping, with 5-room tents, folding tables and chairs and stoves (and kitchen sinks!) and so on, is not really appropriate for motorcyclists – though you do occasionally meet Harley-Davidson and Goldwing owners in the United States who go in for this sort of thing. Having a trailer helps – and who wants a trailer on a motorcycle? Come to that, who wants a trailer on a Honda Goldwing?

At rock bottom, if you go to a warm country, all you need is a sleeping bag. You can eat your food cold, or cook it over a camp fire – though the number of places where camp fires are legal is decreasing steadily. This is cheap, and very uncomplicated, but you run into trouble (a) if it rains and (b) if the local police take exception to you. Getting out of the way obviously helps with the latter.

Roger - Clothes

6 prs. cotton socks
2 prs Damart socks
4 prs. underpants
4 T-shirts
2 sweatshirts
2 prs. jeans
Quilted vest
Waterproof jacket
"   trousers
Gauntlets
Riding boots
Trainers
2 x Indian scarves

Other

Wallet, chequebook, cards,
credit cards, money, Swiss
army knife, KEYS, pen
Washbag (toothbrushes,
toothpaste, dental floss, toothpicks,
pHisohex, shampoo, deodorant, lip
salve, first aid kit, tissues.
Maps. Cameras + film

Clothes – Frances

6 pr. socks – (cotton)
wooly outer socks
6 pr. underpants *
2 bras
2 cotton rollnecks
1 set long underwear
2 sweaters
2 blouses
2 pr. jeans
1 skirt or denim pinafore dress
1 leather jacket
1 set waterproofs
2 prs. gloves
  1 light – 1 heavy
1 pr. riding boots
1 pr. shoes
2 large cotton Indian scarves

* Note: two pairs of underpants are nylon – to be worn only when necessary but easily washed, and dried

The next stage up involves a groundsheet or two to make a bivouac, but most people will prefer a lightweight tent. A Primus or similar stove, or one of those solid-fuel things which take forever but cannot go wrong even when you are hopelessly drunk, completes this scene. You can also get a surprising variety of very edible freeze-dried foods, which just need boiling water to make them ready to eat. The best way to prepare for this sort of trip is to go to a good camping store: if you have not been to one lately, you may be amazed at what they have. A device which intrigued me, and which I use often, is a sort of straw through which you can suck even polluted water, and get something drinkable and safe, even if it tastes fairly unpleasant. *Inodium* are the best anti-diarrhoea tablets I have ever found, if worst comes to worst, but they are *powerful* and not to be taken lightly.

If you have no experience of camping, or if you have not camped out since you were a kid, you would do well to get an up-to-date book on the subject, or better still to go with someone who is an experienced camper. There is really not space to cover the whole camping experience here, so all I can do is to point out a few of the more important considerations.

Good camping gear is surprisingly expensive, and bad camping gear is not really worth having. You have to be reasonably sure that you are going to use the stuff several times if you are going to get your money's worth: otherwise, you might as well use youth hostels and cheap guest-houses, which will cost you about the same as kitting out. Some camping stores will hire stuff out, and you should always cast an eye over government surplus stores: ex-government entrenching tools are useful for burying rubbish, digging toilets, and so on, for example.

If you travel with someone else, you can split the load, and if there are any troubles they can be shared. Furthermore, if you have to go shopping, one can stay at the camp as a guard. If you travel with a lover, you had better be pretty sure about the relationship!

Choose your camp site carefully – or use an 'official' one. Although the Scandinavian countries have something which translates as the 'all-man's-right' to camp on private land, provided you cause no damage, other countries are not so liberal. Ask permission wherever possible; get well out of the way otherwise. Watch out for land that will flood if it rains – even experienced campers get caught out on this one from time to time.

Always pitch camp in daylight; it makes life far easier. It also means that you can read warning signs about private property, wild animals, etcetera. I know deer are harmless; but they don't look harmless at six in the morning when they are scratching themselves on your tent post.

Always try camping with friends on a short trip before you commit yourself to a longer one.

The only real attraction of camping as far as I am concerned is that it is cheap; even the more expensive camp-sites are unlikely to damage your budget much, and if you decide to camp in woods or fields you can live for next to nothing. Some cities even have camp sites within the city, and others provide covered accommodation of various sorts, so you need not be confined to the countryside.

There are some people, however, who like camping for its own sake. I must admit that I cannot agree with them; but if you like to rise early, breathing fresh, clean air, and to wash in a stream, it does have its attractions. In any case, it's better than staying home. . . .

Packing and loading

The traditional motorcyclists' approach to packing and loading was to use a great deal of codline, and to lash things more or less haphazardly to the bike itself. Nowadays, Aerolastics or 'bungies' have replaced the codline, but there are still some diehards who use this approach to fasten bedrolls, pots, pans, parcels, Primus stoves, and indefinable lumps to their machines.

There are, however, three major drawbacks to this approach. First, it is insecure. Things fall off when you are riding along, and are stolen when you stop. Second, loading and unloading takes forever, especially in the rain; you also have to make dozens of trips if you are carrying things up to a hotel room, which by Sodd's Law will be up five flights of stairs with no lift. Third, the load is likely to be aerodynamically inefficient, badly distributed, and dangerous in an accident. If you want to retain fair fuel consumption and handling, and reduce the risk to yourself and others, you are going to need to be a bit scientific.

The first thing to consider is the maximum permitted weight of the motorcycle, which is usually given in the rider's handbook. This is not just an arbitrary number; the manufacturer has calculated what his machine can carry, and this is the result of his calculation. There will be a safety factor in his figuring, you can be sure, and exceeding the maximum permitted weight by a few pounds – even ten or twenty – is unlikely to matter; but in some countries it is technically an offence to exceed the maximum permitted weight (hereafter called the m.p.w.), so it is worth keeping an eye one it.

The m.p.w. of the R100RS is 970 lb. Ready to roll, the bike itself weighs about 500 lb. A solo rider, fully kitted out, might weigh 200 lb, so he could carry 270 lb of luggage – enough for anyone. Even a lightweight pillion rider will eat into this quite dramatically, however: the original '101 pounds of fun' is likely to weigh 120 lb by the time she is kitted out. If she is a bit on the cuddly side, 150 lb is by no means out of the way; this leaves 120 lb of luggage. Even so, this is still plenty of luggage by anyone's standards.

Consider, however, the MZ TS250/1 Supa 5. The m.p.w. is 704 lb; the bike weighs about 330 lb. Add a 200 lb rider and you have 174 lb available for luggage. But a 120 lb (dressed) pillion passenger leaves only 54 lb for baggage; a 150 lb passenger leaves only 24 lb. You can see why smaller bikes are better for solo touring. . . .

It is also instructive to look at the power-to-weight ratios of the machines. A R100RS with a 200 lb rider and no luggage has a power-to-weight ratio of about 225 bhp/ton; at the m.p.w., it is about 160 bhp/ton. The MZ, under the same conditions, goes from about 80 bhp/ton to about 60 bhp/ton. This still has most family saloons beaten hollow (30–50 bhp/ton), but it means you lose a lot of 'zip'.

Next, you need to consider weight distribution. In order to have the minimum effect on handling, you must keep the weight as low as possible, and inside the wheelbase. A moment's thought will show that a big heavy bike with a long wheelbase is best, because the added weight will have a smaller effect on a heavy machine and because it is easier to get the load inside the wheelbase. It is worth remembering that a pillion passenger is a form of luggage, too: on my MZ, I used to carry various girls on the pillion with no problem at all, but when one day I gave a lift to a big (6'4", 180 lb) male friend, the handling terrified me: a 'tank-slapper' threatened every time I braked. He was tall, he was heavy, and his centre of gravity was just slightly behind the wheel spindle.

The best place for luggage is on the tank, because extra weight that far forward rarely does any harm. Furthermore, it is quite easy to insulate whatever you carry in a tank bag from high-frequency vibration, by using a few soft clothes at the bottom. I always carry my cameras there, along with film and paperwork – passport, insurance, and maps – so that I can snap it off the tank and carry it if I leave the bike.

Actually choosing a tank bag is more difficult than it seems, because the temptation is always to get the biggest one possible. You have to keep a sense of proportion here: a bag that is too big may obstruct handlebar movement, make it difficult to see the instruments, and tend to topple or slide off, especially at low speeds. It is better to get a slightly smaller one which is more manageable. Some are more waterproof than others, too: a tank bag cover may be advisable in really nasty weather. The bag itself should be quickly detachable from the bit that holds it onto the bike, and it should have a handle or (preferably) a shoulder strap so that you can carry it. Some bags are fitted with locks, and can also be locked onto the tank; as a stout penknife will soon cut the straps around the tank, or slash into the bag, this seems a bit useless. A few bags can be divided into two sections, either of which can be used on its own or which can be used together. This is sometimes handy, especially if you are staying in a guest-house and only want to carry passports, etc., but it is not a decisive feature. Whatever bag you buy, always try it on the bike before you hand over the money.

The next choice, after a tank bag, is panniers. Like tank bags, these vary widely in quality, but the best sit as far forward as possible without interfering with the pillion's legs, and are reasonably deep from top to bottom: some of the little dinky Hondastyle panniers seem to be far too high and small. The best panniers are generally agreed to be Krausers; they can be unlocked from the pannier frame and used as suitcases, and specially-made inner bags are also available (at a price!) which fit inside the panniers and afford extra protection. The only real objection to Krausers is that the locks are pretty feeble, both on the panniers themselves and on the pannier-to-frame latch.

Cheaper panniers are usually not quickly detachable, but this is not necessarily a disadvantage: it makes them harder to steal, though anyone with a crowbar or a small axe would not have much problem. Some, like Krausers, come with proper fitting kits, while others require a degree of creative bodgery. Their big advantage is that they can be as little as a quarter of the price of Krausers.

Cheaper still are soft throw-over panniers. Although they offer next to no security, they can always be carried over the shoulder, cowboy-style, when you leave the bike. They also have the great advantage that they can be slung as far forward as you can stand, even over the tank: tank-mounted panniers are even better than tank bags from the point of view of weight distribution, though some designs on some bikes may blow around a bit. Fairings rarely leave room for tank-mounted panniers, always assuming that your knees do!

The third standard way of carrying luggage is the rear rack, with or without a 'top box'. If you have a tank bag and panniers, you will probably do best without a top box, just lashing lightweight stuff such as bedrolls and warm jackets to the rack with bungies; use those ugly nylon stuff bags, with an extra spray-over of waterproofing, to protect them. The risk with a top box is that you will overfill it with heavy things, because it is so convenient and (usually) the most secure place on the motorcycle. The most dangerous from this point of view are those huge hampers which are advertised as being able to take two full-face helmets, and have a rail and grid on top so that they can be even more overloaded. On a big bike, like a Goldwing or even a CBX, they are still within sight of the rear wheel; on a CX500, the rack is already hung out well behind the rear wheel, and a big top box is a recipe for disaster. If you look at police motorcycles, you will usually find that they have single seats, and the top-box is mounted where the pillion would normally sit, inside the wheelbase.

As a rough guide to the weights you can carry in these ways, the tank bag should normally be up to anything that you can get into it – say a 20 lb maximum, given that you have to carry it. Panniers should not be too heavily loaded: about 25 lb per side is the normal limit. Finally, the rear rack should be very lightly loaded indeed: even a big machine is likely to feel funny with any more than 20–25 lb on the back, *including the top box itself* (most weigh 4–6 lb), and on a smaller bike, 15 lb is more realistic. This gives you a total carrying capacity of close to 100 lb on a big machine, perhaps 60–70 lb on a smaller one.

Once you have exhausted these three possibilities, you are going to be reduced to lashing things on with bungies, in the way described at the beginning of the chapter. If you do not have a passenger, you can obviously carry a lot on the pillion seat – but remember that you may have problems with security. A traditional place to carry a bedroll is under the headlamp, but not all machines are big enough for this: if it looks even slightly dangerous, don't do it. The same goes for other lash-ons; beware of sharp spiky bits which could damage you or someone else in the event of an accident. If you are carrying a Primus stove, billy-cans, and the like lashed to the outside of the bike, keep them well to the rear and consider using sleeping bags or something similar to pad the sharp edges.

There is also, of course, the possibility of carrying things about your person. If your riding gear is bulky enough, this is usually an excellent way to protect your camera: wear it round your neck. The danger is that if you do fall off, you will not only damage whatever you are carrying: you may also damage yourself. For this reason, it is better to carry strawberries, soft cheeses, and sandwiches in your pockets than bottles of wine, cans of beer, or tent-pegs. On the other hand, there is the story of the really hard case who fell off when he had two litres of red wine in his pockets. He looked at the slowly spreading red pool around him, dipped his finger in it, tasted it, and said, 'Thank God. It's only blood.'

However you pack stuff, your main considerations will be the same. First, you will need to keep things clean and dry: for this, plastic bin-bags are invaluable. They are also useful for carrying dirty clothes. Second, you will need to have some things more accessible than others. Maps, documents, and camera should live in the tank bag; the panniers should be packed with the wash-bag and underwear on top, so that you do not have to unpack the whole thing for an overnight stop. Third, keep the weight as low as possible – pack heavy things at the bottom – and finally, try to keep the bike reasonably balanced, with the panniers and lash-ons of equal weight either side. It does not matter so much once you are moving, but it does make the bike much easier to manhandle.

Last of all, I would repeat what I said at the beginning of this chapter. Unless you are certain that you cannot live without something, leave it behind. Excess baggage is tiresome to pack and unpack; it adversely affects performance, handling, braking, and fuel consumption; and it is just something else to get stolen. Most people are surprisingly honest – but not all!

6　　Food and Shelter

If money is no object, you are unlikely to be faced with many difficulties over food and accommodation. Even if your chosen hotel or restaurant is fully booked, a well-lubricated palm will suddenly cause someone to discover a cancellation, or a mistake; you will have no problems.

At the other end of the scale, if you are cutting expenses to the bone, there are equally few difficult decisions. You find somewhere you can camp for free, and you eat bread and cheese and perhaps a little *wurst* from the nearest supermarket, washed down with wine or beer from the same source or (if you must) water.

It is the in-between traveller who has the decisions to make, and this means most of us. Your choice of accommodation ranges from the expensive hotels, through more modest hotels, guest houses, and inns, to private houses, youth hostels, YMCAs/YWCAs, and then on to camping. The different types of accomodation are not mutually exclusive: you can camp for two nights, stay in a guest house on the third, and go to a youth hostel for the fourth. The same goes for food. You can enjoy a really good restaurant meal, and then make up for it by eating your next five meals as cheaply as possible; you can cook over an open fire; or you can adopt the easy course of having a picnic style lunch and a modest restaurant dinner in the evening. The permutations of good food and accommodation are endless.

What will be obvious to the English or American traveller, though, is that the choice available is both different from what is available at home, and very much greater. Riders from Continental Europe, however, will have some rather unpleasant surprises when they come to England.

Most English people have very little experience of hotels. It is a fairly small country, and there is simply not the need to cater to a travelling population that is covering large distances, as there is in Europe and the United States. As a result of this, hotels and similar institutions are thinner on the ground, except at recognized holiday resorts. They are also, as a rule, insanely expensive by European standards.

At the time of writing, a cheap hotel room in the United States was under $20. It would be basic and boring, the standard motel room of a thousand movies, but it would be clean and supplied with its own bathroom. Again at the time of writing, this corresponded to £14 or less. The prices that are quoted here will of course change, but they have remained fairly constant in their relationship for several years; you can soon make your own adjustments to allow for inflation.

In England, a similar room *without bath* in a guest-house, or private house which let out rooms, would not be much less. A cheap hotel room, in anywhere which called itself a hotel, would be unlikely to cost less than £18/$25 *without bath* – a comparable room, with bath, would probably cost £10/$15 more, and it is far from difficult to find rooms costing £40 or even £50 in what appear to be very modest hotels. Admittedly, your £40 room may have a lot more character; it may be Georgian, or Elizabethan, or even older. But it is still a lot of money!

In most of Europe, you have the best of both worlds. In the big cities, unless you know where to go, you can find yourself being stung quite badly: but even in Zurich, you can get a good room with bath for under £30/$45, and in Paris, which everyone who has not been there (or who has been to the wrong places) believes to be very expensive, you can get a perfectly agreeable room with bath for well under £20/$30. In the country, you should be able to find a room with bath for £10–15/$15–22, or a room without a bath for £5–10/$7–15. You can even stay in Paris for under £10/$15, if you are not too fussy. There won't be any bed-bugs, but it can get pretty seedy! All these prices are for *double* rooms; in most European hotels, the charge is by the room, not by the number of occupants, and you can sometimes get triple-bedded rooms which really bring the per-person cost down.

What is more, most of these places will have real character: they will be run by individuals, and they will reflect the character of those individuals. As a rule, it is only the more expensive hotels in Europe which sink into the kind of bland anonymity which characterizes American motels.

There is, however, one consolation which can make up for staying in English hotels: the English breakfast. Traditionally, this was always included in the price of the room, and it would usually consist of breakfast cereal; fried bacon, eggs, tomato, and bread; tea or coffee; and toast, butter, and marmalade. Sometimes you are allowed substitutions, such as fruit juice (almost invariably canned) for the cereal, or poached or scrambled eggs instead of the fried course. Whatever you eat, it is considerably more filling than the traditional continental breakfast of a couple of rolls or croissants, a little butter and jam, and coffee.

The only trouble is that fewer and fewer English hotels are including a proper English breakfast in the price of the room. Paradoxically, it is the more expensive hotels which do not provide it: the cheaper hotels and guest houses still do, for the most part. It has come to the point that you should always check whether breakfast is included or not.

On the other hand, an increasing number of Continental hotels do seem to include a breakfast in the price of the room – albeit a modest one, as described above – so it is also worth asking if breakfast is included in *their* prices. The only country where a hearty breakfast is regarded as normal in a hotel seems to be Holland, where you will quite likely get cold meat and cheese along with your bread.

Finally, on the subject of breakfast, standards can vary wildly. Do not expect Dickensian breakfasts in England as a matter of course; you will often be disappointed with a few slices of cold toast made from English sliced bread (the worst bread in Europe), a foil-wrapped pat of butter, and an individual serving of jam, together with a greasy and scanty fried breakfast. You may, however, be equally surprised at a spectacular meal, with fresh bread, good butter, home-made jam, sausages, ham, etc. It is all the luck of the draw, but you are likely to draw a bit luckier if you go out into the country, off the beaten track.

When it comes to finding a room to stay in, you have a number of options. As already mentioned, hotels are much more common in Europe than in England, and generally much more reasonably priced. I could never really tell the difference between hotels and guesthouses (*gasthof, pension,* etc), but the general rule is that guesthouses are slightly less impressive and slightly cheaper – though I have stayed in many guesthouses which would put a modest hotel to shame. Furthermore, each country has its own variations on the hotel scene. In France, for example, there are the *gites*. These are mostly rural and out-of-the-way, reasonably priced (but not cheap), and excellent value for money. There are also the *Relais Routiers*, which are basically transport caffs with accommodation – though a good deal better than this description might lead you to believe, whilst still remaining commendably cheap and very good value. In Spain there are the *paradores* and in Portugal there are the *pousadas*; these are state-run hotels specifically intended for travellers (in summer you may not be allowed to stay more than two or three days), but they are usually excellent. As a matter of principle, I will normally stay away from anything that is state-run; but after experiencing the *pousadas* of Portugal, I would not want to stay anywhere else. Mostly in superb rural locations, with delightful rooms and attached bathrooms, they are comparable in price with a very modest hotel room in England.

In England, and to a lesser extent in the rest of Europe, the tradition of the inn survives. Some inns are now indistinguishable from hotels, both in price and in anonymity, but others can be tremendous value or historically delightful or both. Even if a pub does not look as if it has any accommodation, ask; I remember once sleeping in a room on the Derbyshire moors which looked as if it had last been redecorated in the 1930s, and little used since. It was perfectly clean, and the bed was well aired; but I still had the sensation of being in a time-warp.

Rooms in farmhouses and other private houses are another possibility. Sometimes you may see a sign which says *Accommodation*, or *Chambres*, or *Zimmer*, but often you will simply have to ask – in a bar, or a restaurant, or a fellow-motorcyclist that you happen to meet. These will usually be the cheapest rooms of all, and often with an excellent breakfast either included in the price or available at a modest extra cost. If you are not an early riser, remember that most farmers are – and have to be. This may come as a bit of a shock!

As a general rule, the less you pay, the lower the likelihood is that your host will speak English, or indeed any other language except his own. This is less of a problem than you might think. Look at the ten-word vocabularies in the second part of this book for *room* and *how much?*, and try (by sign language) to get the price written down: 125 is 125, whether you pronounce it *one hundred and twenty five* or *cent-vingt-cinq*. If he just holds up fingers, write it down yourself and show him, just to make sure. Of course, finding out if baths, or breakfast, are included is another matter; you will just have to exercise your ingenuity. Remember, though, that if he is in the business of letting rooms, he is going to want your custom; he is going to try to communicate with you.

It is always a good idea to look at the room before you take it. Only very rarely will you get somewhere truly awful, and even then you may decide to take it because you cannot face going any further, but if you do have time and you don't like the room, do not be afraid to say that you think you will go a little further and look for somewhere else.

Apart from this, there are two good general rules about finding accommodation. The first is to start looking reasonably early: the higher the holiday season, the earlier you start looking. In early spring, or late autumn, you can safely leave it until eight o' clock or even later; in the height of the season, even four o'clock is not too early to start. The second rule is to stay out of the big towns as much as possible: prices will be lower, and availability will be higher. Frances and I were in Köln once for Photokina, and rooms were almost impossible to find; when we did find one, it was alarmingly expensive. An hour outside the city – say forty miles – we found a much better place at just over a quarter of the price. With a motorcycle, staying outside a city and visiting it for the day is practical in a way that it could not be in a motor-car.

You may have noticed that so far, I have not said a thing about booking in advance. This is because I have never found it necessary (though there have been a couple of close calls), and because I don't like being tied to a schedule. The only exception I will make to this is if I am travelling between two places which can pass on bookings – the *paradores*, for example – when I can ask the place I am staying to book the next night or couple of nights for me. I might also consider it if a local tourist office offered to book me in somewhere that night; many will do this. Otherwise, the whole idea of booking in advance turns me off, the more so because it involves letters and telephone calls in foreign languages to places I have never seen, which may not be too attractive, and which are probably more expensive than the kind of place I could find if I went there in person. If you must book in advance, there are plenty of guide books which list places to stay, prices, addresses, and telephone numbers; this is something we just do not have the space for here.

These guide books are, however, very useful in two ways. First, they give you a good general idea of prices, especially relative prices for different countries and areas. Second, they tell you where to look, as already described in Chapter 2. You do not even need a current edition of the guide to get this information; often, you can pick up last year's edition in a discount bookshop for a fraction of the price of the current one. If you add 10% or so to the prices, you are unlikely to be far out, and you may even get some pleasant surprises.

If even modest hotels are outside your budget, but you still want to sleep between four walls with a roof over your head, the next thing to consider is youth hostels, YMCAs, and the like. I say 'and the like' because there are often other ways of getting a roof. Amsterdam is well-known for its 'sleep-ins', which provide really basic accommodation very cheaply, and (for example) at Sagres in southern Portugal there is a 'camp site' which is actually indoors. You only get a stone floor to sleep on, but it is dry and reasonably clean, and certainly cheap; well under £1/$1.50 at the time of writing.

On the other hand, it is also worth knowing that some Ys operate more like hotels than like basic dormitories, and consequently the price range can be enormous. Again at the time of writing, a Y could cost you from £3 to £15 ($4.50 to $22.50), depending on whether you stayed in a dormitory or in a private single room. Youth hostels tend to be at the bottom end of that price range, but some of them still have the old system of sharing chores like washing, sweeping, etc.

If you have never stayed at Ys and youth hostels, you may find that they are not quite what you expected. The Ys, for example, are nothing like so offensively Christian as you may have imagined. It is true that they have talks, and sometimes religious services, for anyone who is interested; but they do not stuff their religion down your throat, and indeed on most occasions they will improve your opinion of Christianity by their open, honest, and friendly behaviour.

The Ys tend to be concentrated more in city centres, and (as already mentioned) to afford quite a range of accommodation. Many are now co-educational, especially the YMCAs (actually, I've never come across a YWCA that

admitted men). You do not need to belong to any
organization, or even church, to use them; you can usually
get their addresses either from the tourist office of the
country concerned before you go, or from local tourist offices
while you are travelling. If you go for the dormitory
accommodation, then you will have to sleep alone, but it
may be possible to share a room with your lover if you take
a private room or if it is out of season. The only real catches
with the Ys are that they are patchily sited – you can find
large areas without a Y for miles – and that they can fill up
quite quickly; a phone call ahead may be a good idea.

Youth hostels are more inclined to be rural, because
they were originally founded for hikers in the last century; in
fact, it is only recently that some have been prepared to
accept people who arrived in cars or on motorcycles, rather
than on foot or by bicycle. They are usually very basic
indeed, but they are also very cheap – often less than the
cheapest accommodation at the Y. What you get is a bed in
a dormitory, (usually) the use of cooking utensils, and
blankets. You will need your own sheet sleeping bag, which
is nothing more than a sheet sewn into a bag shape, with a
space for a pillow, and your own cutlery. Many of the
hostels will have sheet sleeping bags for hire: some
of them actually make it compulsory to hire them, though
the cost is very low.

If you want to use the youth hostel network – and there
are about 4,500 in 49 countries – you have to join your
national Youth Hostel Association. This costs very little, no
more than the price of a couple of gallons of petrol, and
after that you need only show your card to get really cheap
accommodation. Despite the name, there is no age limit,
except in Bavaria – and even there, it is not always enforced.
There are, however, *minimum* age limits in some countries,
whilst some hostels in some countries have facilities for
families. Out of season, you may even be able to arrange to
share a room with your lover: it depends on the space
available, and the disposition of the Warden. The best way to
get an idea of the youth hostel scene in the various countries
is to buy the International Handbook of the YHA, which lists
them all together with addresses, facilities, and regulations.
Volume 1 is the one you want; it covers Europe and the
Mediterranean. Volume 2 covers the rest of the world. They
are very inexpensive.

One thing which is worth knowing, though, is that the YHA in Britain and some other countries is currently undergoing something of a shake-up. The traditional users of youth hostels are becoming fewer and fewer, and the hostels themselves are being forced to change and adjust to late twentieth century conditions. Unless they can attract more users, they may not survive; it is worth patronizing them while they are still there. They can be dank and gloomy, with wardens like sergeant-majors; they can also be very friendly, with a club-like atmosphere and a lot of swapping of travellers' tales and useful hints. Fortunately, the latter is more usual.

The cheapest form of accommodation is undoubtedly camping, but if you use official camp-sites with all facilities it is very little cheaper than youth hostelling, and much harder work. On the other hand, you are your own master. You have a wide choice of places to stay; you can move at a moment's notice; and there are few if any rules and regulations.

If there are two of you, then camping begins to look a lot cheaper than youth hostelling. This is because most (but not all) camp sites charge on a per-site basis, or only add a very small supplement for a second person, whereas youth hostels charge on a per-person basis. If in addition you camp 'wild', away from the authorized sites, you can really save money. As already mentioned, the right to camp is enshrined in the law in some countries, and in most countries, it is perfectly legal to camp on private land if you have the landowner's permission. In few countries, notably the Communist ones, you *must* camp at official sites. It is true that what the police don't see, they can't grieve after, but if they do catch you, you may have trouble.

If you are already an experienced camper, there is little to learn about combining camping with motorcycling; your only real problem is going to be finding the best way to stow the tent on the motorcycle. If you are not an experienced camper, then there is not enough room here to tell you all about it. Camping is not as easy as it looks: you really do need a bit of basic knowledge first, and I would recommend that you read a book on the subject.

Actually finding campsites is not difficult at all. They are normally well signposted, and various national tourist offices and guide-book firms put out lists – though not all lists describe the facilities available. Finding unofficial sites is another matter; I refer you back to the books again.

One specialized branch of camping is the rally scene. The big European rallies, such as the Starfish at Zandvoort and the Faelke Treffen in Denmark, are a rare opportunity to meet other motorcyclists and eat, drink, and sleep bikes (preferably along with food, booze, and women!). There are endless others: one-make rallies, bad-weather rallies, Poser's rallies, and so forth. The best way to find out exactly where and when these are held is to read the motorcycle press: more and more rallies nowadays are pre-book only (to avoid gatecrashers), and many shift their location from year to year for the same reasons. Conditions vary from the slightly primitive to the extremely primitive, and there are some which have few attractions unless you are into heavy metal rock and beer-throwing; but you'll never know until you try one. When addresses are given in the magazines, either send the money as requested or send a stamped self-addressed envelope (or an International Reply Coupon, available at post offices) to be sure of an answer.

Going on from accommodation to food and drink, the range of choice is again tremendous. What you eat, and where you eat it, depends on your budget, your personal tastes, and where you are: it also depends, enormously, on which meal you are talking about.

We have already looked briefly at breakfast. If the hotel does not provide it, and if you still want breakfast, you have three main choices. The first is to carry your breakfast with you, and eat it in your hotel room: yoghurt, bananas, and biscuits are useful here. If you are of a more heroic constitution, try cheese, bread, and beer. The second is to go out and eat breakfast. This is difficult in England and Ireland, but in most of Europe you will be able to find a little cafe that serves a continental breakfast, and often an omelette or something similar as well. Unless you want to sit down and eat an omelette, it is usually much cheaper to have some coffee and a roll or croissant at the counter. In some countries, you may also care to try a 'heart starter' – a small cognac or something similar, either on its own or in your coffee. Puritans may be shocked; others may like the idea. The third option is to have some sort of picnic brunch, at ten or eleven, after you have been riding for a while. I must confess that this is my favourite, but unfortunately my wife is inclined to get downright evil if she does not eat shortly after getting up, so I don't do it any more.

Lunch is another matter. A picnic, with bread and cheese and fruit and wine, is almost invariably the best option if the weather is even half-way decent. It is cheap; it is delicious; and it is fun. In beer-drinking countries, such as Holland, Belgium, and Germany, you can substitute beer for the wine. In England, however, the English pub can be an excellent place for lunch. A pint or two of beer and a 'ploughman's lunch' (bread, cheese, and pickle, usually with a little salad) is reasonably priced and very pleasant; alternatively, you can try pork pies, various kinds of rolls, or even hot food served at surprisingly reasonable prices in many pubs. Standards and prices of pub food vary enormously, though, so it is as well to wait until you have caught a glimpse of what someone else has got before you order. In particular, avoid tourist-traps. For example the Jamaica Inn at Bolventor is a beautiful building – but it is overcrowded with tourists, and the food is overpriced and underwhelming, or it was the last time I was there. A few miles down the road, at Roche, there is the Victoria. The 'Vic', as it is known, provides better beer; a superb range of food (including handsome pasties) at very reasonable prices; a roaring fire in winter, which you can actually get near; and really friendly service. Mind you, I come from St. Denys myself, so I'm biased. . . .

You can, of course, eat a heavy lunch, but then the ground-rules are the same as for dinner. I find that a proper restaurant lunch, except in the winter, is not only hard on the wallet; it also slows me down more than I like in the afternoon, and it makes me even fatter than I am now.

For dinner, though, I do like to eat well. A good meal in a modest restaurant anywhere in Europe is likely to be a lot cheaper and a lot better than anything you could find at a comparable place in England, and quite a considerable improvement over most American restaurants. The thing to do is to go for the local food: that way, you get whatever is freshest, cheapest, and (usually) best cooked, because it is a traditional dish. If you insist on English or American-style food, you will pay handsomely for it and it may well be indifferent. Do not be afraid to try some of the more unusual dishes; I remember once surprising a French waiter by ordering *steak tartare*. He said, 'But m'sieu, you know eet is raw?'. When I told him that I did know, he beamed all over his face: he liked having an English customer who appreciated French food.

All this assumes that you can afford to eat like this. If you cannot, then your likeliest bet is to eat the same for dinner as for lunch; satisfy your need for hot food by ordering a bowl of soup in a *Relais Routiers* or somewhere else cheap. If you are youth-hostelling, you will normally have cooking facilities at the hostel; obviously, you are going to be restricted to fairly simple fried or boiled food (or reconstituted freeze-dried stuff, or cans), but at least you can eat hot food cheaply. Campers can of course try cooking boy-scout-style over an open fire, or with a portable stove. I would back the portable stove, every time.

There is a knack to finding the right wood; to building the fire and getting it to burn; to getting anything to cook on top of it; and to not setting fire to the surrounding countryside. Unless you have mastered all of these, in the Boy Scouts or elsewhere, you may find yourself going hungry a lot of the time, and eating half-charred, half-raw food the rest of the time. Seriously, do be careful about lighting any kind of fire in dry woodland or dry grass. You can do millions of pounds' worth of damage, and possibly kill yourself and other people.

However you decide to eat, do try to eat at least some of your meals at local restaurants. Good food is one of the great attractions of a holiday, as far as I am concerned, and if I have to restrict myself too far, I'd rather stay home. Remember too that there may be local 'fast food' or other ways of eating, which can be much cheaper than a usual restaurant meal. In München, for example, restaurants are fairly expensive, but if you eat in the *Bierstadt* that is maintained by one of the breweries as a showpiece, you will not only get excellent beer: you will also get (comparatively) cheap food. Again, local tourist offices are full of this sort of information, especially if you make a point of asking them to recommend somewhere cheap to eat.

One last note on food and accommodation. In most of Europe, motorcyclists are (as I have said) treated just like anyone else. In England, however, they are sometimes regarded as hooligans, yobs, and bad financial risks. Personally, I resent this very much when I have outside a motorcycle which probably cost more than half the cars in the car park. If I am refused service, I begin by being very

polite, and asking why. Sometimes, this will work; a
particularly good trick, if they tell you that they have no
rooms (and you are certain that they have) is to explain that
you have come a long way, and ask them if they can
recommend anywhere else nearby. Only if they persist in
being awkward is it worth becoming rude; ask them who the
hell they think they are, running some little tin-pot hotel or
bar and turning away custom. Call them fools to their faces,
and tell them that you will make sure that everyone you
know gets to hear about them. It probably won't do any
good – it may even make things worse – but you will feel
better for it, and it may even make them begin to think.

7   Formalities

In theory, the formalities required before one member of an EEC country can visit another are almost negligible. In practice, the old national pride and prejudices still apply; unless Your Papers Are In Order, you may be delayed, refused entry, or otherwise hassled – even thrown in jail. If you are not a citizen of an EEC country youself, or if you want to visit non-EEC countries, the formalities may be even more stringent.

On the other hand, border checks in most of Western Europe are now casual to the point of laxity. Most of the time, you will simply be waved through from one country to another. But it only takes one customs or immigration officer with a hangover, or a chip on his shoulder, to turn a minor oversight into a major event. It is not worth skimping on the formalities.

It is also worth remembering that if anything does go wrong, you will probably be struggling with a foreign language; you will have no idea of your rights, or of whether you have been told the truth; and your main ambition will be to get out of trouble as fast as possible.

Fortunately, it is very easy to avoid trouble – at least in Western Europe. In thousands of miles, I have only had a spot of trouble once. It happened because I went into Portugal late one night, just before the border closed for the evening (only the major crossings stay open all night), and the border guard was somewhat the worse for brandy. He had considerable trouble in focusing on the forms, let alone on filling them in, and although he was perfectly friendly about it, he evidently forgot to give me some vital piece of paper which I was supposed to hand back on the way out. The border guard on the way out clearly did not believe that I had never had this piece of paper; he thought that I had lost it. On the other hand, it would have been a lot of trouble for him to do anything about it. What he did, therefore, was to fill in a duplicate copy of this form, carefully marking it DUPLICATE, and to hand it to me. I handed it back to him, and he filed it with all the other pieces he had collected. Honour was satisified.

Although ignorance of the law is no excuse in any penal code (except possibly Bermuda), if you are a foreigner who appears to have made a genuine mistake, and who is polite and willing to answer questions, you are unlikely to run into any trouble. So don't worry: the things that you have to do are simple enough in the first place, and if you do accidentally screw up, you should be all right anyway.

For convenience, the formalities can be divided into three parts. First, there are those which affect all travellers: these might be called the 'personal' formalities. Second, there are the ones which affect you as a motorcyclist: these I have called the 'vehicle' formalities. And finally, there are those precautions – such as holiday insurance, as distinct from vehicle insurance – which make life easier if anything does go wrong. I have called these the 'desirable' formalities.

Personal

The first thing which everyone thinks of is the passport. In fact, it is quite possible to travel without one, but it does make life very difficult.

British subjects have a choice of two types. The more useful is the full passport, the hard-covered deep blue variety. Application forms are available from main post offices, passport offices, and some travel agents. In addition to the form, you will need two passport-specification photographs and (at least) a birth certificate. If you are not kosher British-born, you may also need to produce other documents listed on the passport application form notes. If you are a woman, and are, or have been, married, you will need your marriage certificate or divorce documents. Once you have filled in the long and inquisitive application form, you will need to have it countersigned (along with the photographs) by a 'Member of Parliament, Justice of the Peace, Minister of Religion, Lawyer, Bank Officer, Established Civil Servant, School Teacher, Police Officer, Doctor or a person of similar standing who has known you personally for at least two years' and who is also kosher British or a citizen of a Commonwealth country.

It will take anything from three weeks to three months for the bureaucrats to send you your passport, so apply in plenty of time. It is good for ten years from the date of issue. These passports are surprisingly valuable, so people try to steal them (it's not worth trying to sell them yourself, because you wouldn't know where to look for a buyer – and besides, it's very, very illegal). If you do lose yours, report the loss immediately to the local police and then to the British Embassy or the nearest British Consulate. Usually, they will give you a temporary passport which is good for up to 12 months, and which can be extended to the full validity of the lost passport once you return to the UK. This will happen very much faster if you know the serial number and date and place of issue of the passport, so make a note of it somewhere or even memorize it. Rarely, you may be given a Single Journey Emergency Passport, which (as its name suggests) is a get-you-home measure, or a short-term passport. Either the Consul or the local police may also insist that you go straight home immediately, but this would normally only be in very unusual circumstances.

The second type of passport is the British Visitor's Passport. This is about half the price of a standard passport, and can be obtained on demand at any main post office from Monday to Friday. Again you need two pictures, plus the following documentary evidence: a birth certificate OR adoption certificate OR National Health Medical Card in your present name OR a DHSS Retirement Pension Book or Pension Card BR464 in your present name OR an uncancelled Standard British Passport or British Visitor's Passport in your present name (or husband's / wife's if included on it). You do not need the counter-signature for these.

Although the BVP is cheaper and easier to get than a 'real' passport, its short life is one drawback, and another is that it is only good for some countries – basically, Western Europe plus Tunisia, Turkey, Greece, Bermuda, and Canada. It is no use in any Communist Bloc country, not even for travel through East Germany to West Berlin. There are also other restrictions: depending on how you acquired your British nationality, you may not be entitled to a BVP even if you are entitled to a full passport; you cannot use a BVP if the journey involves any paid business travel; and you cannot spend more than three months in any one nine-month period in the following group of countries: Denmark, Finland, Iceland, Norway, Sweden. Children under 16 years of age cannot travel on a brother's or sister's passport in Belgium, Luxembourg, or the Netherlands. All in all, the only reason for getting a BVP is if you run out of time to get a real passport.

Americans and other non-Europeans will, of course, require their own passports, which take about as long to order as British ones. The American variety, for example, takes between two weeks and two months to arrive, and lasts five years.

Visas are not required for most non-Communist countries, at least for the holders of Western European and American passports; Americans do particularly well out of this, given the vicious nature of their own visa requirements. On the other hand, most Communist countries do insist on visas: it satisfies the socialist love of control and paperwork, and brings in a useful amount of hard currency. Charges for visas vary, and so do the formalities: some can be issued at the border, and others require anything up to a couple of weeks' advance application at the embassy of the country in question, before you leave. Visa requirements can change, so check before you go, but the requirements for English and American passport holders given under each country heading were accurate at the time of writing (mid-1984).

Whether you have a visa or not, it is usually illegal to work in a foreign country unless you have a special visa which permits you to do so. Inside the EEC, residents of the EEC can theoretically work freely – but even then, the practicalities of the situation are rather different. If you plan on working, I suggest that you either read another handbook, or take only casual work and stay out of sight. This book is concerned mainly with touring; there are others which deal with work.

Some countries may also insist on inoculation certificates for certain diseases, though this is unlikely to affect travellers from the UK, the US, Canada, or Australia – unless they have been through a country known to be infected with a particular disease. For example, British travellers were required to have smallpox certificates a few years ago, as a result of a laboratory accident in Birmingham, which shows how arbitrary the whole system is. Remember too, that you may not be able to get back into your own country without one of these certificates, if you have been in an infected area. British travellers can (eventually) get a copy of the DHSS leaflet '*Notice to Travellers*', by writing to the Department of Health and Social Security, Alexander

Fleming House, Elephant and Castle, London SE1 – or, if
they are lucky, from a local DHSS office. American travellers
will have a more difficult time, because most American
doctors seem to be completely ignorant of (and indifferent
to) anything that happens outside the United States. Ring
the Immigration Service for advice, if desperate.

A passport (with visas, if necessary) is normally all the
documentation you will need to carry with you – inoculation
certificates are very rarely needed. At the borders, however,
there will be additional formalities.

Leaving your own country is rarely a problem. They will
inspect your passport, and that is about it.

Entering another country may involve any or all of the
following: passport inspection and immigration control,
health control, customs inspection, and currency inspection.
Immigration, customs, and currency control may also apply
as you *leave* some countries, especially Communist ones or
those which have had problems with an outflow of antiques.

Passport inspection is rarely a problem – just a quick
look – but immigration control may involve filling out a bit of
paper which is either retained by the immigration officer or
stuck in your passport (or both). If you are given any bits of
paper, don't lose them, because it will almost certainly slow
you down on the way out. Keep them in your passport. You
may be asked why you are visiting the country, how long you
intend to stay, and where you are staying. For the first,
always answer 'Tourism', and (If you feel like it), throw in a
bit about visiting their beautiful country. For the second, tell
them the *maximum* you intend. Always give them a number,
rather than being vague. Usually, it is not entered anywhere,
and there is never a penalty for leaving early, but staying
longer than you said can be a problem if it is entered in your
passport. The third is the trickiest. In most free countries,
'Just touring' is enough; in Communist countries, pre-booked
accommodation may be essential. If they hassle you too
much, decide whether you really want to visit the place
anyway.

Health control is usually a matter of noting where you
came from, and asking for an inoculation certificate if
necessary. Usually no problem – but if you need to be
inoculated, it can usually be done at this point.

Customs inspection is concerned with two things:
dutiable items, and prohibited items. These vary from country

to country, but as a general rule, anything that is genuinely for personal use will not be subject to duty. Even if there are rules, they are usually flexibly interpreted for tourists. For example, many countries limit the amount of film you can carry for your camera, but few actually apply the limit. In very rare cases, you may be asked to leave a deposit equal to the duty, which is refunded when you export the goods again. The only things you will be charged on in most cases are booze and tobacco (and perfume) over the duty-free limit set by the country. These duty-free limits are given in the country-by-country guides.

Prohibited and restricted items are another matter, and here the rules will be strictly applied. There are some things which may not be imported (such as switchblade knives into the British Isles), and others which may only be imported in limited quantities, and then subject to strict controls. Some of these restrictions are a matter of public health: for example, foodstuffs for private consumption may be OK, but quantities will be restricted. The most important example of this is the restriction on the import of animals into the UK. There is no rabies in Britain, and anyone in their right mind intends to keep it that way, so animals have to spend a long time in quarantine if they are to be imported at all.

The only prohibited and restricted items which will affect most motorcyclists are drugs of various kinds and (in some Communist countries) 'pornography'. I use the inverted commas because even *Playboy* is banned in some countries; you might also have some trouble with some of the heavier motorcycle magazines. Penalties for smuggling will depend on what you are trying to smuggle, and the country in question. At the least you can expect to have the offending material confiscated and destroyed; after that, there may be a fine, deportation, or even prison. If you have any reason to believe that you may be carrying prohibited or restricted items, read the notes at Customs (an English-language version should be available).

A special class of prohibited and restricted items is made up of things which may not be *exported* from a country. Old religious ikons in Greece are one example, but if you buy any reasonably valuable antiques, it is worth getting a letter from the dealer saying that their export is not prohibited. That way, if he does sell you anything that you cannot export, he will be fined. Again, this should not be a problem for most people. Some Communist countries will also inspect your baggage on leaving, in order to make sure that you have not left behind anything which could be used to overthrow the state. Believe it or not, even typewriters must be registered (with a sample of the type) in some countries, so that they cannot be used for publishing underground magazines. Tape recorders may be subject to the same restrictions. These things will be entered on your passport as you enter the country. If they are stolen, notify the police IMMEDIATELY, and expect a hard time both then and at the border.

Currency control may be concerned with four things. First, there is the amount of money you can bring into the country. Some will restrict the amount of their own currency that may be imported, and many will require that you declare the amount of money you are carrying if it is over a certain amount, no matter what form it is in. This is to make sure that you do not work in the country, or act as a courier to get money out. The amounts for these restrictions are listed country-by-country. Second, some countries may specify a *minimum* amount that you can bring into the country. This is to keep out hippies and anyone else who will not be able to support themselves. Few European countries insist on a set amount, and those that do so will only require a fairly nominal sum, but unless you have enough money to support yourself during your stay, you may be turned back under vague vagrancy laws. You would have to be fairly poor for this to happen, though. Again, the sums are in the country-by-country guide. Third, some Communist countries will insist that you change a certain amount of 'hard' currency – in other words, Western European or American, Canadian, or Australian money – at an official exchange rate, for each day that you are there. Often, there are three main exchange rates: the official rate for natives of the country (which is worst), the official tourist rate (which can be twice as high, in the tourist's favour), and the unofficial or black market rate which is always the highest, but also the most dangerous. You will get the tourist rate; if you want to try the black market rate, which may be several *times* better, be aware of the risks, which include confiscation of the money, additional fines, and deportation or prison. Never change more money than you have to. You can always change more money as needed, but changing surplus 'soft' currency back into 'hard' can be difficult or impossible – and, like any currency exchange deal, the rates always work against you. Finally, some countries place restrictions on the amount of money you can take *out* of the country. Again, this will often apply to their own currency, but it may also apply to any other currency which you failed to declare on entry, so if you are carrying large amounts of (say) dollars or pounds sterling, be sure to declare them on the way in. You would also be well advised to keep any currency exchange forms, because you may need them in order to change money back again, or to prove that you really have changed some money in their country. All this is covered in the country-by-country sections.

Vehicle formalities

The basic rules for vehicle documentation are the same in all countries; the exact details are given in the country-by-country sections. As a rule, however, you will need your driving licence; your insurance; and the vehicle registration document ('log book').

With the exception of a few countries, where no licences are required at all for mopeds, you must have a full licence for the size of motorcycle which you intend to ride. A British licence is all that is required in most Western European countries, but an international driving permit (IDP) is required for Andorra, Cyprus, Hungary, and Spain. Actually, a British licence is sufficient in Spain if it is accompanied by an official Spanish translation, but as these cost more than an IDP, the IDP is a better buy. Irish licence holders will also require an IDP in Austria and Greece. American requirements vary from state to state: some state licences are apparently more acceptable than others. Your local AAA office should know.

In practice, an IDP is a good idea anyway, as it tends to be more acceptable than a national licence, and gives the cop something he can read in his own language. It also has a picture of you in it; the British licence, with no photograph, upsets some people. They are not expensive, and they are valid for a year, so they are worth getting. In England, the AA and the RAC issue them. You will need two passport-type pictures (machine ones will do) and your British licence, and the IDP can be issued on the spot.

A fruitful source of confusion, however, lies in age limits.

As a general rule, most countries will honour the licences of other countries (or IDPs issued in those countries) even if the licence-holder would be too young to drive under the laws of the country which he is visiting. For example, a 17-year-old British full licence holder can ride in Germany, even though the age limit in Germany itself is 18. In some countries, though, the national age limits apply even to visitors; for example, in Norway, a visitor must be 18 if the *vehicle* is Norwegian registered. Just to add to the fun, the age-limits for different capacities of machines may vary even inside one country. Thus, in England, you can ride a 50cc low-powered moped at 16, but are forced to wait until 17 for a real motorcycle. In France, you can ride some mopeds at 14. Details are given in the country-by-country guide.

Age limits may also affect speed limits. Again in France, any driver who has passed his test within the last year, or who is 18, is restricted to 90 kph (56 mph) on all roads, and must display a black-on-white '90' sticker.

Moving on to insurance, there is more room here for confusion than you might think. Basically, anyone who holds a policy issued anywhere in the EEC is covered to the minimum legal requirement in all other countries of the EEC; but those minima vary widely. In the UK, for example, this is 'Road Traffic Act' coverage, which restricts the insurer's liability to paying damages for personal injury to third parties. Note that 'personal injury' bit: it means that if, for example, you dent someone's Rolls Royce and are found liable, *you* pay for repairs to the vehicle. In France, there is no such restriction on property damage claims, but there is an overall liability limit (at the time of writing) of Fr. 5,000,000 per claim; in Germany, it is DM 1,000,000, or DM 1,500,000 if more than one person is involved. These are very high limits, but it is worth knowing that they exist. As a result, it is worth getting a *green card*; these are also compulsory in several countries, including some in the EEC (Greece, Portugal, and Spain).

Green cards are not expensive; at the time of writing, the basic rates were £11/month for riders of 22 and over, and £15 a month for 21 and under. There are loadings for some countries, though: Czechoslovakia, Hungary, East Germany, and Yugoslavia are 50% more, and Turkey is 100% more. Bulgaria, Romania, and Poland are at standard rates, but give only third party cover. Malta and Cyprus are not signatories to the relevant convention, and special cover has to be arranged for these.

Most insurance companies will only willingly give three months' overseas coverage in a twelve-month policy, but you can usually arrange a small extension – perhaps even to four months – if you ask them nicely, or are an old and valued customer. Beyond this, you may decide to rely on mimimum cover in those countries where a green card is not required at the border, or you can insure yourself at the border in most cases (though not in Austria). This is an expensive option, but can be useful.

Americans, Canadians, and Australians may be able to arrange insurance at home, but if not, they should be able to take out a policy in England, and get a green card. English insurance is among the cheapest in Europe, but getting a policy for less than the standard one-year contract may be very difficult, especially if much of the time is to be spent touring. The easiest bet is to buy a one year policy, and resign yourself to the fact that you are going to throw away some of it.

The registration document is perhaps the simplest to deal with, but there are a couple of things worth knowing. One is that if the vehicle is not registered in your name, you will need special forms (obtainable from AA, AAA, and RAC) for Portugal, and a letter of authority from the owner *countersigned by a motoring organization* for Yugoslavia.

In fact, if you are riding a bike that is not registered in your name, it is a good idea for *any* country to have a letter of authority from the owner. Even if it is not compulsory, it will make life very much easier.

If Swansea has swallowed your log book, the DVLC may give you a V379 form, which serves as a temporary one, or a V204 for vehicles which have not been registered but which have been submitted for registration, if the DVLC holds the application papers. If you have trouble with Swansea, an International Certificate of Motor Vehicles (obtainable from motoring organizations again) may be easier than dealing with the computer or its slaves. It looks like an IDP and costs a couple of pounds.

Some countries also insist on International Distinguishing Signs (GB plates, for the UK), which must be affixed to the rear of the vehicle. The standard size is $6.9 \times 4.5"$, but a smaller version is acceptable for motorcycles. In Italy, Luxembourg, Holland, Norway, Portugal, Spain, and Switzerland you can theoretically be fined for not having an appropriate national plate, so you might as well get one. Incidentally, the plate refers to the country in which the vehicle is registered, not to the nationality of the driver.

Apart from this paperwork, there are also various other legal requirements which fit in here as well as anywhere else. To begin with, crash helmets are now almost universally compulsory, but there are no other legal requirements about protective clothing (goggles, gloves, boots) that I have been able to discover except in Czechoslovakia, where goggles are compulsory. The French insist that crash-helmets should carry a band of reflective tape, but this seems to be widely ignored; besides, only fibreglass helmets should have anything stuck to them.

In those countries which drive on the right-hand side of the road, headlamps should dip to the right. A stick-on mask is the easiest way to ensure this – or ignore it, if this cuts down your lighting too much. I've never heard of anyone being prosecuted, though there is the argument that left-hand dimming could be dangerous. Although French vehicles have to have amber lamps, foreign ones do not; this annoys the average French driver, who flashes his lights at anyone who uses white light, but that is their problem. I'd rather have the additional light. Besides, in England, side-lights *must* be white: if they are incorporated in the headlamp, as many are, you will be breaking the law if you put yellow nail-varnish all over your lamps. The countries which insist on daylight riding lights are listed country-by-country.

Other requirements, such as carrying a first-aid kit in Austria or a spare set of light-bulbs in France, are dealt with in the appropriate sections.

Desirable formalities

There are two kinds of desirable preparations which, although not compulsory, are a good idea. One kind will only matter in an emergency; the other kind will make life easier even if nothing goes wrong.

To begin with the second, it is worth getting a Eurocheque card, which will allow you to cash cheques on your own home account at foreign banks. This is extrememly useful, especially in emergencies, and it also saves you having to carry too many travellers' cheques, or an excess of cash. Otherwise, travellers' cheques are probably the most useful form of currency. In Europe, Thomas Cook's cheques are probably the most useful, followed by American Express.

If you are camping, it is worth getting a camping *carnet*, which acts as a sort of camper's passport. You can get one from the AA or RAC, or from various camping clubs. It is compulsory for camping in French national forests, or camping anywhere in Portugal or Denmark, but it is very useful elsewhere. It provides third-party and personal accident insurance in much of Europe while you are actually on the camp site, and it is an acceptable deposit in place of a passport at other places – a very good idea, as you never want to let go of your passport if you can possibly avoid it.

If you intend to travel during the high season, consider booking accommodation in advance, by phone or by letter (enclose an International Reply Coupon). Otherwise, don't leave it later than 3–4 pm to find somewhere to stay.

Moving onto the lifesavers for emergencies, one word says almost everything: insurance. In Britain, you can buy insurance policies against cancellation, personal accident, repatriation of yourself or your bike, third party liability, medical expenses, and duty indemnity (which covers duty payable if the bike is stolen abroad – though only rarely would anyone try to charge you duty if this happened). Read a specimen policy CAREFULLY, not just believing what you are told, and check carefully that motorcycling is not excluded or loaded – some policies charge 50–100% extra for motorcycling risks, or exclude them altogether. This sort of insurance is not particularly cheap, but nor is it very expensive, and the peace of mind it brings is worth the money. If anything does go wrong, the cost can be repaid ten or a hundred times over.

For both this insurance and your bike insurance, make sure that you know exactly what you have to do in order to claim. If you know beforehand, it is much easier to keep calm in the event of an accident; and if you can keep calm, it is much easier to avoid making things worse. The general drill for bike accidents is the same the world over: stop; never apologize or admit liability; get medical assistance if necessary; call the police if anyone has been hurt, if an unoccupied vehicle or property has been damaged and the owner cannot be found, or if required to do so by law (see the country-by-country sections). Get the names and addresses of witnesses, third parties, etc., and make a sketch, or take photographs, or both – these can be invaluable in settling claims. Notify your insurers, by letter, usually within 24 hours (check your policy), and give the names and addresses of any injured parties to them.

Finally, don't worry. Only very rarely does anything go wrong, and the chances are that it won't be you. If you are unlucky (or careless), be prepared – but don't be obsessive. You're supposed to be enjoying yourself, remember?

PART II

Introduction

Obviously, not everyone is going to visit every country in
Europe. What I have done, therefore, is to divide the various
countries into groups, on the basis of geography and
practicality, and put them roughly in the order in which most
of you will visit them – though some small countries, such as
Liechtenstein or even Malta, are grouped with their
geographical neighbours regardless of the fact that very few
motorcyclists will actually go there The groups are as follows:

1   The British Isles
2   France and Monaco
3   Western Europe
4   Southern Europe
5   South-Eastern Europe
6   Scandinavia
7   The Communist Bloc

I have followed roughly the same format for each of the
countries, beginning with why one should want to go there,
and what the country is like, then moving on to the practical
preparations for getting there, followed by customs and
similar formalities at entry. Next comes a brief appraisal of
what it is like to ride there, with speed limits, parking
regulations, and so forth, and finally there is a ten-word
capsule vocabulary and a guide to food, drink, and
accommodation.

Customs

The countries of the EEC are moving towards standardized customs allowances, and in order to save repeating the same information for each EEC country, the basic customs information is given here:

Item	Goods bought tax-paid in EEC	Duty Free or non-EEC goods
Cigarettes	300	200
or		
Cigarillos	150	100
or		
Cigars	75	50
Tobacco	400 gm	250 gm
Spirits	1.5 litres	1 litre
Sparkling or fortified wine	3 litres	2 litres
Wine	4 litres	2 litres
Perfume	75 grams	50 grams
Eau-de-Cologne	$\frac{3}{8}$ litre	$\frac{1}{4}$ litre

In addition, all countries have an 'other goods' or 'gifts' allowance, allowing goods to a specified value. All normal personal goods are allowed in duty free provided that they are re-exported, but watch out if (like me) you habitually travel with more than a few rolls of film; some countries impose limits, but I have never had any trouble. I just keep quiet!

If you are flying in from outside Europe, you *may* in some countries be entitled to twice the tobacco allowances given under 'duty free' above. There is usually an age limit for both booze and tobacco allowances, and where I have been able to discover it, I have given it.

As a general rule about customs, you can assume that they are looking for three things. One is full-scale commercial smuggling; one is dope; and the third is contraventions of the duty free booze and tobacco allowances. Stay clear of the first two, and inside the third, and you are very unlikely indeed ever to have any trouble. Note, however, that customs alowances can be changed or abolished at any time, so *read the instructions* when you get to the border.

Many people like to combine their touring holiday with a trip
to at least one of the great European races. The usual
sequence in the Grand Prix circuit is something like South
Africa, Italy, Spain, Austria, West Germany, France,
Yugoslavia, Holland, Belgium, Britain, Sweden, and San
Marino. The other two great races are the 24 Heures du
Mans and the Isle of Man. Sometimes, it may be possible to
combine two races in a single holiday. For example, in 1984,
the Dutch GP at Assen was held on June 30th, and the
Belgian Grand Prix at Francorchamps on July 8th; as always,
on consecutive weekends.

Usually, there is camping land available near a Grand
Prix or other major race, and this is the form of
accommodation that most people will choose; otherwise, any
form of hotel can be prohibitively expensive, unless you book
well in advance. Rules and facilities at the camp site will vary
widely, not only from site to site but even from year to year.
For a general guide to attitudes, see the notes on police
attitudes for the various countries concerned.

Several companies organise holidays based around
Grands Prix, and they invariably advertise in the weekly and
monthly magazines. There are advantages to using their
services, of course: they take care of a lot of details, and the
tickets, etc., are often included in the price. On the other
hand, they tie you in to someone else's schedule, and they
do have their own profits to make. Usually, the bare
minimum of preparation is enough: just roll up the day
before the race, look for the rest of the motorcyclists, pitch
your tent, and lay in a supply of booze and food. On that
point, it is worth buying provisions as far from the race as
possible, as prices will go through the roof on race day, and
the junk food on the course will be nothing like as good as
the picnic you can bring with you.

At the race itself, and probably at the campsite, expect
all facilities (or 'any facilities', in some cases) to be
overloaded – toilets, water supply, anything – and to live
rough for a while. Beware of rip-offs; carry any valuables with
you, and put them in the bottom of your sleeping-bag at
night. It's not other motorcyclists you have to worry about –
it's the professional thieves who attend all the races.
Likewise, if you ride anything very desirable (or anonymous
and easily saleable), chain it up thoroughly, or, better still,
use a good proprietary lock such as Citadel or Kryptonite.

Observe these simple precautions, as the warning always goes, and you'll probably have one hell of a party, acquire a really evil hangover, and even see a little racing.

There is no point in trying to give any more exact details here, because the dates vary from year to year, the races are sometimes held at different circuits (e.g. both Montjuich and Jarama in Spain), and the circuits themselves may be lengthened, shortened, or otherwise altered. For detailed planning, consult the motorcycling press; most magazines publish the full racing calendar at the beginning of the season, and then list the remaining races after the report of each Grand Prix as it happens. You may also find special offers on ferry crossings!

The British Isles

Introduction

Everyone realizes the distinction between the United
Kingdom and the Republic of Ireland, but few people are
aware just how many real legal differences there are between
the various parts of the British Isles. Scottish law is often
quite different from English (though not, mercifully, the law
relating to motorcycling), and the Channel Islands enjoy a
measure of independence in tax-gathering which makes
them a sort of internal tax haven. The Isle of Man is home to
the famous Tourist Trophy because racing on English roads
(but not Manx) is illegal. Even those formerly sovereign
countries which are all but completely absorbed still have
strong independent feelings – ask any Cornishman or
Welshman!

The variety to be found in the British Isles is truly
extraordinary, and anyone coming from outside Europe
might do well to start their tour there; if nothing else, the
language makes life easier for Americans, Australians,
Canadians, South Africans, and New Zealanders. This
section may also be of interest to the native English, as a
guide to the approach and prejudices underlying the other
sections.

Great Britain

'Severe storms in English Channel – Continent Cut Off.'
Whether that headline ever really appeared or not, there is
no doubt that the British Isles are both a part of Europe and
separate from it. For English-speaking non-Europeans, Great
Britain is a natural starting-point for a European tour, though
English English and (for example) American or Australian
English can display some surprising differences. For those
from Continental Europe, England is certainly somewhere
different; and for the British themselves, the United Kingdom
is a good place to get some experience at touring (albeit at
very high prices) before crossing over to Europe.

There is no need to say anything about the historical
and cultural attractions of Great Britain, and there are many
other reasons for visiting. There is a surprising range of
scenery, from the garden-like or park-like South-East to the
moors of Scotland, Yorkshire, and the West Country. The
North Cornish coastline is truly spectacular, and so are the
Scottish Highlands. Many people do not realize that there
are ski resorts in Scotland, too.

The British pub is the spiritual home of many
motorcyclists – some are hosts to regular meetings of
motorcycle clubs – and there is still a strong sense of
camaraderie among riders, although this may be due in part
to the way in which motorcyclists are regarded in British
society. The British Ministry of Transport seems determined
to persecute them, their image in the press is poor,
motorcycles are widely castigated as dangerous (despite the
fact that the real accident rate, adjusted for the increase in
the number of riders, has been falling for a decade or so),
and there are still hotels, pubs, and restaurants which have
signs outside saying NO MOTORCYCLISTS. Fortunately, this
attitude is not widespread, but it is fair to say that the social
standing of motorcyclists is lower in England than anywhere
else in Europe – though still better than the United States,
where deliberate attempts by car drivers to kill motorcyclists
are not unknown.

In general though, the British are far friendlier than their image abroad might lead you to believe, and riders of old British machines will find that they are well received, sometimes by old men who remember the great days of the British motorcycle industry. The names roll off the tongue: AJS, Brough, Matchless, Norton, Panther, Rudge, Triumph, Vincent. . . .

Motorcycles are popular, from mopeds and small commuter bikes to the biggest available; at the time of writing, 16-year-olds could ride mopeds and learners of 17 and above were restricted to 125cc bikes until they passed a test. Visitors from abroad are subject to the same age limits; most national licences are acceptable. Because there are so many machines, and such a great tradition of motorcycling, British mechanics can compare with the finest in the world; but they are also very variable, both in quality and in price, so it is as well to go to one that is personally recommended rather than to the first that catches your eye. The spares situation is probably as good as anywhere in the world, though if you are in (say) the Scottish Highlands, you may have a rather longer wait than if you were in a big city.

The **road network** is excellent, whether you want fast toll-free motorways, good open roads, or winding back lanes. The only exceptions to this are in towns, where roads may be very narrow, congested, and badly maintained, and in few places where motorways have not been built to relieve heavy traffic, so that it is forced to use roads laid out hundreds of years ago for horse-drawn traffic and scarcely improved since. A really powerful motorcycle is useful on these roads, where the opportunities to pass may be extremely limited. The only tolls are on a few bridges and tunnels, and, of course, on ferries (now increasingly rare), but they are never very much, and in some cases motorcyclists are exempt.

Similarly, **petrol** is widely available at about average prices for Europe, though it may confuse some people because metrication is far from complete, so petrol may be sold by the Imperial gallon (about $4\frac{1}{2}$ litres, $1\frac{1}{4}$ US gallons). The usual grades are two-star (92–93 octane), three-star (94–95 octane), and four-star (96–98 octane). No form of discount vouchers is available for tourists.

Choosing **when to go**, and how long for, is not easy. The warmest weather is unquestionably in late June/July/August, but only in high summer can you rely on temperatures going much above 70° (80° is a 'heatwave'), so 'warm' is a relative term. Rainfall is highest in late autumn and winter, so if you want to avoid summer crowds (especially at the better-known tourist resorts), spring is a good alternative; even as early as early as mid-March it can be very attractive, though daytime temperatures in April are seldom likely to exceed 60°. Allow plenty of time; people who reckon to 'do' Britain in (say) five days before going on to Europe almost invariably regret it. Allow at least ten days to see a representative sample of England, and two weeks or more if you want to include Scotland or Cornwall or Wales as well.

Papers, preparations and legal requirements are not very demanding. You will need a pasport, but very few countries are subject to visa requirements: you are normally given a 6-month entry stamp when you arrive. For the bike, you will need the registration document, known to the British as the log book, your national licence, and proof of insurance. Insurance is not sold at the frontier, and you will not be allowed to ride until you have it, but it can easily be arranged at innumerable insurance agencies within the British Isles. If you have EEC insurance, you will be covered to the minimum limit required by British law, but this is not very much: although your insurers' liability to third parties for injuries is unlimited, there is no legal requirement to insure against property damage. A Green Card is, therefore, extremely desirable.

Helmets are compulsory, but that is all. Daylight riding lights, first aid kits, spare bulbs, etc., are not required. The helmet law *is* enforced.

The British Isles are served by several rather overpriced **ferries** from the European mainland; the Boulogne, Calais, and Oostende routes are fastest and cheapest, though there are exotic options such as Santander (Spain) and Roscoff (Britanny) to Plymouth, the Hook of Holland to Harwich, and various Scandinavian ports to Hull, Goole, and the like. The hovercraft is easily the best bet, being cheap, fast, and convenient. On many occasions I have arrived with only a few minutes to spare, but still been able to get on, because there is almost always room for a motorcycle. At the ports, customs tend to be perfunctory; the EEC allowances are the standard, with the 'other goods' allowance at £28 for goods bought duty free or outside the EEC, £120 for goods bought and taxed within the EEC. There are all kinds of forbidden goods, but two of the more important ones are self-defence tear-gas canisters and switchblade knives. On the way out, the only customs difficulties are with valuable antiques. There is no form of currency control on either entering or leaving, and all currencies are freely exchangeable.

British **currency** is the pound sterling (£), divided into 100 pence (p); the exchange rate is usually something less than $1.50/£, or say 70p/$. **Bank hours** are 9.30 am to 3.30 pm Monday–Friday, though a few banks also open on Saturday morning. Most shops open at around 9 am and close at about 5.30, Monday–Saturday, but there is usually one early closing day (12.30 or 1 pm) which varies from place to place, and increasing numbers of shops are now keeping longer hours. As a rule, only the smaller shops close for lunch, and not all at that. **Credit cards** are widely accepted, especially at petrol stations, but by no means always at cheaper hotels and inns. Sales tax is charged on most things except food; at the time of writing the VAT (Value Added Tax) rate was 15%. Some shops operate a scheme whereby single large purchases can have the tax refunded, but this normally applies only in tourist traps. Tips are 10–15%, and may not be added into restaurant bills: look carefully. It is not necessary to give any more if a tip (or 'service charge') has already been added in.

The standard of **driving** is fairly high, though as in any country there are inexperienced and incompetent drivers and riders. Riding in London can be dangerous, because the despatch riders who work there are often so dangerous and stupid that all motorcyclists are suspect; watch out particularly for the big black taxis, whose drivers often resent the loss of the business that the despatch riders have taken from them, as well as the carving-up that the riders are noted for. Of course, the British drive on the **left** which for some reason is much easier to get used to on a motorcycle than in a car.

Speed limits are in miles per hour. Maximum limits on the various sorts of roads are as follows, although lower limits may be posted on the open road and higher limits (usually 40 mph or 50 mph) may be posted in built-up areas. On motorways and other dual carriageways (divided roads): 70 mph (113 kph). On the open road: 60 mph (97 kph). In towns: 30 mph (48 kph). Villages on the open road are not automatically 'built up areas' unless there are either signs indicating a speed limit or regular street lighting. In practice, exeeding the speed limit by a few miles an hour (up to about 10%) is normal, and many riders achieve thoroughly illegal speeds without getting caught; the police will nick you if you are riding dangerously, but let you off with a caution as often as not if it is merely a technical offence.

Right of way is, of course, priority to the **left**, but in all but the very smallest junctions in towns, priority is clearly marked on the roadway. The priority road has no markings; the minor road may have a dotted line or a solid line. If it is a solid line, you must stop before proceeding; with a dotted line, slowing down is enough if you can see that the road is clear. Traffic **on** a roundabout has right of way.

Overtaking is governed largely by common sense, and by road markings in the centre of the road. A single line may be crossed if it is safe to do so. A double solid line may never be crossed, except in an emergency or to pass an immobile obstruction. A double line, one side broken and the other side solid, may be crossed from the side which is broken only. The international NO OVERTAKING sign (see inside cover) may also be used. An important thing to note is that you may **only** overtake on the **right**, except in slow-moving traffic in town. The British are very well disciplined about this, and overtaking 'on the inside' is therefore very dangerous, as a vehicle may swing back in wihout even looking. Unfortunately, they are much less disciplined about lane use, especially on motorways. In theory, you are supposed to keep in the leftmost lane except when overtaking, but in practice the inner lane is left for lorries and slow vehicles, with cars and bikes in the middle lane. Infuriatingly often, there will be someone in the fast lane who sees no reason why he should pull over; he is going quite fast enough, thank you, and you should be content to do the same. These people drive you up the wall, but you will be in the wrong (and may well be nicked) if you overtake on the inside.

Parking restrictions are indicated by yellow lines painted at the side of the road, and by written notices on poles. Broken yellow lines mean that there is some form of parking restriction for less than the working day; a single yellow line means that parking is prohibited during the working day; and a double yellow line means that parking is prohibited at all times. An added sophistication is the presence of one, two, or three lines on the kerb, which restrict waiting during the same periods ('Waiting' being defined as loading or unloading, waiting for someone who has gone into a shop, etc.) There are free marked bays in most town centres, and it is usually legal to tuck the bike in between two cars at parking meters – ask a traffic warden or policeman if in doubt. It is **not** legal to park on the pavement, except in marked bays.

Other roads signs follow the European international standards. (See inside covers.)

British **police**, as already intimated, are more concerned with catching real villains than with traffic work, though speeding in towns (and sometimes on the open road) is checked with radar guns. Most are polite, though you do meet the occasional cocky young copper, and if you are polite back, you are unlikely to run into any trouble. Because they cannot impose on-the-spot fines, they are inclined to let foreigners off with a caution; they know that the chance of the foreigner turning up for the trial is negligible anyway. The same goes for fixed-penalty parking tickets, issued on the spot by parking wardens but not payable to them – you have to go to a magistrate's court, usually, and no one is going to catch you if you leave the country anyway. Of course, severely illegal parking may result in your bike being removed, when it will cost you plenty to get it back. The police have only to be called to an accident if someone is injured, or if the owner of property damaged in the accident cannot be traced; failing to report such an accident is an offence. The number for the police and other emergency services is 999.

In the event of **breakdowns**, both the Royal Automobile Club (PO Box 92, RAC House, Lansdown Road, Croydon CR9 6HB) and the Automobile Association (Fanum House, Basingstoke, Hampshire RG21 2AE) operate 24-hour services, but these are only available to members of affiliated clubs. Service is free: parts are paid for. The number to contact varies from place to place. Otherwise, try the Yellow Pages.

Eating in Britain is something of a problem. Normally, the only decent meal is breakfast, and that is usually served only as part of a bed-and-breakfast deal in a hotel or guest-house (or pub), though a few grand hotels offer very expensive but absolutely excellent buffet breakfasts, in the all-you-can-eat style. Lunch is best eaten in a pub; the 'Ploughman's lunch' (bread, cheese, and pickle) is usually a good buy, especially in the less pretentious pubs. In the evening, ethnic restaurants (Chinese, Indian, or Greek-Cypriot) are mostly the best and cheapest bet, though you may be lucky enough to find a 'carvery', where you have a help-yourself style buffet at fairly reasonable cost. Traditional British restaurants are either unbelievably expensive or extremely poor, or frequently both. Eating out in England is not the pleasure it is in, say France. Picnic food is a much better buy, because it is not subject to VAT, so buy some good bread from a small baker, some beer or cider, a little cheese, and eat that.

Drinking Britain is a beer-drinking nation, though wine was reduced in price in 1984 to bring it down to a more realistic level, and traditional British beer is drunk at room temperature without added carbonation – or warm and flat, if you are used to cold fizzy beer from other countries. The standard measure is the pint (20 fluid oz., about 600 ml), and it is good value. Cider is also widely drunk, though it varies from the insipid to the ferocious. In really good cider, there are not only bits in it: the big bits chase the little bits. Cider is at its best in the West Country (ask for 'scrumpy'), and superb with a Ploughman's. Spirits in pubs are expensive; and in liquor stores ('off licences'), except for fine Scotches, which are cheaper than most other places in the world. One big problem is the licencing hours: pubs are only open from about 10.30–11 am to 2.30 pm (3 in London), and then from 5 or 6 or even 7 pm to 10.30 or 11 pm. Many Scottish pubs are open all day. Fortunately, off-licences are not so restricted, and it's quite legal to drink in the streets. The blood alcohol level is 80 mg/100 ml, and the police are ready and willing to test you, so be careful. Should you be reduced to drinking water, it is safe everywhere (but tastes disgusting in London).

Accommodation is, if anything, even more absurdly expensive than food. A decent hotel room costs 2–3 times as much as the European average, and even an indifferent room in a bed-and-breakfast establishment will cost you as much as a hotel room elsewhere in Europe. Admittedly, you usually (but not always – check first) get a pretty good breakfast thrown in, but so you should at those prices. Often, it is a good idea to stay in a pub, where prices are no higher than a bed-and-breakfast place, and you can drink until closing time and then stagger up to bed.

A realistic alternative is a youth hostel or a YMCA, neither of which has age limits, and both provide very cheap, if rather basic, accommodation. Hostels tend to be rural, Ys urban. Finally, camping is legal anywhere with the landowner's permission, and you will not be troubled if you pick a reasonably out-of-the-way spot on public land. Camp sites vary widely in quality, but are cheap, and if you can face the climate, sleeping rough is possible but not desirable – the police tend to wake you up if they find you, so get well out of the way.

Eire

The people, and the blarney, have to be the reason for going to Ireland. The weather is, if anything, milder and even wetter than England, which accounts for all the greenery of the Emerald Isle, so that is no particular attraction, and Irish food is (on average) about as dull as English. There are, however, other attractions. There are miles of roads, with hardly a car to be seen, stretching across all that emerald scenery. There is Arthur Guinness's excellent Dublin Extra Stout, and 'the crathur' from John Jameson, Powers, Old Bushmills, and others; but ultimately it is the willingness of the Irish to sit around and make friends, having a 'crack', that makes the place so delightful.

It is important to lay the lie that the Irish Republic is dangerous because of IRA or other terrorist activity. It isn't. There are a few areas close to the border which it is wise to avoid, but over the majority of the country you would never think that the 'troubles' were anything but a thing of the past.

Motorcyclists are regarded as eccentrics, but not looked down upon. As the charming lady at the Irish Tourist Board put it, 'Oh, everyone thinks they're lunatics.' I asked her how that distinguished them from other Irish drivers, and she said, 'Ah, well, there's lunatics and lunatics.' All driving and riding in Ireland tends to be enthusiastic, often to the point of falling off and hitting things, but most accidents are minor, and minor accidents are regarded as Acts of God, so no one worries very much. You will see truly alarming numbers of bent and scratched cars and bikes, and no one seems concerned. The fact that the Irish have the highest blood-alcohol limit (100 mg/100 ml) among those nations which have a limit may have something to do with this. Bikes are popular, but spares are expensive, so Irish mechanics tend to be masters of improvization; if they can't bodge it, or get a second-hand part, expect cheap labour rates and sky-high parts bills.

The **roads** are all but deserted, well-surfaced but narrow and winding – the perfect country roads. Of course, they also have country hazards, such as cow-pats, agricultural vehicles, and animals in the road, so make sure that you can see where you're going. Petrol prices are higher, and the three grades (available everywhere) are 'lower', 'middle', and 'top' – about 90, 94, and 98 octane respectively.

The **time to go** is summer or spring, as for England, but you can expect to get rained on anyway; the Irish equivalent of Scotch mist is 'a soft day'. Because of the pace of life in Ireland, anything less than a week may not let you sample the full flavour of the place, though if you only want Dublin and environs, three or four days may be enough.

Papers The English don't even need a passport, just some form of identification (a driving licence is fine), and visas are not required from most other nationalities. For the bike, you need the registration document or log book; your licence (most national licences are accepted); and insurance. EEC policies automatically give the minimum cover required by Irish law, namely unlimited cover for personal injury and £1000 for damage to property. *Injuries to pillion passengers are not included* in the compulsory insurance. You also need to wear a helmet, and display a nationality plate.

To get to Ireland, you take the disgracefully expensive **ferries** from North Wales or South-West Scotland. When you arrive, customs allowances are higher than elsewhere in the EEC: 2 bottles of spirits, 300 cigarettes, 75 gm of perfume, 375cc of toilet water, and other goods to the value of IR£120, provided no one item exceeds IR£52. You *don't* get the same allowances if you enter from Northern Ireland by road. Meat, dairy, and poultry products are prohibited, and they are very touchy about weapons – even imitation ones. Export problems will only arise with antiques and works of art worth more than you're likely to want to carry on a motorcycle. You can import any amount of money in any currency, but declare large sums on entry, because you will only be allowed to take out IR£100 (in £20 notes or smaller) plus foreign currency up to the amount declared on entry. The Irish pound, or *punt*, is worth about 20% less than the English – little more than a dollar, in fact (say 10% more). The punt is divided into pence, and the coins are the same shape, size, and weight as their English equivalents (but are not accepted Britain) **Banking hours** are 10 am – 12.30 pm and 1.30 pm to 3 pm (5 pm on Thursday), often less in the country (where they may be open only on certain days), weekdays only. A warning: Irish bank clerks strike a lot. Other shops open from about 9 am to about 5.30 pm, Monday to Saturday, with one day's early closing a week, which varies from place to place. **Credit cards** are moderately useful, but mainly in big towns, near tourist attractions, and at the larger petrol stations. Irish VAT (at a variety of rates, up to 25% at the time of writing) is recoverable on some purchases through some shops, which will display a sign. Tips are not usually added into the bill (but check just in case); the usual 10–15% is expected. As in England, tips are not expected in pubs – but you could always buy the barman a drink.

The general standard of **driving** has already been mentioned, but there are other things to consider, too. For example, bicycles are not required to carry lights, and as cyclists are neither invariably sober nor invariably on the correct (left) side of the road, this can be fun. **Speed limits** are in miles per hour, with an overall 55 mph (89 kph) limit on the open road and 30 mph (48 kph) in town, unless otherwise signed. The distances on signposts may, however, be in miles or kilometres – and they rarely tell you which. But it's a small country, and you begin to realize that the stories about the Irish do have some foundation in fact.

The Irish drive on the LEFT, like the English, and the rule of the road is very much the same – except that there is less traffic, and drivers can grow forgetful, or drunk, or both. Never rely on your right of way, and use the horn to wake someone up if you have to. When it comes to **parking**, the same state of gentle anarchy prevails (though bikes may not be parked on the pavement); only if you are thoroughly badly parked is there likely to be a problem. On the other hand, the Irish are always aware of the danger that a 'badly parked' car may be there with some alternative motive. A friend was asked if it was his car that was blocking the gates of Trinity College, Dublin. He told the porter it wasn't, and asked why, and received the magnificent answer, 'It's terrible awkward parked, and the Gardai are after blowing it up.' The Irish also use yellow lines at the side of the road, as in England, which leads to the old joke that a single line means no parking, at all, and a double line means no parking at all, at all. Other road signs are as in England; it is only rarely that you find signs which are not duplicated in English if they are in Erse, because not all Irishman speak good Erse anyway. You will never meet an Irishman who speaks only Erse; the natives really do speak English, for once.

The **police**, or Gardai (gar-dee) are the subject of mixed reports. Neither I, nor anyone else I know, has ever had any untoward trouble from them; but a few books suggest that they can be quite heavy, especially about speeding. My view is that you'd need to be very unlucky indeed to run foul of them. Dial 999, as in England, for emergencies. The police need not be called to an accident unless there is personal injury, or the parties cannot settle matters amicably. One odd little legal side-light is that it is illegal for any Irish national to ride your bike, except a mechanic, and he will need your written permission.

Breakdowns The Automobile Association, 23 Suffolk Street, Dublin, telephone 779 481, provides a free 24-hour breakdown service to members of affiliated foreign clubs, but will not help non-members; they can use P.M.P.A., Long Mile Road, Dublin 12, telephone 508 930, but they will have to pay.

Accommodation Staying in Ireland is much like staying in England, but rather cheaper. The food is similar to English – at its best, simple but excellent ingredients simply cooked, and at its worst, good food ruined by overcooking. You can eat in pubs, too, but you will find that restaurants are relatively rare: the Irish are not great eaters-out. The hotel or guest house may also provide a meal, if asked. Simple picnic food is cheap and excellent. When it comes to the drink, this is excellent too, but not cheap; the Irish learned all too well about excise taxes from the English. Porter (Guinness) is, of course, the thing, and one of their great attractions of Ireland is sinking a few jars in a convivial pub. The Irish, even more than the English , drink in 'rounds': half a dozen (or more or less) friends drinking together, each buying a drink for the whole group in turn, which obviously leads to some serious drinking. Licencing hours only exist in Cork and Dublin, where the pubs shut for an hour in the afternoon in order to get people back to work. The blood alcohol limit, as already mentioned, is a high 100 mg/100 ml, but remember that you can be done for drunken driving if you are obviously incapable under this limit.

Hotels are not particularly common, nor even remarkably cheap (though they are usually a good deal cheaper than in England), but they usually include breakfast in the English style; an Irish breakfast is frequently even more impressive than an English one. Bed-and-breakfast deals, on the other hand, are everywhere – and prices are usually a fair bit lower than England, so most people find this the most convenient form of accommodation. There are also 61 youth hostels, run by *An Oige*, 39 Mountjoy Square, Dublin (an address to conjure with!), telephone 745 374. They are cheap, basic, and good, varying in price according to the location and the age of the guest (there is no age limit). There are many camp sites, again cheap, and no one is likely to object if you park on out-of-the-way public land. On private land, get permission from the landowner (usually freely given).

France and Monaco

Introduction

For most British or British-based motorcyclists, France is the first country they consider for touring abroad. It is cheap, easy, and quick to get there, and indeed it requires a certain amount of determination if you are not to go through France on your way to almost any other European country. For the same reasons, most Continental motorcycle tourists also spend a fair amount of time in France.

But even if France were not so convenient, it would still be a country worth visiting. It is true that there are still many Frenchmen who are deeply suspicious of all foreigners (especially English and German foreigners), but there are many more who extend a genuine welcome; and the general feeling in France is one of extreme tolerance, so that a tourist is neither looked down upon as a necessary evil, from whom as much money is to be extracted as possible, nor the subject of curiosity and conversation. I must confess that for me, the prime attraction of France is not the people – though I do not dislike them, despite my John Bull attitude to life – but the food, the wine, the countryside, the architecture, the weather, and the general sense of *civilization* which pervades the whole country.

France

France dominates Europe by size alone. No fewer than six European countries have a land border with France, and the Channel coast is England's main route into Europe; frequent ferries, from Calais, Dover, Newhaven, Southampton, Folkestone, Bournemouth, Weymouth, and even Plymouth make this almost a land border in its own right. If the long-awaited Channel Tunnel ever comes to anything, perhaps there will be a real land border.

Because of her great size, the range of attractions in France is tremendous. The city of Paris is one of the most beautiful in the world; to the north-east of Paris is champagne country; to the west are Normandy and Brittany, home of superb scenery and truly wonderful food; to the south, particularly, are old and beautiful towns; and on the Mediterranean coast are the famous (if expensive) Riviera seaside resorts. Everywhere, the French care about their culture: their language, their *cuisine*, their history, their way of life.

Furthermore, France is tremendously good value. You can eat an excellent meal almost anywhere in France for no more than the cost of an indifferent repast in England, and a reasonable French hotel will cost no more than an English bed-and-breakfast. And you are not looked down upon if you ride a motorcycle; to British and American riders, this may come as something of a revelation, though it is typical of most of Europe. My wife and I have arrived at superb restaurants, tired and travel-stained, and after we have hung our riding waterproofs out of the way, we have been shown to first-class tables with sparkling linen tablecloths, and treated as if we had arrived in a Rolls-Royce. In Paris, expensive motorcycles are a real status symbol. Many are just poseurs' toys, such as Paris-Dakar replicas and massive Kawasakis which will never be ridden to half their limits; but a big, beat-up, dirty BMW like ours commands real respect, because we are riding the way that they would like to in their dreams. Playing boy racers up and down the Champs Elysees is a wonderful experience, though I have a theory

that an out-and-out race would be won by a grocer's delivery
boy on a 50cc Velo Solex, weaving in and out of the traffic
at full throttle with absolutely no braking whatsoever. If you
do have an expensive bike, incidentally, it is worth chaining it
to something really solid in Paris; the theft rate is apparently
appalling.

Outside Paris, it must be admitted that the French are
users of motorcycles, rather than motorcyclists. By this I
mean that they will thrash small machines mercilessly, riding
them into the ground with no thought of maintenance, in
very much the same way that they drive their 2CVs. Big bikes
are also discriminated against by stiff taxation laws, based on
a curious 'fiscal horsepower' system which actually
corresponds closely to cylinder capacity; thus, people will say
admiringly of my R100RS, 'Ah, c'est 10 CV, non?'. It is no
use telling them that the actual power output is 70 CV
(CV = HP); they just look blank. Nevertheless, this all serves
to reinforce the mystique of big motorcycles. It does have the
effect, however, that spares for large bikes can be very hard
to get outside the larger towns, and that mechanics are more
at home with tiny clapped-out Mobylettes than with Honda
Goldwings, so repairs to big bikes can be expensive, even if
the price is not loaded on the assumption that anyone who
rides a big bike must be rich.

French **roads** vary enormously, from the extremely fine
and very fast toll motorways (look for the word PEAGE, which
means TOLL), through indifferent free motorways, country
roads which vary from the delightful and uncrowded to the
truly awful, and roads which are little more than cart tracks.
Watch out particularly for the dreaded *rainurage*, parallel
grooves scratched in the concrete surface of a road (usually
a toll-free motorway) *in the direction of travel*. This can result
in truly frightening handling; the sign for it shows a
motorcycle with the word RAINURAGE underneath, but you will
usually have been frightened silly by the road surface before
you see the sign. Toll motorways are quite expensive for cars,
and prohibitive for trucks, which makes them admirably
uncrowded, but motorcycle rates are not all that high –
certainly a bargain if you want to get from A to B as fast as
legally possible. Petrol comes in two grades, *ordinaire* (very
ordinaire – about 90–92 octane) and *super* (97–98 octane),
at about average European prices, and both grades are
available everywhere.

When to go Again because of the size of France, the best time to go varies considerably. The climate of northern France is similar to that of southern England, though warmer in the summer and cooler in the winter, which means that even spring and autumn are quite reasonable bets. The summer months can also be as damp as England, but the rain normally falls in more concentrated bursts. The further south you go, the better the weather gets, until at the Mediterranean coast only December, January, and February are less than desirable. The summer in the south can, however, be too hot for some people – especially a few miles inland, where it can hit 100° (though not often). It is, in any case, worth avoiding France in August, which is the traditional holiday month. Almost everything is closed, except in the resorts, the roads are crowded, and France is not seen at her best. In August the south will, however, be hot and dry, though I would rather go in the early spring (the autumn tends to be slightly wetter, though still very attractive). The mountains add a whole new dimension, of course; from November to March, you may well find snow on the high passes, so the high summer is the best time to go.

You can spend as much or as little time as you like in France, because you can go there at every opportunity that presents itself and still only see a small part of one aspect of life on each trip. I cheerfully go over for a day or two, or for several weeks; it just depends on how much time you have. Choose a particular part of France or French life, and explore that. For maps, the flimsy but cheap and comprehensive Michelin series are probably best.

Papers Visitors to France need a passport – the French cut up funny about identity cards in early 1984, especially where black Britons were concerned – but no visa for most countries. For the bike, you need the registration document or log book (plus letter of permission if it is someone else's bike), your national licence (IDP not required in most cases), and insurance. The minimum requirements for insurance in France are better in many ways than in Britain: you are covered for liability for both personal injury and property damage, and the limits are sufficiently high that you would need a pretty severe accident to exceed them: five million francs per vehicle per claim for injury, three million francs per vehicle per claim for property damage. Any EEC policy will extend this cover in France.

You will also need a **helmet**, which must (in theory) be decorated with a strip of reflective tape – though I have never been picked up for not having this, and a member of the CRS riot police I talked to said that foreigners would rarely be prosecuted. You must carry a spare set of light bulbs, but daylight riding lamps are not compulsory. There are no other special requirements. You do *not* need to stain your lights yellow, though French-registered vehicles do. Getting there is no problem; avoiding France is more difficult. Easily the cheapest, most frequent, and most convenient services are from Dover and Folkestone; it is only worth considering another route if it saves you a great deal of riding time, because fares on the other routes are much higher. The hovercraft ferries are wonderful, cheap and fast, but they only run during the day; several sea ferries run all night as well, often with considerable discounts. Once in France, you may wish to consider shipping your bike on the train, but do not go through Paris, or anywhere else that a change is involved: if you are lucky, your bike will arrive only 24 hours after you and in one piece, but if you are unlucky it can take three days and have a lot of dents.

Customs on the way in are the EEC standards; the 'other goods' figure is 1030 francs for EEC travellers, 140 francs for those entering from other countries. On the way out, there are no problems apart from the usual ones about antiques and works of art. As for currency, you can import all you like, but there is a 5000 franc limit on exports unless more has been declared at the time of entry. The unit of **currency** is the Franc, which oscillates between 10–11 FF/£ sterling, say 7 to the dollar; divide by ten for a good guide. The franc itself is divided into 100 centimes. The **bank hours** are 9 am to 4 or 4.30 pm, but in some areas this will be Monday-Friday, in others Tuesday–Saturday. There may or may not be a lunch break – likelier in small towns – and there is a sneaky custom of closing at mid-day on the day before a bank holiday. Shops vary widely; bakers and other food shops may open as early as 6 am, though 6.30 or 7 would be more usual, and they may not close until 8, 9, or even 10 pm, but they may well take 2–4 hours off in the afternoon. Other shops will usually open about 9 am and close at about 6 pm; small shops may take two hours for lunch, large ones may stay open. Surprisingly, for a strongly Catholic country, quite a lot of shops open on Sunday.

Credit cards are quite widely accepted, but only in the larger petrol stations. Visa is vastly more use than Mastercard/Access. French VAT, called TVA, is reclaimable on purchases of over 1030 francs for EEC residents, 400 francs for others. Tips, the other percentage deal, may be included in restaurant bills (look for *service compris* or S.C.) and in some bars; it is then the custom to round the bill up to the nearest 10 francs or so. Otherwise, allow 10–15%. It is customary to leave a small tip (5–10%) in a bar, and to tip the usherette in a cinema a couple of francs. The French are into tipping, but they do not expect extra tips if they have already made it clear that *service* is *compris*.

On the road, **driving** is strictly 'up-and-at-'em', but not particularly dangerous; the worst single thing is the passion for *priorité a droite* (priority to the right) which will be relentlessly enforced except when you are on a priority road (*Passage protegé*), and sometimes even then, by elderly farmers who have no truck with modern roadsigns. It is fairly said that the French often allow logic to triumph over reason, but at last they have changed the rules so that traffic **on** a roundabout has right of way – you used to have to stop on the roundabout to admit cars on your right. Even so, some roundabouts are now marked with road-markings showing that this still applies! Street cleaning vehicles, as well as emergency vehicles, have right of way (and will take it), and on steep hills, *ascending* traffic has right of way.

Speed limits have all kinds of unexpected complications. To begin with the limits for experienced drivers on dry roads (!); they are 130 kph (81 mph) on toll motorways, 110 kph (68 mph) on non-toll motorways and other dual carriageways, 90 kph (37 mph) in built-up areas. If, however, you have held a full licence for less than one year, you must display a '90' disc, and you may not drive faster than 90 kph on any road, ever. If the road is wet, the limit is 110 kph (68 mph) on toll motorways, 80 kph (50 mph) elsewhere. All these limits may, or course, be varied by signs, and a particularly sneaky trick is not using speed limit signs at the beginnings of built-up areas: the little sign with the place name is considered sufficient warning that you are in a built-up area, which ends when the placename sign appears again, this time with a line through it. Speed limits are observed quite well in towns, but on the open road they are only important when there is a *gendarme* handy: this is especially true of the 90 kph limit on ordinary roads. On the other hand, the police can and do impose steep fines – frequently 500 francs or more – so speeding is risky. These fines are payable on the spot, and you will not be allowed to go until you have done so.

Overtaking is forbidden where it would involve crossing a double *or single* continuous line in the middle of the road, where the NO OVERTAKING sign is displayed, when the vehicle to be overtaken is already overtaking someone else (which says a lot about French driving!), or subject to the usual observations about brows of hills, curves, or blind intersections. **Parking** is easy: it is legal anywhere that it is not forbidden, including on the pavement provided it does not obstruct the passage of pedestrians. There is no need to take any risks in parking (near junctions, etc.) because you can always find somewhere within a few yards to push the bike out of the way. It is, however, illegal to park for more than 24 hours in one place in Paris. Road signs are mostly international, though there are some funnies. *Chaussée deformée* means (loosely translated) 'appallingly bad surface, especially near the edge of the road' (literally 'road shoulder deformed'); *Nids de poules* means not 'chickens' nests' but 'potholes'; a sign like castle battlements means that you may park in lay-bys; and the following are less exciting but still useful:

Haute tension	Electrified line
Route barrée	Road closed
Attention travaux	Road works
Gravillons	Loose chippings
Allumez vos lanternes	Turn on your lights
Interdit aux pietons	Forbidden to pedestrians
Fin d'interdiction	
de stationner	End of prohibited parking

The **police** are nothing like as bad as their popular image, especially towards motorcyclists, but it is still as well to be extremely polite to them. They have the power to demand some form of identification, and may give you a difficult time if you are not carrying your passport or something similar. They can also pull you in for vagrancy if you have less than 10 francs on you, but this is unusual. Dial 17 in emergencies, or look them up in the phone book for non-emergencies, and do not expect them to speak even a word of English. In the event of an accident, call them if someone is injured, if traffic flow is impeded, or if you think that the other guy is drunk. They can request a deposit against possible fines, returnable if you are not found guilty (or if you are fined less). Otherwise, complete a *constat a l'amiable*, a sort of agreed version of the accident, and get the other guy to sign it. *Vehicles must not be moved until this has been done.* If you cannot reach agreement, get a written statement from a bailiff (*huissier*) immediately; bystanders will tell you where to find one, but it will cost you anything up to 500 francs. Alternatively, try the police, though they may refuse to come unless the accident sounds interesting.

The general state of French mechanics in case of **breakdown** has already been mentioned, and the Touring Club de France offers only a very incomplete breakdown service; a local garage is really your only chance. The TCF is at 65 avenue de la Grande Armee, Paris 16; the general phone number is 553 3959, and the 24-hour breakdown number is 704 8888. There is also the Automobile Club de France (ACF), 6 place de la Concorde, Paris 8 (265 3470), and the Royal Automobile Club, 8 place Vendome, Paris 1 (260 6212).

France is the one country where most Englishmen should have some idea of the language, but the problem is that some Frenchmen refuse to listen to French in an English accent; Americans will fare far better.

please	*s'il vous plait* (seel voo play)
thank you	*merci* (mare see)
yes	*oui* (we –or 'ouais', way, for 'yeah')
no	*non* (surely you can remember this one: naw)
where is	*ou est?* (ooh eh?)
room	*chambre* (shombre)
toilet	WC (vay say)
more of	*plus de* (ploo duh)
how much?	*combien* (kom byen)
eat	*manger* (mon-jay)

Eating in France is, of course, a delight, whether you go to a restaurant or have a picnic. In restaurants, though, there are four things to beware of. One is really superb, but horrifyingly expensive, places. Check the menu (displayed outside) first. The second is expensive but bad restaurants, aimed at the tourist trade. These are easy to spot – the menu will usually be in English and German as well as French. The third is trendy places. The French are suckers for fads, and there are some really awful but still expensive American-style fast-food places. Only a fool would eat at MacDonalds in France. The fourth is unfamiliar things on the menu. A pocket dictionary will help, or ask.

Drinking In some restaurants, wine is included. This is normally clearly stated on the *menu*, which is not the same as what we call a menu. The French for menu is 'carte'. Do not be confused! The *carte* lists all the food, and will usually have one or more fixed-price meals. Each fixed-price meal is called a *menu*, and typically there might by a 50-franc *menu*, a 65-franc *menu*, and a 90-franc *menu* for example. In each one, you will have a limited choice from the items on that *menu*, usually with extra courses, better food, or more choice in the more expensive *menus*. As a general rule, go for the *menu* as far as possible: it will be the best value, usually because it is made of whatever was cheap and fresh in the market that morning.

If you want to picnic, go to a specialist baker for the bread, and buy everything else in a supermarket, where prices for cheese, wine, etc., will be lowest. Unless you buy the wine in a throwaway plastic bottle, there is usually a deposit on the bottle. This does not apply to the more expensive wines, which are very poor value compared with the cheap stuff. Most French beer is indifferent, though the biere d'Alsace is pretty good, and you can try cider in Normandy – usually rather sweet for my taste, because the French do not understand about cider apples (or any other sort of apple). If you like brandy, try *armagnac* as a change from the usual cognac. Spirits on sidewalk cafes are expensive (so are beers, teas, etc.), but drinking inside a cheap bar is very cheap indeed. There are no licencing hours, but you must be over 18 to drink. The blood alcohol limit is 80 mg/ 100 ml, as in the UK. Watch out for this if you are touring in the wine country, where free *dégustation* (tasting) is the order of the day; visit two or three vineyards and you can rapidly get sozzled enough to fall off the bike, for free, if the police don't catch you first. If you drink water, *eau non potable* means 'water not drinkable'; the best advice is to do as the French do, and buy mineral water. Perrier is reliable, but Vichy water's soapy taste is something that many people (me too) do not like.

Accommodation is wildly variable, but can be very cheap indeed. As recently as 1982 I stayed in a really basic, shabby, but still clean (no wildlife) room in central Paris for about £4 (under $6), and a decent room with your own bathroom costs no more than an English bed-and-breakfast (though usually without breakfast – ask). Even in Paris you can stay cheaply; get one of the excellent cheapo guidebooks, which also tells you the cheapest restaurants in Paris. Put it this way: at the time of writing, I had never paid £20 for a double room with bath in Paris, or as much as £15 outside. A really basic single room, no private bath should cost no more than half that! The French National Tourist Office gives away a marvellous guide called *Auberges et Logis de France*, listing one- and two-star hotels, and inns with no stars at all, all over France. There are youth hostels at reasonably modest fees: contact *Federation Unie des Auberges de Jeunesse*, 6 rue Mesnil, Paris 75016, phone 553 1695 for information. France also has about 9,000 camp sites, ranging from the very basic to the extremely luxurious (they are officially graded, one-star to four-star), at very reasonable rates indeed; or camping 'wild' is perfectly legal, provided you get the landowner's permission first (or get well out of the way on public land). *All* accommodation, hotels, camping, the lot, tend to be jammed in August, and July is often not much better, so book ahead if you plan on travelling then.

Monaco

The Principality of Monaco, just outside Nice, is about two
square miles of semi-independent state rule by the Grimaldi
family. There are no border formalities with France, and
French currency is used (though Monegasque currency
cannot be used in France). It attracts gamblers to the casino
in Monte Carlo, and philatelists with a weakness for gaudy
stamps, but Cousteau is the director of the Oceanographic
Museum, and it's worth going for that. There are one or two
places which are not too horrifically expensive, but they are
rare; this is a playground for the rich, and with the highest
VAT in Europe, small wonder. It is a place to visit for the
day, rather than to stay.

Western Europe

Introduction

Many people find that their first tour can be confined to France alone: it is a big enough country, with enough variety, and despite traditional English-French rivalry, the people are actually very friendly. But other people want to go further afield, and the countries which border on France are a natural choice. The astute geographer will notice that Austria does not actually have a French border, but is included, whereas Spain has a long French border and is not included. It just seemed more reasonable this way.

Border formalities with most of these countries are unlikely to consist of much: as often as not, you will simply be waved through. Which country you like most will depend on your own personality; Southern Germany and Austria are my favourites. Because the area covered by these countries is so large, it is not possible to generalize, except possibly to say that the south is warmer than the north, and that I have always found southern people friendlier than northern.

Austria

Again and again, when writing this book, I was seized by the idea of putting aside the typewriter, locking up the house, and heading back to the places I was writing about. There were two places which were especially hard to resist: Portugal, of which more later, and Austria.

I have not spent much time in Austria, but the Austrian Tyrol sticks in my mind as one of the most beautiful places that I have ever seen. Still, dark lakes reflected snow-capped mountains; cows grazed in meadows of grass that looked like velvet, their bells clanking and tinkling; the pure clean air filled the clear blue sky; it was utterly beautiful. It was what I had always imagined Switzerland would look like, but having seen both I believe that Austria is even more beautiful, and I certainly prefer the Austrian people and the Austrian lifestyle to the Swiss.

Austria rests on its Imperial past, from the days of the Austro-Hungarian Empire, and to tell the truth, it has not always made the effort to modernize. Just as southern Germany is more laid back than the north, so is Austria more laid back than southern Germany. The great old city of Vienna, the capital of an empire that has gone, is a place that I have never seen; yet all that I hear makes me want to go there. It is true that the Austrians are sometimes stiflingly old-fashioned, but even that has its charm – and old-fashioned they may be, but repressive they are not. Everyone is entitled to his point of view, even motorcyclists; it is assumed that you have considered your choice, earned the money that you need to run your motorcycle, and are now enjoying the fruits of your wise decision. This may sound formal, and it is – but that is the way that Austrians are. Who says you cannot be formal and still enjoy yourself?

You will not be able to ride in Austria unless you are 18, but your national licence is enough. Because Austria is an affluent country, you will have no difficulty with spares and repairs; you will also find that labour rates are somewhat lower than in Germany, which is welcome. The **roads** are excellent, even if they do charge tolls on some of the motorways and mountain passes, and both *normal* (92 octane) and *super* (97 octane) are available everywhere at fairly average European petrol prices.

When to go Because of the altitude, Austria is rarely very hot; and even on those days when the mercury hits 90°, there is usually a cooling breeze. The summer months are, however, the wettest (another consequence of the altitude), and lightweight waterproofs are a good idea. Personally, I would go for the autumn and spring, even if it does mean wrapping up a bit when you are actually riding, in order to avoid the crowds and enjoy the sparklingly sunny days. The winters are cold, though; you would do best to avoid November to January, especially because the passes will be snowy (though rarely blocked for more than an hour or two at a time) during those months.

Papers You do not need a visa for most nationalities; a British passport entitles you to stay for 6 months, most others for 3 months. You will need your registration document or log book (and letter of permission from the owner, if necessary), your national driving licence (minimum riding age 18), and insurance. Most European policies (certainly British) cover you to the minimum extent required by Austrian law: ten million Austrian schillings (AS) – say £300,000 – for personal injury and property damage, but not passenger insurance. You must also carry a first-aid kit. Failure to produce one at a spot-check will not be treated as an offence, but if you are asked to give assistance at an accident (which is legal obligation), it is an offence not to have a first-aid kit.

Getting to Austria is easy. The quickest route, Oostende-Köln-Frankfurt-Nurnberg-Wien, is about 778 miles, or you may prefer to go through Strasbourg, Stuttgart, München, and Salzburg, or (scenically most attractive), via Basle, Zurich, and Innsbruck. No matter which route you take, allow at least three days to do it in comfort. On any of these routes, border formalities are quick and easy at each country. When you reach Austria, the **customs** allowances are the EEC standards listed in the Introduction to Part II of this book, (see p.96) with an 'other goods' limit of only 400 schillings; you must be over 17 for the tobacco and booze allowances. There is no **currency** control on entry, but there is an export limit of AS 15,000 plus US $1000 (which does not apply to travellers' cheques). The Austrian Schilling is divided into 100 *groschen*; for rough calculations, allow AS 30/£ sterling, AS 20/$ US.

Banking hours are Monday to Friday, 8 am–12.30 pm and 1.30 pm–3.30 pm (5.30 pm on Thursdays), and shops are typically open from 8 am to 6 pm Monday to Friday, half day Saturday, though food shops in particular may keep much longer hours and open every day of the week. Sales tax at the time of writing was 18%, and items over AS 2000 were eligible for a refund if exported; ask at the shop. Tips are usually figured into the bill (at 10%), and this is sufficient for hotels, but eating and drinking places expect the tip to be rounded up a bit, to about 15% overall. **Credit cards** are fairly useful, especially in larger towns, but do not rely on them anywhere.

Riding in Austria bears few surprises; **driving** standards are high, though you find quite a lot of Germans driving just as fast as they do at home, and the Austrians are no great respecters of speed limits. **Helmets** are compulsory, of course, and so are daylight riding lights. Road surfaces are mostly first class, even in the Alps, but expect frost damage in the spring. The tolls, where charged, are not high – certainly not high enough to put you off using toll roads – but the non-toll roads are so beautiful that it seems a bit pointless to pay good money to hurtle along on a motorway that is indistinguishable from any other. The **speed limits** are 130 kph (81 mph) on the motorway, 100 kph (62 mph) on other roads, 50 kph (31 mph) in town.

Right of way is the usual priority-to-the-right, except on main roads or where there is the international priority sign, but trams and emergency vehicles *always* have right of way. **Overtaking** is illegal where it would involve crossing a single yellow line in the middle of the road, within 80 metres (say 85 yards) of level crossings or pedestrian crossings, or anywhere that visibility is obscured or it might be dangerous. Do not use your horn unless you have to; throughout Austria, the horn may be used only when necessary in the interests of road safety, and in Vienna its use is banned at all times!

Park in marked bays (not on the pavement unless marked), and take note of the following list of restrictions: where the road narrows, on the brow of a hill, on a bend, on or under bridges, tunnels, and underpasses, on or near level crossings, within 5 metres (16 feet) of crossroads or 15 metres (say 50 feet) of bus or tram stops, anywhere that obscures traffic lights, road signs, etc., or on motorways except in designated lay-bys. The Austrians distinguish between 'parking' (over 10 minutes) and 'waiting' (under 10 minutes). Both 'parking' and 'waiting' are illegal under the above conditions, but you may 'wait' (but not 'park') as follows: where there are crosses on the roadway, in front of entrances to houses, public buildings, petrol stations, etc, in two-way streets less than 7.5 metres (25 feet) wide, on the left on one-way streets less than 5 metres (16 feet) wide, on priority roads outside built-up areas in reduced visibility. You must use parking lights unless the vehicle is visible at 50 metres (55 yards).

Road signs are mostly international, but the following written signs may be important:

Ausweiche	Detour
Fahrbahnschäden or	Damaged road
Frostschaden or	surface
Schadhafte	
Fahrbahndecke	
Lawinen Gefahr	Danger of
	avalanches
Strasse Gesperrt	Road closed
Steinschlag	Falling rocks
Beschränkung für Halten	(literally) Restricted
oder Parken	for Waiting or
	Parking
Halten Verboten	Waiting forbidden
Hupverbot	(literally) Horn-
	forbidden
Querstrasse	Crossroads
Schneeketten	Snow chains
Vorgeschrieben	compulsory

In case you're wondering what motorcyclists do when car drivers have to use *schneeketten*, the answer is that they fall off a lot. Snow chains are obviously impractical for most motorcycles, and *as far as I could discover*, you do not have to have either chains or special tyres. However, riding in snow on mountain roads – and falling off a lot – is not my idea of a vacation.

Austrian **police** are polite and old-fashioned, and very formal; follow their lead, and you will have no problems in most cases. They prefer to caution visitors rather than to give them a ticket, but they can impose heavy on-the-spot fines. Beware particularly of drunken driving: the **minimum** penalty is a fine of AS 5000 and loss of licence, or a week inside! The police must be called if anyone is injured in an accident, or if traffic flow is severly obstructed, but not otherwise. The police number is 113, and ambulance is 114. For **breakdowns**, the Österreichischer Automobil-, Motorrad- und Touring-Club (ÖAMTC), Schubertring 1-3, 1010 Wien, operates a Touring Breakdown Service on all motorways and main roads and can be called to breakdowns on other roads; dial 9540 in most areas. This is far from free, and depends on time of day, help rendered, whether or not towing is required, and so forth, but members of affiliated overseas clubs do get a discount on production of the membership card.

Food and drink German, of a sort, is spoken in Austria (though the accent may confuse you), so the German vocabulary will do. Food is not particularly cheap, but the quality is usually very high indeed, as Austrians are enthusiastic eaters. *Pâtisserie*, or *Konditorei* as the Germans render the art of cake-making, is superb, especially with the usual lashings of whipped cream. There are also about four million different kinds of coffee for sale in the cake-shops. Picnic food is not expensive, and Austrians drink wine and beer interchangeably, so you can suit yourself. The English should be pleased to see that many Austrian bierkellers have a beer-warmer, in case you don't like your beer too cold! The blood alcohol limit is the standard 80 mg/100 ml; the water is drinkable everywhere.

Hotels are officialy classified as A-1, A, B, C, D. At the time of writing, you should be able to find a double room in a D hotel for under AS 250 if you look hard enough: like most places in Europe, you are charged by the room and not by the person, and breakfast is rarely included. Vienna tends to be more expensive than the rest of Austria, inevitably, and out-of-season rates can be 25–40% cheaper than peak. Rooms in private houses, like an English bed-and-breakfast, are good value, and youth hostels started at well under AS 100 per night at the time of writing: contact the Austrian Youth Hostel Association at Gonzagagasse 22, 1010 Wien, telephone 6353. Camp sites are very good value indeed, and you can also camp 'wild' if you have the permission of the landowner; for public land, ask at the local municipal offices. Note, however, that fires are banned in or near woodland.

Belgium

To be quite honest, Belgium does not strike many people as a place to visit; more a place to be passed through, preferably as quickly as possible, on the way somewhere else. This image is not improved by the Belgian Tourist Office, which describes the chilly and dreary seashore as 'the coast with the most', calls Durbuy (an attractive little place with an oversize castle) 'the biggest little town in Belgium', and refers to one place as 'nestling beneath peaks 325 feet high' – more a large molehill, than a small mountain.

Nevertheless, Belgium does have its good points. Alone in Continental Europe, they seem to understand the idea of the pub; there are several historic towns, including Brugge, Antwerpen, Gent, and even Bruxelles; and the French-speaking part, Wallonia, is beautiful. There are winding roads through gentle hills and woodland, lakes, grottoes, caves, and castles and chateaux from all periods. The ferry to Oostende makes it easy to get to, the roads are good and well-maintained, Belgian driving is nothing like as bad as you may have been led to believe, and at the very least, it is worth taking a look at the place. Some people grow to love Belgium, and return there year after year, but the pleasures are not easily described: you have to see it for yourself.

For some reason, Belgium is much less infested with tiny worn-out motorcycles than France, and late-model megabikes are surprisingly common: it is an affluent little country, and consequently sometimes rather expensive, though it must be said that **petrol** is as cheap as almost anywhere in Europe (except Luxembourg), with 92-octane *normal* and 98-octane *super* at well under UK prices. Riding motorcycles is regarded as a perfectly normal activity, and motorcyclists are no more and no less welcome than anyone else. You will have few problems with spares, but labour rates are quite high – another good case for insurance. There are plenty of good **roads**, no matter what your definition of 'good' may be: fast motorways, well-surfaced secondary roads which range from fast and open to winding and twisty, and intriguing cobbles in the older towns. Quite honestly, I do not

know why Holland's popular image is so much better than
Belgium's; I would rather go to the Belgian Ardennes than to
any part of Holland.

The **climate** is much like England's (or Holland's),
which means that the summer is mild and the winter is damp
and miserable; but the spring is a good alternative to
summer, when there are likely to be crowds, and autumn in
the Ardennes can be very beautiful.

Papers To get in, you will need a passport but no visa
in most cases (UK, US, Canada, Australia, New Zealand,
etc.), a driving licence (the Belgians only cottoned on to
these a few years ago), insurance, and a registration
document or log book. Your national driving licence is fine,
and most policies will meet the Belgian minimum
requirements: unlimited liability for both personal and
property injury, except in those cases where property
damage is caused by fire or explosion, in which case the limit
is five million Belgian francs. **Helmets** are compulsory,
daylight riding lights are not, and although the girl at the
Belgian tourist office in London (a dozy crew) said that first
aid kits were compulsory, I have found no confirmation of
this anywhere else, and she wouldn't put it in writing.

To get there, you can go straight in to Oostende or take
the shorter, quicker, and cheaper ride over to Calais and ride
up. Alternatives include Dunkerque (very nearly on the
border), Zeebrugge (a bit south of Oostende), or even
Antwerpen. Ports of departure from the UK include Dover,
Tilbury, Southend, Harwich, and Felixstowe; Northerners
might consider going to Holland from Hull or Immingham,
and riding south.

Customs are the usual EEC allowances – Bruxelles is,
after all, the capital city of the EEC – with an 'other goods'
allowance of 6250 BF for goods bought tax and duty paid in
the EEC, 1250 BF otherwise. There are no controls on the
export or import of currency of any kind.

Currency The Belgian Franc (BF – honestly!) is not the
most valuable variety of franc; allow 80/£ sterling, 50/$ US
as a rough guide. **Credit cards** are not particularly useful,
although some stores and petrol stations take them. **Bank
hours** are 9am to 4 pm, Monday to Friday, though many
may close for lunch from noon to 2 pm. Shopping hours are
variable, basically 9 am to 6 pm, with or without a lunch
break, but there is an increasing tendency for big stores to

stay open to 9 o'clock at least one night a week (Thursday) and often all week. Most shops are open six days a week. The sales tax varies widely, from 6% to 25% at the time of writing, according to the type of goods, and as usual you can apply for exemptions on single high-value items shipped out of the country. Tips are a great Belgian custom; they aim for 16% (about a seventh) and can be quite anti if they don't get it. In hotels and restaurants it is often added into the bill – look carefully. Don't give them any more!

Riding holds no surprises. Belgian **driving** is fairly cutthroat, though not as bad as you may have heard (but the accident rate is very high, so maybe I've just been lucky, or good). The motorways are fast and toll free, with a maximum speed limit of 120 kph (75 mph) and a minimum limit of 70 kph (44 mph). Other roads outside built-up areas are limited to 90 kph (56 mph), and the limit in built-up areas is 60 kph (37 mph). Most Belgians take these more as guidelines than as absolute limits, and a few mph over is unlikely to land you in trouble, though like anywhere else you may catch a policeman on a bad day. Fines can be imposed on the spot, but you do not pay the policeman; buy stamps at the post office (or do a bunk – but the fines are not high, and if they *do* catch you, you will be in real trouble). In town, watch out for the dreaded Belgian *pavé* -really chunky cobbles, which can get very slippery when it rains after a long dry spell, and dump you without warning.

Right of way is theoretically priority-to-the-right, unless otherwise indicated, and trams and emergency vehicles always have priority. Do not enter a junction unless your exit is clear, either – this is an offence. NEVER try insisting on right of way in Belgium, though; the Belgians just don't drive that way. As the old saying goes, 'He was right, of course – dead right. But he's just as dead as if he'd been wrong.'

Overtaking is to the left, except when a vehicle is turning left, and it is illegal when there is a no overtaking sign; at intersections, unless they are controlled by traffic lights or a policeman, or the road in question is marked as a priority road; at level crossings; if the guy in front is about to overtake on his own account; where visibility is restricted in any way; or (and I can't figure this one, but everyone ignores it) when other traffic is approaching.

Parking is subject to an interminable list of restrictions, most of which come down to common sense. The main

ones are: on cycle tracks or in cycle lanes; opposite another
vehicle in a one-way street, or in any street where it might
cause an obstruction; under bridges; on roads crossed by
tram or railway lines; within 5 metres (16 feet) of an
intersection, 12 metres (40 feet) of a bus or tram stop, 10
metres (33 feet) of a road sign (except one regulating
parking or stopping), 20 metres (66 feet) of traffic lights, or
within 1 metre (39") of another vehicle; on corners, or
brows of hills, unless there is an unobstructed view of 100
metres in open country or 20 metres in town; in gateways;
on portions of roadway having lane markings; or where a
pedestrian might be forced to leave the pavement in order to
avoid an obstacle. Parking on pavements is generally
forbidden, unless there are marked bays. Having said all this,
parking is still pretty anarchic, and you can usually find
somewhere to stick the bike along with a few others, even if
it is not actually marked as a bike bay. Parking lights are not
required if the vehicle is visible at a distance of 100 metres
(110 yards) without them.

The **horn** is enthusiastically used in Belgium, but should
only be used with discretion (in an emergency) after dark, or
in built-up areas at any time. As for road signs, a problem
arises in that the Dutch-speaking part uses only Dutch signs,
whilst the French-speaking part uses only French signs, so
you have to be alive to the possibilities of both.

The Belgian **police** are amiable enough, and although
they do not have to be called to an accident unless there is
injury or damage, it is usual to do so. They can request
blood samples from all parties if summoned, and everyone is
required to stay at the scene of the accident until the police
have finished, so decide whether the rules work for you or
against you (and the other party!). The emergency number,
for all services, is 900.

For **breakdowns**, the Touring Club Royal de Belgique
offers a breakdown service from 7 am to 11 pm, and minor
attention will normally be rendered free to members of
overseas automobile clubs – though there is no obligation on
the Touring Club Royal de Belgique to do so, and it is a
matter of courtesy on their part.

There are two official languages in Belgium, Flemish (or
Dutch) and French; the main problem is knowing which to
use, but French is likely to be more widely understood if
even less popular with the supporters of the opposite camp.

Belgian **food**, similarly, is influenced by both Dutch and French *cuisine*; there are also numerous ethnic restaurants, including Chinese, Italian, Balkan/Yugoslav, Indian, Greek, and South-East Asian. I have (on admittedly limited acquaintance) found Belgian food (and drink) to be very expensive, but everyone else I know who has been there tells me that I went to the wrong places; you can actually eat quite cheaply if you know where to go, or take the trouble to hunt around a bit. The **beer** is very good, even if all the brands taste pretty much the same, and there are Belgian pubs which look and feel very much like British ones, but keep much more civilized hours. The permitted blood alcohol level is (as far as I could discover) 80 mg/100 ml, and the tap water is safe to drink if you need to sober up. If you are asked to blow into a breathalyser, you can claim a 30-minute sobering-up time first, but this will obviously make the police suspicious. Try deep breathing and drinking plenty of water.

Accommodation is apparently quite reasonable, much like France, though once again I must admit that I have not tried it; Belgium is not a very big country, and you can easily cross into France if you can't find anything that you like in Belgium. Indeed, if you are under 21, or are travelling with a member of the opposite sex under 21 to whom you are not married, you may well have to do so; it is said that under Belgian law, it is a criminal offence for a couple meeting these requirements to share a room *or tent*! To cheer you up, many Belgian hotels and guest houses do provide breakfast, included in the bill. Check when you book.

For historical reasons there are two youth hostel headquarters, namely *Centrale Wallone de Auberges de la Jeunesse*, 52 rue van Oost, 1030 Bruxelles, and *Vlaamse feugdherbergcentrale* at Van Straalenstraat 40, Antwerpen; as you might guess from the names, one is for the French-speaking bit, and one for the Dutch-speaking bit. Belgian youth hostels are basic but *cheap* – they were only about £1 a time in 1982/3, and I do not think that they have gone up much since. Camping is another bargain, with over 500 official sites to choose from and 'wild' camping quite legal if you get permission from the landowner; stay well out of sight on public land, though.

West Germany

Germany is the most important country in this group, by reason of size, cultural influence, wealth, and strategic importance. But unless you have studied the history of Germany, or visited the country, it is easy to forget that little more than a hundred years ago it was not a single country at all, but a collection of imdependent kingdoms, principalities, city-states, and free towns.

With the present division of the country into East and West, it is also important to remember that West Germany may also be divided into North and South – or if you like, into Bavaria and the Rest.

Most people visit Bavaria. It is not hard to see why. As the southernmost kingdom that went to make up Germany, it is milder in climate and rather easier-going than the northern states. Although the Germans as a whole are much friendlier than they generally given credit for, there is little doubt that the Bavarians are friendliest; maybe it is that excellent Bavarian beer that keeps them in such good humour. The Bavarian Alps are, of course, very beautiful, though for my money those on the Austrian side of the border are even more stunning, and there are also the mediaeval towns and fairytale castles (such as Schloss Neuschwanstein) for which southern Germany is famous.

This is not to say that the north is not worth visiting. The big industrial towns, such as Köln (Cologne) are much like any other big city, and frighteningly expensive, but once you get out into the countryside you will find traditional German hospitality and lower prices, together with a landscape which may not be to everyone's taste, but which has a bleak charm of its own – especially on the North Sea coast. There is also the divided city of Berlin: if you want to take your 'bike there, you will need a full passport; a return transit visa (available at the border); and modest paranoia. The roads (non-Germans may use only the E6 and the E8) are patrolled by *Vopos* (*Volkspolizei*) from East Germany, and they are on the lookout for anyone trying to escape from their socialist paradise. To be on the safe side, stop only at service areas, never stray from the main road, do not

give a lift to East Germans, do not even talk to them at
length (the police may hassle them afterwards, though you'll
probably be OK), and remember that chucking an old
newspaper or (worse still) copy of *Penthouse* into a trash-bin
can be construed as 'disseminating subversive or
pornographic literature'.

In most of Germany, motorcycles are reasonably
popular, but the high cost of passing the test for a large bike
and the heavy taxes that you pay for the privilege of running
one are enough to put many people off. As a result, owners
of large *motorraden* are respectfully regarded as citizens of
some substance; an amazing turnaround from British and
American practice. The minimum riding age for Germans is
18, and they have to pass a graded series of tests in order to
be able to ride increasing capacities of machine, but valid
licences from outside Germany are recognized even if the
rider is only 17. Mopeds may be ridden at 16, and *mofas*
(even lower-powered mopeds) at 14; for these, insurance is
required, but there is no driving test. A side-effect of the
prestige of big bikes, however, is big repair bills. Labour costs
are high in Germany, and although you will have no
difficulties either with repairs or with spares, you may need a
bullet to bite on when you see the bill. Insurance is an
excellent idea!

German **roads**, as you would expect, are of a high
standard and well kept, but there are several surprises to be
faced. The first is that the much-vaunted *autobahnen*, the
last roads in Europe not to be saddled with a speed limit, are
usually only two lanes wide; German discipline in keeping to
the nearside lane except when actually overtaking is all that
makes them work. Mercifully, you do not find the horrible
British phenomenon of some elderly gnome blocking the fast
lane at 70 mph and refusing to move over. And do not stay
in the fast lane yourself, even at 100 mph: you will soon
have an annoyed Mercedes or Porsche on your tail, eager to
do 120 mph. In the early morning, when there is no one
around, you can legally (if not entirely safely) explore the
limits of both your bike's performance, and your own. The
second surprise is finding large military vehicles, and even
tanks, exercizing in country roads; this can be a nasty shock
when you come around a corner a bit quickly, so watch out
for warning signs, soldiers, and fresh tracks. The third
surprise is a pleasant one: there are still many unspoiled

mediaeval towns in Germany, with correspondingly tiny and windy roads through overhanging houses on cobbled roads. Exercise a fair amount of care.

The *autobahnen* charge no tolls, and are excellent for getting quickly from A to B, but there are many other attractive roads in Germany, whether you want open country roads or twisting mountain ones. There are frequent rest stops on the *Autobahns*, and adequately frequent petrol stations. **Petrol** is sold in two grades, at average-to-high prices for Europe: *regular* at 91–92 octane and *super* at 97–99 octane. My BMW always seems to like going home, and runs most sweetly on German *super*.

When to go The best time to go will, as usual, depend on where you are going. The north will be snowy throughout much of the winter, and so will the mountains in the south, but otherwise the north is best in summer (June/July/August) whereas the southern season extends well into spring and autumn – certainly May to September, and quite possibly April to October. Summer months are wettest, and spring and autumn are about equally dry (or wet). The German Tourist Board may not house the friendliest people in the world, but they do give away an excellent map of the country, quite sufficient for most route planning unless you have very obscure destinations in mind.

Papers No visa is needed for most countries, for at least up to 3 months. Take your registration document or log book (plus letter of permission if necessary), and an EEC licence or one from Austria, Finland, Hong Kong, New Zealand, Norway, Sweden, Switzerland or Senegal – an odd selection. Otherwise, either get an IDP or a German translation of your national licence (the IDP is usually easier). Insurance is compulsory, and any EEC policy gives the minimum legal cover of DM 1,000,000 for personal injury (DM 1,500,000 if more than one person is hurt) plus DM 400,000 for material damage and DM 40,000 for property damage; passengers are automatically insured. Green cards are, therefore, only needed in order to extend Fire, Theft, and Comprehensive cover. You can buy insurance at the border, for 15 or 30 days, and renew it at any branch of either the Allgemeiner Deutscher Automobil Club (ADAC), 8 Am Westpark, D-800 München, or the Automobilclub von Deutschland (AvD), 16 Lyoner Strasse, D-600 Frankfurt-Neiderrad.

Nationality plates are compulsory, and you must wear a **helmet** if your machine can exceed 25 kph (about 16 mph), but otherwise there are no special requirements which will be enforced against visitors. The unfortunate German rider is subject to ferocious construction and use regulations, which require type approval of the machine itself, *any* accessory, and *any* modifications, but unless a visitor's bike is obviously dangerous, there is nothing to fear. Daylight riding lights are advised, and widely used, but not compulsory.

The quickest way to get to Germany is probably via Oostende, Bruxelles, and Bonn, but a more agreeable route if you are going to the south may be through Reims, Metz, and Strasbourg to Stuttgart and then on to München (Munich). München itself is nearly 600 miles from the French Channel coast, so allow three days to do it in comfort, two days if you are pressing on. Border crossings at each country are easy, and German customs regulations are the EEC standards; the 'other goods' figure is DM 460 for entry from EEC countries, DM 100 for non-EEC countries in Europe, and DM 100 again for visitors from outside Europe. There are no restrictions on currency import or export, unless you are planning to invest large sums in industry or the like.

Currency The Deutschmark is one of the archetypal 'hard' currencies, divided into 100 Pfennig (Pf). For very rough calculations, allow just under DM 4/£ sterling, just under DM 3/$ US. **Banks** are open at about 9 am, but after that, there are all sorts of local variations. Some close at 1 pm; others may stay open to 4.30 pm (5.30 pm on Thursdays), and there may be a lunch break at 1 pm to 2 or 2.30 pm – all Monday to Friday. Other shops open from 9 am to 6 or 6.30 pm, with a half day on Saturdays, but there is an increasing tendency in big towns to stay open later and all day on Saturday. Throughout Germany, **plastic money** is less use than you might expect; as a rule, rely only on the larger establishments in major towns. Most useful is Visa.

German VAT (*Mehrwertsteuer*, MWST) stood at 12% at the time of writing, and refunds on single expensive items could be obtained by having the receipt stamped at customs, then sending it back to the shop. Service is included in all hotels and restaurants, but in the latter a small tip (say 5% maximum) is normal. Tips are not usually given in bars and beer halls, but lavatory attendants expect a pfew pfennings if you use their conveniences.

Once you are in Germany, and riding, you will soon discover that German **drivers** are highly disciplined and *quick*. The only time that you are likely to run into problems is when you are in the wrong lane, when the gentleman in the next lane may well refuse to let you in, because he is in the right, and you ... well, that is your problem. As already mentioned, never block the fast lane, and expect everyone to break the speed limit. Watch out for cop cars, because they can impose fines, but the usual way of catching speeding motorists is to photograph them with a remote-controlled camera and send the picture (with radar readout) to their home address. Motorcyclists, with no front number plate, are hard to catch at the best of times; foreign motorcyclists have little to fear.

Not that **speed limits** are usually a problem. There is an advisory limit of 130 kph (81 mph) on motorways, dual carriageways, and other roads with at least two marked lanes in each direction, but it is almost universally ignored. If there is an accident, and it can be proved that you were exceeding the advisory limit, it will tell against you in establishing liability – but that is all. On ordinary public roads, the speed limit is 100 kph (60 mph), and in towns it is 50 kph (31 mph). Guessing what constitutes a 'town' or 'built-up area' is not always easy, but there is usually a speed limit sign as you enter. All speed limits may, of course, be varied by appropriate signs.

Priority is usually clearly marked, with vehicles on the right taking precedence if there is any uncertainty. Trams have invariable right of way (even over pedestrians on pedestrian crossings), buses have right of way when they are pulling away from a bus stop, and traffic on a roundabout always has priority. So, too, do all emergency vehicles, as anywhere. One thing to watch out for is complex sets of traffic lights, operating in no detectable sequence, letting different streams of traffic through at different times.

Overtaking is always on the left, except for trams: in one-way streets, or where there is no room to the left, they may be overtaken to the right. It is illegal to overtake when there is a NO OVERTAKING sign, where overtaking would be dangerous (brows of hills, etc.), or near crossings and intersections. It is also illegal to stay in the overtaking lane any longer than is necessary. The police can and will impose on-the-spot fines for these offences, but will normally only do so if you actually are driving dangerously (including obstructing traffic), or if they got out of bed on the wrong side that morning.

Parking restrictions are generally posted, but there is also a long list of general restrictions which turn out to be common sense upon examination: on a main road, or one carrying fast-moving traffic; on a motorway, except in marked lay-bys; on or near tram lines; within 15 metres (49 feet) of a bus or tram stop; over manhole covers. You must park with the flow of the traffic, but you may park on the pavement so long as you do not obstruct the passage of pedestrians. There are marked and free motorcycle bays on the pavement in many cities.

Unusual or written road signs include the following:

Rollsplit	Loose grit
Frostschäden	Frost damage
Glatteisgefahr	Icy road
Radweg Kreutzt	Cycle track crossing
Strassenschäden	Road damage
Fahrbahnwechsel	change traffic lane (literally) drive-way-change
Baustofflagerung	Road works material store
Seitenstreifen nicht befahrbar	Use of road verge not advised

A picture of an eagle inside a green triangle means that you are inside a wildlife reserve, and may only park in marked bays.

By and large, you should have no trouble with the German **police** unless you go looking for it. They are friendly and helpful, and remain so even if you have broken the law – but only so long as you are polite back. Otherwise, they do not hesitate to react, as witness their behaviour at political demonstrations. They must be called to an accident if anyone is hurt, or if there is more than minor damage – it is up to you and the other guy to agree what is 'minor'. Telephone numbers for police and ambulance (110) and fire (112) are not completely standardized, but these numbers will work in over 95% of the country. Otherwise, look in the phone booth.

Breakdown services are operated by the ADAC and the AvD (for addresses, see above), as well as by two smaller German automobile clubs. As far as I was able to discover, anything more than the briefest attention of a passing patrolman must be paid for, even by members of affiliated clubs, but you might try waving your RAC or AA card.

It is worth knowing that in German law the concept of 'pure accident' does not seem to exist; blame must always be apportioned, and someone has to pay. As a result, many Germans take out third-party personal liability insurance, to cover non-motoring accidents. Such cover is very cheap, and normally forms a part of any holiday insurance package.

The ten-word vocabulary for Germany ist:

please	*bitte* (bitt-uh)
thank you	*danke* (dan-kuh)
yes	*ja* (ya)
no	*nein* (nine)
where?	*wo?* (voe)
room	*zimmer*
toilet	*klosset* or *abort*
more	*mehr* (mayr)
how much?	*was kostiert?* (vass koss-tea-urt)
eat	*essen*

German **food** is more filling than elegant, and not particularly cheap – better than England, worse than France on both counts. The cheapest places to eat are department store cafes and snackbars (*Schnellimbiss*, 'quick-snack', or *Imbissstube*, with three esses, 'snack-room'), with an ethnic restaurant for the evening meal – Greek, Italian, Yugoslav/Balkan and Turkish are all likely to prove cheaper than German restaurants. **Beer** is the cheapest drink, at little more than English prices, and very good it is: you can get *dunkel* (dark) or *helle* (light). Bars cost much more than *Bierstuben*, and supermarket beer is cheaper than either. Making friends in a *Bierstube* is usually easy, if thirsty work, and the Hofbrauhaus and the Bierstadt in Munich take beer-swilling to an art. Alternatively, time your visit for late September, which is when the crafty Bavarians hold their *Oktoberfest*. There are no problems with licencing hours, the blood alcohol content permitted by law is 80 mg/100 ml, and the water is always drinkable.

Accommodation costs depend very much on where you are. The big cities are expensive, with prices similar to England – worse if there is a trade fair, and the Germans are strong on trade fairs. On the other hand, go a few miles outside, and the prices drop to half or less, comparable with French rates. Look out, too, for rooms in private houses, or on farms; often, these will throw in breakfast for the same price as a *Gasthof* or modest hotel, and you get to sample real German hospitality. Otherwise, breakfast is not normally included.

Youth hostels are widespread and cheap, because the Germans practically invented the idea, and you can get a full list by sending five International Reply Coupons to *Deutsches Jugendherbergswerk*, Bulowstrasse 26, 4930 Detmold. Alternatively, Tourist Offices will have maps. For basic hostel-type accommodation in the mountains, try *Naturfreundejugend* (literally, 'Naturefriends-youth'), Grossglocknerstrasse 28, 7000 Stuttgart.

Camping on sites is cheap, and there are about 1900 official ones to choose from, though only about 400 stay open all year. 'Wild' camping is legal, but only if you get permission from the landowner or (for public land) the local police. If you don't get permission, and you do get found, you can rely on being hassled.

Luxembourg

The first time my wife and I visited Luxembourg, we thought it was some sort of festival. We went to bed early – it had been a long ride, and besides, we had not been married long – but we were kept awake by the disco and the revellers in the bar, who stayed until three in the morning. When we got up, at ten the next morning, they were boozing again; by the sound of it, they had been at it for hours already. The next time we went, we found that it was always like that (though we found a quieter hotel). What really amazed us was that although the bars open at first light, we couldn't find anywhere that sold food for breakfast. . . .

Apart from being a very thirsty little country, it is also an extremely attractive one. The north is wooded and hilly, like the Ardennes, the south is rich farming country, and the eastern border is the wine-growing country of the Moselle. Prices are agreeably low for food, drink, and accommodation – possibly even better value than France in some cases – and petrol is the cheapest in Europe: at the German border, there are long queues of cars at the weekends, waiting to fill up with cheap petrol and cheap booze. There are all the usual historical attractions – castles, old villages, monasteries, etc. – but the actual town of Luxembourg can be something of a disappointment, apart from the food and the booze.

From a practical point of view, most of the information for Belgium applies, with the following amendments: you must be 18 to ride there; daylight riding lights are compulsory; the green card is essential; the police actually collect on-the-spot fines, instead of just imposing them; and the law about couples one or both of whom is or are under 21 does not apply. The Luxembourgeois franc is on a par with the Belgian franc, but most places will accept not only their own and Belgian currency, but also French francs and German marks as well. Note that although you can use Belgian francs in Luxembourg, Luxembourgeois francs are not much use outside the country. Use 012 for police and general emergencies, 44 22 44 for fire and ambulance. You can park on the pavement if you do not cause an obstruction.

Food is good, and cheap – a rather solid and filling variation on French cooking, for the most part – and **booze** is particularly good value, though much more expensive in bars than at liquor stores. Beer is the usual tipple, though wine is also drunk and there are several rather intriguing liqueurs. **Hotels** are comparable with France, and the Luxembourg YHA (18 place d'Armes, Luxembourg-Ville) can give you the addresses of all nine **youth hostels**; at the time of writing, the standard fee at eight out of the nine was 110 francs for those under 26, 130 francs for those over 26 – not excessive! There is no age limit, but YHA members over 35 with a valid national ticket will only be admitted if there is a room after younger members have been accommodated. There are over 130 licenced camping sites, at modest rates, and you will find some bed-and-breakfast accommodation in private houses at good rates.

The Netherlands

Holland enjoys a curiously mixed reputation. On the one hand, it is held up as *the* place for rebellious youth, with all kinds of 'alternative' accommodation, entertainment, etc. Most things are legal: booze, dope in reasonable quantities, hard-core pornography, sleeping rough (except in a few prohibited areas), prostitution – you name it. But there is also an air of boredom, of indifference, and of suppressed violence, especially in Amsterdam. You can almost rely on seeing someone up against the wall, being frisked by the police, if you take an evening stroll; and the urban decay is depressing. The country side is deadly boring, though there is a certain amount of attraction in the architecture, and the roads are crowded and slow, even if most Dutch drivers do treat the 100 kph (62 mph) speed limit on the motorways as a minimum rather than a maximum.

Overall, unless you want to explore the 'alternative' scene, composed mainly of over-age hippies with a few teeny-bop hangers-on who may be good in bed but are not much use for anything else because they're too wasted on dope, there is not much to commend Holland. It's too far north, it's not particularly cheap (though not particularly expensive either), and it's very nearly as boring as north Belgium, from which it is indistinguishable. At best, it's a Scandinavian country that didn't quite make it.

You can ride at 17 on a full bike licence, though the Dutch have to be 18 and you can't ride a Dutch-registered machine unless you are 18. There are an awful lot of mopeds, a few Hell's Angels, and not much else; the average Dutch rider is pretty staid, not to say dull, and most of the people who would normally ride bikes in other countries are too stoned to stand up in Holland. The general attitude, to riders, repairs, spares, and everything else, is one of quiet efficiency – which looks very like dullness if you don't like the place. The only people I've met who do are real heads, who don't really notice what's going on anyway. The **roads** are good (but flat and crowded), and **petrol** is expensive; the choice is 91–92 octane *normal*, or rather good 98–99 octane *super*.

The Dutch **climate** is consistent across the whole country, though the coast is a little wetter than the inland parts, and can best be described as mild to the point of boring. Maximum average day temperatures only exceed 60° from May to September, and never reach the magic 70°; from June to September, minimum daily temperatures average something in the 50–55° range. In winter, by contrast, the minimum daily temperatures rarely get as low as freezing (though it is not much warmer). February to May are the driest months, with under 2″ of rain, but the monsoon sets in during July and August with over 3″ each month. May and June offer the best compromise, with the most sun (over 200 hours/month) combined with moderate temperatures (about 45–70°) and average rainfall.

The quickest way to get to Holland from the UK is via Oostende (Belgium) if you are coming from the south-east, or Harwich to the Hook of Holland if you are coming from the north, though it may be cheaper to go through Calais or Boulogne and ride a bit further. **Customs** are EEC standards, with an age limit of 15 for the booze and tobacco allowances. The 'other goods' allowance is fl. 450 for goods bought duty-paid in the EEC, fl. 90 otherwise. There is no form of currency control for non-residents.

Papers You will need a passport, but no visa if you are European, Canadian, or American (bad luck Australia and New Zealand). Your national licence is OK, and so are most European insurance policies: the minimum cover required by law is 1,000,000 guilders, which covers both personal injury and property damage but does not cover the policyholder, owner, or driver of the vehicle or their wives/husbands or any blood relations – so take your girlfriend rather than your wife! Don't forget the registration document or log book, and letter of permission from the owner if appropriate. **Helmets** are compulsory, daylight riding lights are not, and you do not have to carry spare bulbs, first aid kits, or other impedimenta.

Currency is the guilder, rather confusingly abbreviated to fl. (for *florin*), divided into 100 cents. **Banking** hours are 9 am to 4 pm, and many shops take foreign currency anyway. **Plastic money** is useful, but by no means infallible: don't rely on petrol stations accepting it. Shop hours are 9 am – 5.30 pm (5 pm on Saturdays) on weekdays, though some shops stay open longer and there may be a late opening night on Thursday or Friday (to 9 pm). There are also various half-day closing customs, usually Wednesday afternoon, but watch out for Monday mornings or other afternoons. Dutch VAT is called BTW, and there are various rates – high for luxuries, low for necessities. Refunds are normally only possible for business travellers, and then only on some things. Tips are usually added into the bill (*bediening inbegrepen*), and no extra is given; otherwise, reckon on the usual 10–15%.

Dutch **drivers** are a curious blend of the stolid and the manic, but the general standard is not too bad. The **roads** are well surfaced, but (except for the motorways) bicycle-infested, a result of the flat countryside. **Speed limits** are 100 kph maximum/70 kph minimum (62/44 mph) on motorways, 100 kph on dual carriageways, 80 kph (50 mph) on other roads, and 50 kph (31 mph) in built-up areas. **Right of way** is normally governed by common sense, tempered with priority to the right, but there are a few clever exceptions. One is that trams, funerals, and military convoys have priority along with the usual emergency vehicles, and another is that motor traffic has right of way over cycles except where specially signposted, or when you want to turn right across a cycle path (which is usually the case).

Overtaking is not permitted if it involves crossing a white line in the middle of the road – you are not allowed to do that, even to make a left turn – but otherwise, there are no overtaking restrictions for motorcyclists, except for those manoeuvres which would actually be dangerous, even when there are clear signs prohibiting other vehicles from overtaking.

Parking is prohibited in the following circumstances, most of which come down to common sense: where there are STOPVERBOD (no parking) signs; in front of driveways, etc., or in such a way as to obscure road signs, signposts, etc; on pedestrian crossings and bicycle crossings, or within 5 metres (16 feet) of the approach to such crossings; on access roads to and from main highways; on clearways (which say STOPVERBOD and display the international clearway sign); on cycle paths or footpaths; under bridges or viaducts, or in tunnels; on bends, curves, or the brows of hills; on the carriageway near a traffic island or a solid line, unless there is 3 metres left clear; in the fast and slow lanes near the exits of motorways (!); within 12 metres of a bus stop, or beside the black and white line painted at the kerb by such a stop, except to disembark or pick up passengers, and then only provided the bus is not obstructed; on level crossings; in the centre of the road, unless in a marked bay (!).

The road signs are the standard international ones, heavily supplemented: there is even a sign showing a dog crapping, with a red line through it. It means (you've guessed), 'Don't Let Your Dog Foul the Pavement'. There are so many signs that it is sometimes impossible to read them all if you are riding at more than a walking pace. Watch out especially for WOONERVEN, sleeping policemen, aka motorcyclist-killers. Other written signs are:

Tegenliggers	Oncoming traffic
Pas Op: filevorming	Attention: lane control ahead
Langzaam rijden	Slow down
Werk in Uitvoering	Road Works in Progress
Wegomlegging	Detour
Doorgaand verkeer gestremd	No thoroughfare
Opspattend Grind	Loose gravel (upspitting grit?)
Rechtsaf toegeslaan	Right Turn Permitted.

The Dutch **fuzz** are, for the most part, kindly family men with absolutely no pity. Break the law and they will nick you. The remainder are the same, only worse. They are particularly inclined to turn you over if you are young, and they turn very nasty very quickly: most sensible Dutchmen stay out of their way. The police emergency number, which you will need for all accidents, is 22, 22 22, and the emergency number for ambulances is 13 13 13. If there is a serious accident, or if it looks like apportioning blame might be difficult, call the police before the vehicles are moved.

In case of **breakdown**, members of affiliated foreign clubs can get free help from the *Koninklijke Nederlandsche Automobiel Club* patrols, or call their ANWB breakdown service on 22 44 66 in Amsterdam 63 69 68 in Den Haag. The head office is 4 Sophialaan, Den Haag 2005. Non-members can get temporary cover for fl. 61 (at the time of writing).

The basic ten-word vocabulary is given below, but almost all Dutch people speak English, so try that first.

please	*alstublieft*
thank you	*dank je* (dank ee)
yes	*ja* (yah)
no	*nee*
where is?	*waar is?*
room	*kamer* (kammer)
toilet	*WC* (vay-say)
more	*meer*
how much?	*hoeveel?* (hoy feel?)
eat	*eten* (ay-teh)

Dutch **food** is influenced by both German and Scandinavian cuisine, as well as by their colonial past: there are many Indonesian restaurants, which are usually cheaper than Dutch, but seem to offer the same dish (something cooked with peanuts) under ten different names. Indonesian food is a bit like Thai or Vietnamese, but (in my experience) nothing like as good as either. Eating is expensive, so try University canteens (*Mensa* – no ID normally required) or a *broodjeswinkel* (sandwich bar). Remember that Dutch hotel prices often include breakfast, which is usually cold but may offer cold meat and cheese as well as the usual continental roll-and-coffee. Picnics are reasonable value, and a canal-side location in town can be quite attractive; otherwise, why not go into the next country?

Beer is the national drink, and very pleasant most of it is. Heineken's do a free brewery tour, too. If you want a change from the usual light *pils*, ask for *bockbier*, which is darker and (usually) sweeter. I drink bottles rather than draught, because Dutch bartenders are even worse than the worst Germans when it comes to giving you six inches of froth and an inch of beer. There are no licencing laws to speak of, and the blood alcohol limit is a surprisingly low 50 mg/100 ml. The water is safe everywhere.

The range of **accommodation** available is wide, with the cheaper hotels comparing favourably in price with an English Bed and Breakfast (and including breakfast in many cases – check!). The VVV (Tourist Offices) in over 90 cities and towns offer a booking service for local rooms, both hotel and private, and for rooms in other parts of the country.

Staying in private houses is a good idea, because the Dutch people are mostly very nice; it's just the hippies and the police, and their amazingly flat country, that gets them a bad name.

Youth hostel prices typically include breakfast, and run at about half hotel prices. Contact *Nederlandse Jeugdherberg Centrale*, Prof. Tulpstraat 2–6, Amsterdam. Amsterdam is also famous for 'alternative' accommodation, often extremely co-educational, but don't blame me for anything you catch – and the choice is wide. Prices may be about the same as a youth hostel, maybe lower.

There are well-equipped and reasonably priced camp sites, and camping out is quite legal if you get the landowner's permission; camping on public land can be a hassle, unless you get well out of the way, and on the flat Dutch landscape a tent can be seen for miles. Sleeping out is legal, but the police may wake you up in the middle of the night if you are in a very public place, or if they are feeling bored.

Switzerland

After several false starts, I gave up trying to be nice about Switzerland. I will say that the countryside is attractive (but I prefer the Austrian Tyrol), I will admit that I have met some charming Swiss (though most go about with a face like a wet weekend), and I will say that there may be much in favour of Berne, which is the only part of Switzerland to which I have any desire to return. The roads are good, and fast, and toll-free, and the country is as clean and fresh and attractive as you wish, apart from near-terminal air pollution in places. It is even possible to find affordable accommodation, at least by English standards. Oh yes; and the police are polite, friendly, and helpful. So why don't I like the place?

It is viciously, staggeringly, blindingly money-minded: where else would they count the bread rolls on the table and charge you per roll? Even the cheapest place in France provides free bread. It is expensive, and the food is (to be charitable) indifferent. There may be excellent restaurants; but unless you have a Swiss Bank-sized expense account, you will not be eating at them. The inhabitants are grotesquely old-fashioned – last time I checked, women still had no vote, though that was a long time ago – and acutely self-satisfied: they are just beginning to get the rumblings of disaffected youth, and living in Switzerland you can begin to sympathize with the Baader-Meinhof Gang. They love rules and regulations; a Tibetan friend who lived in Switzerland told me that it was written into the lease of his flat that he should not take a bath after 10:00 pm, or flush his toilet after midnight. On the subject of toilets, the public ones seem to close on Sunday. The Swiss complain about rates of unemployment and inflation which would ensure instant re-election for any other government anywhere in the world. It is illegal to drink standing up (!). Even push-bikes have to be registered. I could go on ... and on ... and on.

But let's look on the bright side. It is worth visiting Switzerland, if only to check on whether it really is that bad, and if you camp out (very cheap on authorised sites, free and legal on uncultivated land in most cantons, but ask at the local town hall or police station) it need not be too expensive. Picnic food is tolerable in price, and if you find a helpful Swiss (and as I've said, there are many), you will have a charming host. Just don't expect instant friendliness from everyone. Even the Tourist Office in London was so offhand that I had to compile this entirely without their help – and they are supposed to be encouraging visitors! I am told that the Swiss Cyclists' and Motor-Cyclists' Federation, Schaffhauserstrasse 272, 8057 Zurich are helpful though (tel. 469 220).

Climate Summer is the obvious time to go, but spring and autumn can also be attractive, if a trifle chilly; not until May do maximum average daily temperatures rise above 60°, and by the end of September they are back in the 50s again. Rainfall is fairly low and constant, with the spring drier (and sunnier) than the autumn.

Papers Holders of British, US, and Canadian passports need no visa for up to three months (and no one can afford to stay longer!). You must be 18 to ride in Switzerland, but a national licence is sufficient; you can ride on your British insurance, with a liability limit of one million Swiss francs (well over £300,000, or about half a million dollars) covering any combination of personal and property damage; and you will need your registration document or log book.

Getting there is easy; you can make the 425 miles from Calais to Basel in a day if you are a masochist, or take it easy in two days. The **customs** allowance is 200 cigarettes or 50 cigars or 250 gm tobacco; 2 litres of alcohol up to 25°, and one litre of more than 25°; 125 cc of perfume; and 10 unexposed rolls of film (no limit on exposed rolls). Non-European residents flying in from outside Europe are entitled to twice the tobacco and perfume allowances, and there are then no limits on film. Other goods to a value of SFr 100 are also permitted, but the import of firearms, drugs, meat and poultry products are restricted. It is illegal to import absinthe or anaesthetics!

Once you are in, you are faced with narrow, winding, beautifully-surfaced **roads**, lots of tunnels (fascinating things to ride in), and varying degrees of overcrowding. One of the weirdest experiences I have had was riding into a tunnel on one side of a mountain in grey drizzle, and four miles later emerging into bright sunlight and blue sky; the low cloud was actually trapped inside the first valley. Everyone has to use dipped lights in tunnels, but that is no problem for motorcyclists: daylight riding lights are compulsory. So, inevitably, are crash **helmets**. **Petrol** stations are frequent, and most take plastic money; the grades are *regular* (90–92 octane) and *super* (96–98 octane), both normally available. **Speed limits** on the motorways are 130 kph (81 mph); on other roads 100 kph (62 mph); and in town 60 kph (37 mph). They are, of course, enforced. The usual on-the-spot fine for speeding is in the 40–60 franc range (say £15–20), and it is payable *on the spot*. Surprisingly, Swiss **drivers** are law-abiding but not disciplined; there seems to be an informal competition to see how badly you can drive and still remain legal. **Right of way** is priority-to-the-right, with some cunning modifications. Main roads always have right of way, but only in built-up areas do they carry the priority sign; otherwise, blue posts indicate a priority road. Trams and the yellow post buses always have priority, but on mountain roads priority normally goes to the ascending vehicle or (on flat bits) to the larger vehicle. Bloody caravans have priority over heavy vehicles! At junctions, if two approaching vehicles both want to turn left, they must drive around the back of each other – not the front, which is easier. 'Needless and exaggerated' use of the horn is forbidden, and it is banned altogether (except in emergencies) between 11 pm and dawn. **Overtaking** is normally to the left, except that motorcyclists may overtake either stationary or moving traffic on the right if there is room. It is however illegal to 'carve' in and out of queues of traffic. Trams and trains must be overtaken on the right, unless there is no room, in which case the left is OK. Stationary trams may only be overtaken on the right unless a pedestrian refuge is provided, in which case they can be overtaken on the left. Overtaking is forbidden where visibility is restricted (eg on bends, or the brows of hills), and a continuous white line in the middle of the road may not be crossed. Two unusual road signs are a post-horn, and a tyre with snow-chains. The post-horn indicates a postal priority road in the mountains (see the note about post-buses above), and a horn with a line through it signals the end of the postal priority. The tyre with snow-chains indicates that chains are *compulsory* for cars. No one was able to tell me what motorcyclists should do; my advice would be to stay home, or put the bike on the train. **Parking** on the pavement is quite legal, except where it would obstruct pedestrians; you should have no problems. As already mentioned, the Swiss **police** are among the friendliest Swiss that you are likely to meet, and they are unfailingly polite and helpful. Their number is 117; you have to call them only if anyone is hurt. In the event of **breakdowns**, Swiss efficiency at its best will ensure a rapid and high-quality repair, but it will cost you an arm and a leg. The Touring Club Suisse runs a 24-hour breakdown service; their head office is at 9 rue Pierre Fatio, 1200 Geneva (tel. 366 000), but call 140 from anywhere. You are in Switzerland, remember; any work other than a courtesy call has to be paid for.

The Swiss **Franc** is divide into 100 centimes (*Rappen* in Schweizdeutsch); the coins are 5, 10, 20, and 50 c, and 1, 2, and 5SFr, with immaculately clean notes for 10, 20, 50, 100, 500, and 1000 SFr. There are no restrictions on import or export of any currency. Frighteningly, though, the Swiss franc has about the same puchasing power as a French franc, despite the fact that there are about 3FF to the SFr. For conversions, allow 3 SFr/£, 2 SFr/$; in fact, it's a bit more than three and a bit less than five, but it makes calculations easier. **Credit cards** are widely accepted. **Banking hours** are variable, but basically 8.00 am to noon, and 2 pm to 4.30 pm – often longer in big cities. Shop hours are from about 8 or 8.30 am to 6.30 pm, with or without a lunch break from about noon to 1.30 or 2 pm, but many shops close at about 4.00 pm on a Saturday and do not re-open until Monday afternoon. Many towns have an early closing day, which varies just as it does in England, and a few supermarkets, etc., keep longer hours, often with late-night shopping on Thursdays (to 8 pm). Tips are included *by law* on hotel and restaurant bills, and the ever-mean Swiss rarely give more; my wife and I made quite a friend of one waitress by giving her an extra 10% (by mistake, it must be said!).

The Swiss use several languages, with German (or a passable imitation – Germans call it *schwarzdeutsch*, 'black German', the accent is so peculiar) at the top of the list, quite passable French, Italian, Romansch (rare, and not worth worrying about), plus a lot of English. There is, therefore, no need for a vocabulary.

The **food** is undistinguished; a French gourmet of our acquaintance, who is not afraid of spending money on food, declares that it is impossible to eat well in Switzerland at any price, and crosses the border for a meal. It is also hellishly expensive, even by English standards – perhaps 50–100% more than you would pay for a similarly indifferent meal in London. Swiss **beer** is good (but expensive), and Swiss **wine** is indifferent (and very expensive). I was not able to find a blood alcohol level figure, but I do know that they habitually imprison anyone who is convicted. The tap water is safe, and often very pleasant.

Accommodation is also frightening, comparable with the United Kingdom, but standards are higher. Even the cheapest hotels (which are not cheap at all) are immaculate, and the fact that breakfast is almost invariably included does soften the blow somewhat. Private bed-and-breakfast is rare, but cheaper, but the best options are either camping (as already described) or crossing the border and staying in France or Italy whenever possible. Because of the amazingly unhelpful National Tourist Office, I was unable to find out about youth hostels, though I believe that they do exist, and are about the same price as a modest hotel in France.

Liechtenstein

Liechtenstein covers 61 square miles and has 26,000 occupants; the capital, Vaduz, houses about a fifth of them. It is effectively a part of Switzerland, with Swiss border guards on the Austrian border, Swiss currency, and Swiss telephones. It does issue its own stamps, and another way of raising money is as a haven for the registration of merchant shipping, but there are also many light and not-so-light industries and a very high standard (and cost) of living. It is reputed to be very picturesque, more Swiss than Switzerland in some ways, with a touch of Southern German/Austrian romance. From the gazetteers, it looks as if accommodation is a good deal cheaper than in Switzerland, and more on a par with European levels generally, but I have never been there and cannot say.

All the practical details for Switzerland apply to Liechtenstein.

Southern Europe

Introduction

If you want real warmth, you have to go south. This section is something of a mixed bag, embracing the usual reasonably accessible warm countries (Italy, Portugal, and Spain), two minor countries which are often overlooked (Andorra and San Marino), and Malta, which is pretty much out on its own.

With any of these countries, you are talking about fair-sized journeys – 500 miles or more – and although you are not exactly venturing into the unknown, you are going to relatively poor countries in which spares for the bike, and indeed many other things that you may take for granted, are not always available. Consequently, a reliable and simple bike is a major asset; so is a good-sized petrol tank, because I have assumed that you will want to see the less well-known parts of these countries. If you want to have a cheap holiday, with English food and Watneys, take a package instead: it will be a lot cheaper and easier.

If you are not used to heat, be wary of high summer. I love warm weather, but I wilt when it gets over 90° – quite common in the places described. Remember, too, that the bike may not like such high temperatures; take the riding easy, and be aware of the risk of seizure in two-strokes if they are ridden at high revs for long periods.

As will become obvious on reading the section, I believe that Portugal is one of the finest places in the world for motorcycle touring, and if you want to try riding in a warm country, this may be your best bet to start with. Now that Spain and Portugal have joined the EEC, it should be even easier to tour there – but it may also be that the dead hand of the EEC bureaucracy will stifle the place, so go as soon as possible.

Andorra

I want to go back to Andorra,
It's a land I do adore;
They spent four dollars and ninety cents
On armaments for their defence
Did you ever hear such confidence?
It's a land I do adore.

The arms bill may by now have hit ten dollars, for the
ceremonial blanks fired at salutes (the police force is the
army in time of need – or vice versa), but it still gives some
idea of what Andorra is like. Extraordinarily unspoiled, ruled
jointly by the President of France (in his capacity as Prince of
Andorra) and the Spanish Bishop of Urgel (in *his* capacity as
Prince of Andorra), the 188-square-mile country use the
postal services of both Spain and France (depending on
whether you buy stamps in pesetas or francs, either of which
are accepted) and the French phone system. Entry
formalities from either neighbour are non-existent, though
both French and Spanish customs on leaving will be quite
rigorous – there are no sales taxes, and precious few other
taxes. It is not particularly cheap, but it is certainly a very long
way from expensive. It is beautiful, with 9000ft mountains,
deep gorges, clean rivers, and abundant wildlife; it really is
one of those places which is worth going to soon, before
everyone else discovers it. To get the army (or police), phone
21 222, for fire and ambulance ring 200 20.

Italy

Italy is a surprisingly long way from England, but it can be well worth the ride. The climate is excellent and varied; prices, except in the big cities and tourist resorts, are low, even the French admire Italian food and wine (though they still maintain that their own is better, of course!); you can find just about any sort of road that you want, from *autostrade* (toll, admittedly) to winding mountain roads; you can hike in the mountains, or lie on the beaches, though you would do well to choose just where you swim – the Mediterranean is pretty filthy in places; there are unique cities, like Rome and Venice; and fast machinery is admired and looked after. For Italian bike freaks, it is paradise: Laverda, Ducati, Moto Guzzi, Moto Morini. . . .

There are drawbacks, though. Italian drivers are neither as skilled as they think they are nor as considerate as they should be, and Italian roads are not the safest place in the world. The police enforce the law only patchily, but they have been know to pick on tourists as an easy target. Theft is an ever-present danger: a favourite trick is for two men on a scooter to zoom past, so that the one on the pillion can slash a camera strap or shoulder bag strap and make off with it, though this is really only a risk in the major towns; but in the far south, especially in Sicily, there are bandits in the hills, and you are in kidnap country.

Individualism is the keynote to Italian riding; the natives are all convinced that they are the best rider (or driver, or both) in the world, and you are expected to live up to their high standards – or, a cynic might say, to save your hide from their mistakes. Everything is seen as an invitation to a race, but in all fairness, other drivers never try to kill you: they are usually too busy trying to kill themselves. It is easy to be pushed into showing off, and riding a bit faster than is safe, but as long as you bear that in mind, it is an exhilarating place to ride. High-octane **petrol** is freely available everywhere, at fairly high prices, and the Italians have mixed feelings about tourist petrol vouchers; at the time of writing, such vouchers were available, but it is quite possible that by the time of publication they will have withdrawn them again. Again at the time of writing, you could buy 150 litres pre-paid if you were going to Rome or north of Rome, or 350 litres if you were going south of Rome. This not only saves about 40% of the price of petrol; it also gets you five free 2000 lire motorway toll vouchers on the 150 litre deal, eight free 2000 lire vouchers with 350 litres. When you leave, unused vouchers can be exchanged, and even though there is a service charge, this is an excellent way to save money.

The **climate** will depend as much on where you go as on when you go. In the summer, the heat in the south can be fierce, with 100° commonplace even at night; but on the same August day, the temperature in the Alps might be a bracing 70°. As a general guide, unless you like *real* heat, avoid central Italy in July and August, and the south (especially inland) as early as June, except right on the coast. The mountains, on the other hand, are at their best in high summer; with the exception of Venice, the mountains are really the main attraction of northern Italy, which is otherwise pretty flat, dull, and industrialized. In the winter, the mountain passes into Switzerland may be blocked for brief periods, but they are going to be fairly unattractive for motorcycling even if they are open; a better idea is to ride around the side of the Alps, via southern France.

If you want to go to Italy in a hurry, you can ride from London to Rome in two days (it is about 1100 miles), but three would be more comfortable, and I would be inclined to take four. Remember, too, that there is still plenty of Italy left after Rome: Syracuse, in Sicily, is close to six hundred miles more. Because it is so far, and because Italy is so big, it would be foolish to allocate too little time there. A visit to Italy, together with the ride there and the ride back, should take up anyone's vacation.

Papers No visa is demanded for citizens of most countries, provided they are staying less than three months, but you are supposed to register with the police within three days of entering. Hotels should do this automatically, though the Italian Tourist Office guide book adds the sinister warning that the visitor is responsible for checking that it has been done. If you are camping, the camp site may do it, or you can go to a police station – or just not bother, because the chances of trouble are negligible unless you are arrested for something. You need the registration document or log book, plus letter if applicable, and your licence *plus a translation into Italian*, which you can get from most motoring clubs or the Italian Tourist Office, or even from the Automobile Club of Italy at the border, free of charge. You can ride on a full licence at 17, although Italians need to be 18 to ride anything over 150cc, or 16 for bikes under 150cc with a licence. In common with most other European countries, anyone can ride a moped at 16 without a licence. The Green Card is theoretically not required, but you may have difficulty in persuading the frontier guards and police of this. The minimum cover under Italian law varies according to the size of the motorcycle; up to 150cc it is $7\frac{1}{2}$ million lire for material damage, 75 million lire for each person injured, and an overall limit of 100 million lire for any one accident, and for over 150cc it is 15 million lire for material damage, 75 million lire for each person injured, and 150 million lire for any one accident. As a rough guide, 75 million lire is £37,000 or $50,000, so the limits are not excessively generous. Passenger liability is automatic. Apart from this, there are no particular requirements – not even to wear a **helmet**! Italy is one of the last countries in Europe not to require a helmet, and the law may change at any time, but with Italian driving standards it is still not a bad idea to wear one. The Italian authorities also recommend (though do not require) that you carry a set of spare bulbs; Italian police are hot on lighting offences, so this is well worth doing.

At the frontier, **customs** allowances are the EEC standards, with 'Other goods' allowances of £120 (for duty- and tax-paid goods) and £28 (for duty free), and an age limit of 17 for booze and tobacco. There is a limit of 10 films per camera, and two cameras, but this is seldom enforced. Declare any valuable jewellery on entry, in order to avoid problems on exit. Currency control allows the import or export of up to 200,000 lire in Italian currency, plus export of up to 200,000 lire in other currencies provided it is declared on entry.

The **lire** is one of those currencies which leads to telephone-number figures, with (very roughly) 2000 lire to the £ sterling, or 1500 lire to the dollar. Allow for considerable variations; the lire is not one of the strongest currencies in the world. Also, do not be surprised if your small change includes an element of barter, such as chewing gum; there is a chronic shortage of low-value coins. Come to think of it, all coins are low value; the most valuable is 500 lire (25p), and they also have 200 lire (10p), 100 lire (5p), 50 lire (2½p), 20 lire (1p), 10 lire (½p) and even 5 lire (¼p). **Plastic money** is readily acceptable in the big hotels and expensive stores, but virtually useless elsewhere, especially in rural petrol stations. **Bank** hours are 8.30 am to 1.30 pm, Monday to Friday, and shopping hours very variable indeed. Assume roughly 8 am to 8 pm, earlier for food stores, and a long siesta, from about 1 pm to 4 pm, but do not be surprised at variations, especially in the north.

Sales tax varies widely, from 6–35% at the time of writing, depending on the Italian government's view of how much of a luxury the item in question is, but the standard rate is 14%. As far as I know, no refund scheme operates, but no doubt individual stores will tell you if it does. Tipping, the other percentage swindle, is basically 10%, though restaurants will expect 15% *and* charge a small cover fee unless they specifically say that service is included (*servizio compreso*). Everyone expects a tip: lavatory attendants and cinema usherettes (200 lire each), and bars (5–10%) are some of the less familiar ones.

The question if Italian **driving** standards has already been aired, and as you might expect, the speed limits are flexibly interpreted – though this does not stop the police pulling you in if you are breaking them. There are different speed limits for different capacities of vehicles and for different types of road, so the whole thing is horribly complicated.

On *autostrade*, the **speed limits** are 80 kph (50 mph) for bikes under 100cc; 90 kph (56 mph) for 100–149cc; and 130 kph (82 mph) for anything bigger – which is slower than the maximum car limit of 140 kph (88 mph), and the same as for cars of 900–1300cc.

On ordinary country roads, however, the limits for bikes are the same as they are on motorways, whereas cars are limited to 110 kph (over 1300cc), 100 kph (900–1300cc), and even less for smaller vehicles. This means that you can have a lot of fun on this sort of road, legally burning off everything in sight. Watch out, though, for horseshoe nails and other junk, and remember that Italians hate being overtaken, so expect some hairy moments. In built up areas, everyone is subject to the same 50 kph (31 mph) limit.

Right of way is 'Who Dares, Wins', but the theory is that traffic on state highways (*Strade Statali*, numbered and indicated by signs) has precedence, but otherwise it is strictly priority-to-the-right unless otherwise sign-posted. Trams, trains, and emergency vehicles always have right of way, and on postal routes, the buses operated by the Italian Post Office have right of way. An Italian with right of way will always claim it; he is also likely to claim it even when you are in the right.

Overtake on the left, except when someone is turning left and has signalled his intention to do so, or in town when parallel rows of traffic are permitted, and you may overtake trams on the right if passengers have finished getting on and off. Overtaking is not permitted close to or on curves, or in hilly country, where visibility is restricted. On the open road, the horn may be used whenever audible warning of approach is needed (i.e., permanently), and although its use is theoretically restricted to cases of immediate danger in towns, it is enthusiastically sounded whenever possible.

Outside cities and towns, **parking** on the right-hand side of the road is permitted except on *autostrade*, at crossroads, and anywhere that visibility is restricted, traffic is obstructed, or road signs are obscured. In towns, parking is utter anarchy; chain the bike to something big enough to be a part of the landscape, and preferably somewhere that a fork-lift truck cannot operate. No one seems to worry about parking on the pavement, so long as there is no obstruction.

Road signs are mostly standardized, but the written ones which the Italian Tourist Office thinks you ought to know about are listed below. Incidentally, although the London tourist office was unhelpful to the point of obstruction, the Travellers Handbook which they give out is excellent, and updated every year.

Senso Vietato	No Entry
Vietato Ingresso Veicoli	No Entry for Vehicles
Sosta Autorizzata	Parking Permitted
Vietato Transito Autocarri	Closed to Heavy Vehicles
Sosta Vietata	No Parking
Pasaggio a Livello	Level Crossing

Rallentare	Slow Down
Entrata	Entrance
Uscita	Exit, Turn-Off
Svolta	Bend
Incrocio	Crossroads
Lavori in Corso	Road Works Ahead

The variability of Italian **police** has already been mentioned, but you are not obliged to call them to an accident unless there is personal injury. The emergency number (all services) is 113.

Breakdowns can be dealt with by the *Automobile Club d'Italia*, based at 8 Via Marsala, 00815 Roma; if you belong to a foreign affiliated club, you will normally only have to pay a modest call-out fee, but non-members may also use the service and for them the fees are not modest. Dial 116 to get the breakdown service. The other Italian motoring club is the *Touring Club Italiano*, 10 Corsa Italia, 20122 Milano. Otherwise, Italian mechanics are world-famous and (except in the big cities) not expensive, though more accustomed to relatively low-tech European bikes than to Japanese metal. Spares, especially European spares, should be no problem.

The basic vocabulary is:

please	*per favore* (pair fah-vaw-ray)
thank you	*grazie* (grat-zee)
yes	*si*
no	*no*
where is?	*dov'e* (doh-vay)
room	*stanza*
toilet	*gabinetto*
more	*piu* (pee-oo)
how much?	*quanto?*
eat	*mangiare* (manjee-ah-ray)

Food Everyone knows about *pasta* and *pizza*, but there is far more to Italian cuisine than this, including risotto, all kinds of soups, and many kinds of roasted and grilled meat. Seafood can be excellent, but it comes from the often heavily polluted Mediterranean, so beware of clams, oysters, etc. Fish, shrimps, and lobsters are another matter entirely. You can eat filling and sustaining food very cheaply, in the non-tourist *trattorie*; you can eat very elegant food at a fairly high price, in non-tourist restaurants; or you can be ripped off blind and fed pigswill at the tourist spots. Looking at a few menus and prices will soon show you where to go – but the cheapest (and often best) *trattorie* have no menu, so you must be prepared to find out what is available and what it costs, and leave if you don't like it or it is too expensive. One thing to watch out for is that you *must* get a receipt (*recevuta fiscale*), showing the cost of the meal and the sales tax. This curious law was introduced to stop sales tax avoidance, and both you and the restaurant owner can be fined if you cannot produce the receipt as you are leaving! If you want to picnic, the bread, cheese, fruit, salami, and olives available everywhere make an excellent meal.

Wine is the national **drink**, and it is generally much better than you might expect if you have bought cheap Italian wine outside Italy. It is true that the very cheapest can be absolutely vile, like drinking extract of iron filings, but otherwise you should be pleasantly surprised. The beer, on the other hand, is used mainly for thirst quenching, along with mineral water; the tap water is not invariably safe. For spirits, Italian brandy has its adherents, and if you simply want to get wasted cheaply, try *grappa*, which is firewater made from the grape seeds and skins that are left after wine pressing. It is something of an acquired taste, but the more expensive varieties are vastly more drinkable than the cheapest. I was unable to find the permitted blood alcohol level, but assume 80 mg/100 ml (as in most of Europe), and you should not go far wrong.

Like the food and drink, **accommodation** is delightfully inexpensive. There are five classes of hotel (De Luxe, 1, 2, 3, 4), and three of pension or boarding-house (1, 2, 3). The prices are Government controlled, and should be posted inside the room; these are *maximum* prices, and out of season you should be able to get a reduction. Rome is obviously expensive, and so are Venice and some of the industrial towns of the north, but at the time of writing it should still be possible to find a single room in a 3rd class hotel for 5000 lire or so (under £3/$5) in most places. One institution which is, as far as I am aware, unique to Italy is the *albergho diurno* or 'day hotel'. These provide baths, laundry, barbers, and various other facilities, but no sleeping accommodation.

Youth hostels are governed by the *Associazione Italiana Alberghi per la Gioventu*, Palazzo della Civilita del Lavoro, Quadrato della Concordia, Roma (tel. 591 3702), who will send a free map and list of hostels on request (send a couple of International Reply Coupons). There are three grades of youth hostel, with the cheapest starting at under 4000 lire a night. During university vacations, you may also be able to get cheap accommodation in university halls; check with the local *Casa dello Studente*. If you are walking in the mountains, there are also 500 refuge huts in the Alps; talk to the *Club Alpino Italiano*, Via Ugo Foscolo 3, Milano about these.

There are only about 1200 registered camp sites, which are surprisingly expensive (comparable with a really cheap hotel), and it is illegal to camp on public land, though you can camp on private land with the permission of the landowner. If you do, stay out of sight, or the police may hassle you anyway; they don't like wild camping. Sleeping rough is likely to attract the attention of the police (if you are lucky) and muggers (if you aren't).

San Marino

San Marino is a tiny republic, 25 square miles in area, which miraculously escaped the unification of Italy. It is genuinely independent, with its own elected Regent Captains (elected every six months!), but it uses Italian money and is part of the Italian phone network, as well as having absolutely no border formalities with Italy. About the only real distinction is that you have to use San Marino stamps – a major source of revenue.

The other source is of course tourism, and in July and August you can barely move. Ideally, go in the spring, before the crowds start; then, you can admire the superb mountain scenery and the three massive old castles which brood over it. To get there, take the Ancona road out of Bologna, and turn right instead of left at the Rimini turnoff.

Malta

No one can be objective about a country in which he grew up, and as I had the good fortune to spend four years of my childhood in Malta, I cannot be entirely objective about the place.

Despite its tiny size, it is a fascinating place. It is jammed with living history, from the prehistoric tombs of Hal Saflieni and Hagar Qim through the Moorish walled city of Mdina to the 'city built by gentlemen for gentlemen', Valetta. The people are friendly, and everyone speaks English – a legacy of the British naval base which only closed in the 1960s, and which was the biggest single employer on the island. The sister island of Gozo is smaller and more primitive, and the minute island of Comino was still only inhabited in the summer (by goatherds) when I lived there in 1960. Although strongly Catholic, the Maltese culture is as much Arab as Italian, and the language is close to Arabic – which accounts for bizarre spellings like Ghajn Tuffeija, Luqa, Mdina, and Ghaxxar.

Climate As might be expected, it can get very hot indeed – I remember 100°F on the roof at midnight once – and even in January, the average lowest daily temperature is in the high 40s. The summer is bone dry, too, and unless you like dry heat, the autumn and winter are best. From October to February, the rainfall can be considerable, so March, April, May and September are the months to go.

Papers You will need your log book or registration document and national driving licence, but matters are complicated by the fact that Malta does not recognize the Green Card, so you will have to arrange special insurance before you leave, or buy it in Malta. The only other requirement – patchily enforced, but a good idea considering Maltese driving – is that you wear a **helmet**.

Getting there is a slow process. You need to go to the toe of Italy, take a ferry to Sicily, and then another ferry to Malta. You might be able to do this in four days, but it would be much more realistic to allow at least a week. No visa is needed if you intend to stay less than three months, and customs searches are aimed more at serious illegalities than at personal goods, so any reasonable goods such as a bottle of spirits, a couple of bottles of wine, a couple of hundred cigarettes, etc., are unlikely to cause any problems. There are no restrictions on the import of money, but you cannot export more than £M25 in Maltese currency plus £M250 in foreign currency *or travellers' cheques*, though the second restriction does not apply if you have declared more on entry.

Once you are there, the **roads** are small, crowded, and vary from well-surfaced to out-and-out goat tracks. All grades of **petrol** are readily available, at fairly high prices, but there is just not room to ride far. Maltese **driving** is fairly hair-raising, though not as bad as Greek, and the **speed limits** of 25 mph in town and 40 mph elsewhere are fairly academic for most drivers – though the police can and will nick you if you are riding dangerously. One thing that is very important is that **the Maltese drive on the left**, another legacy of the British Empire, and the rules of the road governing **parking, overtaking, right of way**, etc, are all the same (in theory) as in Britain. Readjusting to this after the long ride through Italy can take some doing; it may be a better idea to fly in to Malta and hire something to ride when you arrive.

Maltese **police** are friendly enough, and used to be easily bribed, but since Independence things have improved somewhat (from a moral, if not a practical, point of view). In Malta, call the police on 99, ambulance on 96, and road accidents on 88; in Gozo, the numbers are 899, 896, 888. They only have to be called in case of personal injury, or property damage which cannot be settled amicably on the spot. In the event of mechanical disaster, Maltese **mechanics** are often geniuses of the bodge-it-with-string school, but do not rely on spares availability. Old British bikes are reasonably well served, and Italian spares can obviously be got quite quickly, but big bikes are almost unknown on the island and so no spares are carried – another argument for hiring!

The **currency** is the Maltese pound (£M), which is worth rather more than the £ sterling – almost $2. The notes are £1, £5, and £10, and the coins are 2, 3, and 5 mils (10 mils = 1 cent), and 1, 2, 5, 10, and 50 cents. **Plastic money** is only accepted in the more expensive places, and not in gas stations. **Bank hours** are Monday–Saturday 8.30

to 12.30, 12.00 on Saturdays. Shopping hours are around 9.00 am to 7.00 pm or later, Monday to Saturday (usually latest on Saturdays), with a siesta from about 1.00 pm to 3.00–4.00 pm. In the more expensive places, 10–15% tips are expected; in the poorer ones, 5–10% is fine.

There is little point in giving a Maltese vocabulary, because almost everyone speaks English, and Maltese is pretty difficult (as witness the spellings already given).

Food In restaurants, there is a heavy Italian influence with lots of pasta, but the dishes are still very Maltese. Ask the waiter what is in them. Picnic food is very cheap indeed. **Drink** the local wine, but don't expect it to be anything very impressive, and don't worry about the water – though it tastes pretty unpleasant, and in 1953 I caught diptheria from it (it's much cleaner now). I don't think that there is a blood alcohol level set by law; they give you the old tests like walking along a chalk line, smelling your breath, etc. If you take the limit as being 80 mg/100 ml, you will not go far wrong.

Accommodation There are some expensive hotels, but even quite good hotels are not particularly expensive, and cheap boarding-houses can be very cheap indeed. There is no organized camping, but disorganized camping is perfectly legal; the police will only hassle you if you are (say) in a public park, or too near the shore on a beach. You can sleep out, too. Watch out, however, for scorpions and the like!

Portugal

Portugal is easily my favourite European country for touring. The climate is excellent, the people are wonderful, the food and wine are marvellous, and the prices are low. The Portuguese love motorcycles and motorcyclists; low wages and high import dues make big bikes unusual, but (for example) a road mending gang will stop and wave if they see one passing. The people are honest and friendly, and any attempt to speak Portuguese will be met with enthusiasm.

There is a negative side. Parts of the Algarve, in the extreme south, are so geared to the English tourist that you might as well be in Spain, and the Portuguese are not the best drivers in the world. Normally, traffic density is so low that it doesn't matter, but on the crowded main roads (such as the Porto/Lisbon road), travelling is not pleasant. It is, however, possible to avoid such roads almost entirely, and to have a tremendous range of roads virtually to yourself. The only other drawback is that some road surfaces in villages are more suitable for a trail bike than a tourer, and if you have really hard suspension you may find the cobbles rather hard on the rump – I measured eleven miles of cobbles once, at a stretch! I wouldn't have noticed that there was a problem with cobbles, because the BMW just soaks them up, but a friend on a Honda 450 swore that he'd never ride in Portugal again.

Most people go to the Algarve, the coastal strip at the very bottom of the country, and indeed that is a very fine part of the world, but it is the most expensive and the most spoiled part of Portugal. The very end, from Lagos to Cape St. Vincent, is about the only unspoilt part left, and I wouldn't want to see Lagos again. The Algarve is in season almost all the year around, though late November to early February can be rather wintry, and the high summer can be too hot for some people unless you stay near the coast.

I prefer the other end of the country, though, north of Oporto. There, you can ride through stunning scenery, and see a country almost untouched by tourists. There are mountains, lakes, forests, mediaeval villages, and truly beautiful countryside, and the whole area is so small that you can explore it in some detail in a couple of weeks. The best season is spring or autumn; summer can be very hot (though that is fine by me), and there is snow in the winter.

Wherever you go, **petrol** stations are reasonably frequent, and sell two and a half grades of petrol; usually, you only find 85 octane *regular* and 96 octane *super*, but you sometimes find 98 octane *super especial*, which high-compression bikes digest better. Prices are a bit higher than average for Europe, and plastic money is virtually useless in petrol stations.

Papers British, Canadian, US, and Australian nationals do not need a passport; nor do inhabitants of other Western European countries, though New Zealanders do. The entry stamp entitles you to stay for 60 days, and this can be extended if you apply to the police at least 7 days before its expiry. Note that none of the border crossings is open 24 hours a day; in summer, expect closure from midnight to seven am or so (maybe longer), and in winter, from around 9 pm to 8 am.

For the bike, you will need the log book or registration document (plus letter of authorization if the bike is not yours), your national licence, and insurance. A Green Card is not essential, at least in theory, but it does smooth border formalities and gives reasonable cover: the Portuguese legal minimum is only 700,000 escudos (say £3500) and does not require passenger cover. You will also need to be 18 years old; as far as I have been able to discover, 17-year-olds cannot ride anything over 50cc (for which the age limit is 16), even if they hold a full UK or other licence. Helmets are now compulsory, and the law seems to be fully observed, and you can be fined for failing to display a nationality plate.

Getting to Portugal from England involves either a long ride through France and Spain – allow at least two days, preferably three, to get to anywhere north of Lisbon – or the unimpressive and expensive, but admirably time and energy saving, 24-hour ferry from Plymouth to Santander in northern Spain. From Santander, it is only a few hours to Braganza. When you arrive, you may find that **customs** formalities have been adjusted to EEC standards – it was happening at the time of writing – but in mid-1984 the rules were as follows: 200 cigarettes or 50 cigars or 250 gm tobacco; one bottle of wine; $\frac{3}{4}$ litre (a standard bottle) of spirits; $\frac{1}{2}$ litre eau-de-cologne; and gifts to a value of 2500 escudos. Currency control imposes a limit of five thousand escudos (written 5000$00) in Portuguese currency for import or export, but you may also be required to produce 5000$00 to prove that you are not broke – though this can be in foreign currency. Declare any large amounts of foreign currency (over £500 or $500, say) on entry, if you want to avoid difficulties in re-exporting money.

Currency For rough reckoning, allow 200$00 to the pound (usually, the escudo is worth somewhat more than this), say 120$00 to the dollar. The escudo is divided into centavos, but there is not much use for these; the lowest value coin, the 10 centavo piece, is worth about 0.05 p, or well under 1/10c US. **Banking hours** are 8.30 am to noon and 1 pm to 2.30 pm; **plastic money** is surprisingly widespread, but only in the more expensive places, with Visa the best bet as usual. Shopping hours are roughly 9 am to 7 pm or later, with a long siesta from 1 pm to 3 or 4 pm. Tips are often included in the bill (*servico incluido*, usually at 10%), but otherwise, work on the usual 10–15%. A convenient and acceptable minimum tip is 10$00, though 20$00 would be even more acceptable.

Once you are inside, the **driving** standards are rather variable, as already mentioned; alertness is essential. The **speed limits** are 120 kph (75 mph) on motorways, 90 kph (56 mph) on other country roads, and 60 kph (36 mph) in town. In addition, if you have held a full licence for less than one year, or if you are under 19, you are restricted to 90 kph at all times, and must display a '90' disc on the bike. On country roads you may find very low limits posted sometimes. Often, they are realistic, especially on mountain roads; if the sign says 30 kph (19 mph), you may be able to get around at 35 kph (22 mph) or even 40 kph (25 mph) – but you may wish you hadn't tried. Small tolls are charged on one or two stretches of motorway, notably on the bridge crossing at Lisbon.

Right of way is priority-to-the-right, unless otherwise marked or on motorways, where traffic on the road always has right of way. Fortunately, low traffic density means that this is not important anyway; common sense is enough. For **overtaking**, note that a broken white centre line in the road may be crossed, but a solid white line may not; otherwise, common sense is enough again. Vehicles over 2 metres (6'6") wide must, by law, pull aside to let other vehicles pass.

You are supposed to signal all changes of direction, but most people signal only the pulling-out manoeuvre, and on the open road you should signal your intention of passing with the horn; in the city, use a flash of the lights. The Portuguese are less horn-happy than most Latins, and it is actually illegal to use it unnecessarily, or in built up areas at night. **Parking** is rarely a problem; restrictions are posted in town, and there is always room elsewhere, but several restrictions are worth knowing about. First, you may not park on main roads, or those carrying fast traffic, even during the day. At night, it is forbidden to park on the roadway outside built-up areas; nor is it legal to park on the pavement, but there are usually wide verges. Always park in the direction of the traffic flow unless otherwise instructed by signs. Do not park where visibility is restricted, or within 10 feet of a tram stop, 50 feet of an official bus stop, or 64 feet of a road junction or crossroads, or where traffic or access might be restricted. At night in badly-lit areas, or in poor visibility, use parking lights. As for road signs, the Portuguese are admirably international; the only odd sign I remember is PAVIMENTO ONDULATO, 'waving pavement' or (more prosaically) 'bumpy road'.

The Portuguese **police** are more concerned with a well-regulated society than with nit-picking laws, but they may take exception to hippies and anyone else who looks as if they cannot support themselves. I always found them very friendly, and as a lot of them ride bikes themselves, they are even better disposed towards motorcyclists than to other tourists. Braganza also has the distinction of employing the most beautiful woman police officer I have ever seen – which reminds me, Portuguese girls are beautiful, and the men are better looking than average, but Catholic morality rules. On the other hand, they are much more open and friendly than Spaniards! To return to the police, they are apparently very hard on drinking and driving, so if you are riding badly and smell of booze, don't expect a breathalyser; expect a night or two in an unsavoury jail instead. In the event of an accident, there are no firm rules – but since the police are so friendly, call them anyway if there are even the slightest problems, or if anyone has any injuries beyond a bump or graze. They can, incidentally, impose small on-the-spot fines. The emergency number is 115.

For **breakdowns**, the *Automovel Club de Portugal* (ACP) operates a breakdown service; call Oporto 29271 in the north and Lisbon 777354 in the south. Members of affiliated clubs may get free service for minor calls, but if the breakdown van has to travel any distance, or if major work is involved, a charge is likely. The HQ of the ACP is Rua Rosa Araujo 24–26, 1200 Lisbon.

Otherwise, Portuguese mechanics are very much of the improvising genius school, used to making clapped-out mopeds run forever, and do better with simpler bikes. Spares are a matter of luck, but there is a tradition of British bikes in Portugal, so you may be lucky, and there is a big BMW dealer in Lisbon. Spares for *small* Japanese bikes may be OK, but if you have a big bike it may be the only one in the country, and you will have problems.

Although Portuguese is said to be a difficult language, it is easier than many; and in addition, the slightest attempt on your part will be met with hearty approval.

The ten-word vocabulary is:

please	*por favor*
thank you	*obrigado* (for a man speaking)
	obrigada (for a woman speaking)
yes	*sim* (si)
no	*não* (nang; the 'ng' sound, which is represented in Portuguese by *ão* at the end of a word, is barely audible and not voiced)
where is	*onde?* (on-day)
room	*quarto*
toilet	*toilette*
more	*mais* (maysh)
how much?	*quanto?*
food	*alimento*

The 's' sound is 'sh', sho all Portugueshe shound ash if they're permanently shloshed (and shome of them are!).

I adore Portuguese **food**. The seafood is superb, and comes from the clean Atlantic instead of the polluted Mediterranean, and they also have a good line in roast meat (pork, beef, mutton, lamb, and goat or kid – the last well worth trying). Helpings are generous, and many places offer the choice of soup/meat/pudding or soup/fish/meat/

pudding. A typical hearty meal of *caldo verde* (green soup),
hake, roast kid, and *poudim* (egg custard), with a bottle of
wine per person, could cost as little as 400$00 in a cheap
cafeteria; at one place, I drank draught *vinho verde* at 12$00
– say 6 p, or under a dime – a glass.

Vinho verde literally means 'green wine', but it actually
means 'young wine', with a hint of sparkle. Both red and
white 'green wines' are drunk cold; I prefer the slightly acid
whites. The beer is no more than adequate, but the brandy is
very cheap, and there is always the port.... The water is
usually drinkable, but to be on the safe side, drink *agua
minerale* (mineral water), or more vinho verde. A picnic of
bread, cheese, wine, olives, and fruit is fit for the Gods, and
very cheap indeed.

Accommodation is another bargain. Good hotel rooms
can cost as little as 2000$00 out of season, 3000$00 in
season, for a double with bath; one that Frances and I stayed
in had a balcony overlooking 160° of the Atlantic, and a
bathroom of solid white marble. The state-run *pousadas* are
superb, and excellent value – the exact opposite of what you
would expect from a state-run enterprise – but in the
summer, your stay may be limited to a few days, as they are
meant for travellers. One *pousada* can book you a room in
the next. If you want to spend still less money, a cheap
pensão (guest-house) can cost a half or even a quarter of the
prices given above, and this is actually comparable with a
youth hostel. For hostels, contact the *Associaciâo Portoguesa
de Pousadas de Juventude*, Avenide Duque de Avila 137, 7°
Dto., Lisboa. Organized camping sites are usually primitive,
but can be very cheap indeed (under 200$00, sometimes
under 100$00); alternatively, 'wild' camping is legal on
private (but not public) land, provided you get the permission
of the landowner.

Spain

Spain is a multifaceted country. From the tourist point of view, the best-known parts are undoubtedly the Mediterranean resorts which are so heavily geared to the foreign visitor, but from our point of view these are the least interesting. Because they are aimed at the package tourist, moving in herds for their set two or three weeks, they are not really equipped to deal with the independent traveller. From our point of view, a much more important Spain is the interior, preferably as far as possible from the organized tourist routes with their plastic hotels and Watneys.

There is no doubt that much of Spain has been spoiled by and for tourism. Ripping off visitors has become a way of life for tens, or perhaps hundreds, of thousands. It is possible to find the unspoiled Spain, but not easy. The best places to look are in the north, and the interior. There, you will still find people who are genuinely hospitable and friendly; authentic Spanish food and wine; castles, churches, and other memories of Spain's great past; and a country where a little money goes a very long way. You will also find a ferociously old-fashioned country, dominated by religion, where women are repressed, and communication is virtually impossible unless you speak almost perfect Spanish. The Spanish police are vicious and trigger-happy (though you can hardly blame them when you consider that the Basque separatists spend much of their time shooting at them, and trying to blow them up), and although they are usually inclined to leave tourists alone, the prospects are not good if you do tangle with them.

From all this, it is clear that I do not like Spain very much; I agree with a Portuguese maitre d'hotel who said to me, 'The Spanish are even more proud than the French – with even less to be proud about.' But I must say in all fairness that I have met people who feel the same way about Spain as I do about Portugal (though I have never met anyone who feels about Portugal as I do about Spain); it is all a matter of personal luck. I have met some charming Spaniards, and I like good Spanish food, but mostly I have just been unlucky. In self-defence, I would also add that it has an authoritarian and eccentric legal system, as I think will become clear in what follows; I think that this is a fair guide to the Spanish mentality.

Motorcyclists enjoy quite reasonable status in Spain, and there is a tradition of motorcycle manufacture. The old Sanglas single, beloved of the Spanish police, is no more; but there are several moped manufacturers, and of course there is the Ducati connection. Fast bikes are admired, and they are also fairly safe: there is little danger of their being stolen, unless by another tourist (who will usually be drunk and crash it). Spanish driving is mostly not too bad, though the tourists on the main roads, stampeding to the south, can make these a nightmare. Travel midweek for safety!

Climate Unless you go to the coast – and it must be said that there are still a few unspoiled areas – it is as well to avoid both the high summer (especially August) and the winter; I have ridden through blizzards in November in the north. As a general guide, the warm days of spring can begin as early as March, and even at the end of October, or early to mid-November, you stand a good chance of very pleasant weather, especially in the south. The south is generally warmer than the north, as you would expect, and the interior is hotter in summer and colder in winter than the coast; the temperature range in Sevilla is 43–59° in January, and 68–97° in August, compared with Alicante's 44–61° and 68–90° for the same months. Bear in mind that these figures are averages, spread over many years, so that in Sevilla there can be frosts in winter and 110° heat in summer, whereas Alicante's position by the sea will even things out rather more. In the mountains, temperatures are much lower all the year around.

Papers Spain demands visas from very few foreign nationals, so formalities there are easy enough, but the bike is another matter. Log book or registration document and letter of authorization are as usual, but you must have either an IDP or a Spanish translation of your licence (the IDP is cheaper and easier to get), and you must be over 18 if the bike is over 75cc (under 75cc, the age limit is 16). Furthermore, if you are an unusually hardy 17-year-old touring on a Honda 70, or something similar, you must have a letter from your parents if they are not with you. This will affect very few riders, but it may affect younger brothers/sisters and girlfriends. At the time of writing, unless you have a Green Card, you would be required to buy insurance at the frontier; this may change with EEC membership, but in the light of the very low insurance limits set by Spanish law, you would be mad not to get a Green Card anyway. The insurance is for personal injury *only*, and the limits are as shown in the table.

Death	maximum Ptas 1,000,000 per person
Permanent Incapacity	„ „ 800,000 „ „
Very Serious Disability	„ „
	1,500,000 „ „
(*If the injured person requires the help of another person to carry out the most essential acts of living.*)	
Allowance for Personal and Family Assistance	Up to a maximum of Ptas 800 daily
Temporary Incapacity	Up to a maximum of Ptas 800 daily for a maximum period of 2 years
Medical and Hospital Expenses	The total cost of medical and hospital assistance received in a centre recognised by the National Guarantee Fund – otherwise a maximum of Ptas 50,000.

In translation, that is £5000/$7000 for death; £7500/$10,000 for Very Serious Disability; or £4/$5.50 a day for temporary incapacity. Spanish insurance awards are low, but not that low!

Helmets are compulsory, but daylight riding lights are not only not compulsory; they may actually be illegal in town, where you are supposed to use only your side-lights (parking lights), even in the hours of darkness – though most people do use only dipped headlights. On the other hand, you must use dipped headlights at night on the open road, even if the road is well lit. It is also compulsory to carry a set of spare light bulbs.

The cheapest and best way to get to Spain from the UK is probably via France; you may wish to consider a ferry to St. Malo or one of the other south-western ports, because you can save as much as 200 miles riding that way in return for two or three hours on the ferry and a relatively small increase in the ferry fare. If you are desperate to spend as much time in Spain as possible, there is also a 24-hour ferry from Plymouth to Santander.

Spanish **customs** are a good deal more relaxed than Spanish police, and take a lenient view of 'personal goods'. The allowances (which will change in time, with EEC standardization) are at the time of writing 200 cigarettes or 50 cigars or 250 gm tobacco; two litres of wine and one ($\frac{3}{4}$ litre) bottle of spirits; $\frac{1}{4}$ litre of eau-de-Cologne and 50 cc of perfume; and other non-commercial items to a value of Ptas. 1700, ptas 700 for travellers under 15. The possible areas of difficulty are medicines – carry a prescription, or letter from your doctor, if you want to avoid a drug rap – 'pornography', and 'political propaganda'. The defintions on 'propaganda' are such that it needs to be fairly heavy communist bumf before they will object, but almost any common girlie magazine, even *Playboy*, is classed as pornography. NEVER try to carry dope into Spain – they throw away the key. Currency control is Ptas 50,000 in Spanish notes, plus unlimited foreign currency, on the way in, and 3000 ptas plus foreign currency up to the amount declared on entry when you leave.

Currency The Peseta, abbreviates Pta and ptas indiscriminately, is divided into 100 centimos, but as (at the time of writing), there were rather more than 200 ptas to the £ sterling, or over 150 to the $ US, the centimo is not worth a lot; even 50 centimo coins are rare. **Banks** open at 8 or 9 am, and close at 1.30 or 2 pm, and shops open at 9 or 10 am and close at around 8 pm, with three hours or so of siesta closing at around 1.30–4.30 pm. Tipping is heavy; even when 15% *servicio* is *incluido*, they still expect another 10%, so your bill ends up 26½% higher than it should be (not 25%, because part of the 10% tip is actually a tip on a tip). Fortunately, prices are low enough that this doesn't matter – but it is still irritating. At a bar, it is usual to leave part of the change (say 5–10 ptas). **Plastic money** is virtually useless.

Riding in Spain is fairly peaceful, mostly because of low traffic densities; on busy roads, Spanish **drivers** are not too good, and tourists rushing to get to their holiday villas make matters a whole lot worse. The National Highways are wide and well-surfaced, and subject to a 100 kph (62 mph) **speed**

limit, and they are rather preferable to the motorways which bear most of the traffic. On the other hand, if you are in a hurry and do not mind paying the modest tolls, the motorways are very fast (with a 120 kph/75 mph limit) and get you from A to B admirably quickly, albeit with a certain amount of nervous strain. Back roads vary from the reasonable to the terrible, and are subject to a 90 kph (56 mph) limit, and in town, the limit is 60 kph (37 mph).

Priority is given to vehicles entering from the right, unless their road is marked STOP or CEDA EL PASO. Most major roads do have priority, but the rest do not, and Spanish drivers (like the French) will insist on their right of way. Otherwise, use common sense. **Overtaking** is a very formal business. First, you must signal your intention to overtake, with your horn out of town or your lights in town. Next, you must wait for the person in front to acknowledge this, by switching on his nearside (i.e. right-hand) indicator. Only then can you overtake, and you must use your indicators whilst you are doing so – though motorcycles without indicators are exempt, and you do not have to keep your arm out the whole time. In town, you may only overtake a stationary tram if all the passengers have finished getting on and off. There is a general prohibition of overtaking when visibility is restricted, for example at bends or on the brow of a hill.

Out of town, **parking** is very rarely a problem; as long as you are more than 5 metres (16 feet) from crossroads, intersections, or entrances to public buildings (!), or more than 7 metres (23 feet) from a tram or bus stop, you will be OK. In town, do not park on a two-way street unless there is still room for three vehicles abreast, and if you are on a one-way street, park on the side with the even-numbered buildings on even days of the month, and the side with the odd numbers on odd days of the month. Always park in the direction of traffic flow. In major cities, use marked bays or use a parking disc (available from the town hall, and some hotels and travel agents). Set the time that you park, and return before the limit is up. You often see bikes parked on the pavement, and the police do not seem to mind as long as there is no obstruction, but most Spaniards ride very small motorcycles; a fully laden tourer may attract police attention.

The Spanish use international road signs, and written ones, of which the following are probably the most useful:

Aduana	Customs
Ceda el Paso	Give Way
Cuidado or *Precaucion*	Caution
Despacio	Slow
Desvio	Diversion
Estacionamento de Automóviles	Car Park
Paso Prohibido	No Through Road
Curva Peligrosa	Dangerous Bend
Dirección Única	One-Way Street
Estacionamente Prohibido	No Parking
Obras	Road Works
Peligro	Danger
Llevar la Derecha	Keep Right
Llevar la Izquierda	Keep Left

As I have already intimated, the Spanish **police** are not the nicest people in the world, and they are very fond of exercising their power – many harbour fond memories of Franco's fascist dictatorship – so stay out of their way, and observe the law meticulously. They can impose on-the-spot fines, and will not hesitate to do so; as the sober but excellent RAC *Continental Handbook* puts it, 'The slightest infringement of the Highway Code is likely to be severely dealt with.' They do not have to be called to accidents, but for all but the most minor bumps, it is a good idea to call on them before they call on you. The normal procedure at a serious accident is to impound all the vehicles, and throw everyone involved in jail, indefinitely, until the case comes up – which can be months. As a result, it is near-lunacy not to get a *bail bond* from your insurers when you get the Green Card. It is not expensive, and it means that you will probably be allowed bail unless you were obviously responsible for a serious accident – or drunk. Once you are out, the best course may be to do a bunk. On the same note, although there is a 20% discount for paying on-the-spot fines actually on the spot, you may be able to delay payment. And if you're leaving anyway. ... If you do have to call the police, the number is 091 in Madrid and Barcelona, or call the operator elsewhere.

The only **breakdown** service operated by the *Real Automovil Club de España* (RACE) is in the Madrid area. Call 754 3344; the address is General Sanjuro 10, Madrid 3.

Otherwise, Spanish mechanics are among the best of
Spaniards: friendly, helpful, reliable, inexpensive, and masters
of improvisation. Spares may be a bit of a problem, and can
be very expensive, but even the most provincial of mechanics
should do an excellent job. There are many garages and
petrol stations all over Spain; the **petrol** grades are *normal*
(84–85 octane), *super* (96 octane), and the rarely-found
super-especial (98 octane).

The basic vocabulary is:

please	*por favor* (por fah-bor)
thank you	*gracias* (grathy -ass)
yes	*si*
no	*no*
where is?	*donde esta?* (don-day esstah)
room	*habitación* (habby-tathyon)
toilet	*retrete* (ray-tray-tay)
more	*mas*
how much?	*cuando?* (kwandoh?)
food	*alimentación* (alley-men-tathion)

The *th* is always soft, like a lithp, not like *this* or *that*.

If you don't like olive oil, you won't like 90% of Spanish
food; if you do, you should love it. *Paella*, a rice dish like
risotto, is about the only common non-oily choice on the
menu, and (like *everything else*) it is loaded with garlic. Near
the Mediterranean coast, watch out for mussels, oysters, etc,
but eat the rest of the seafood. If possible, eat where the
locals eat – not easy, unless you can read a Spanish menu –
or you could end up paying 2–3 times as much as necessary,
though it will still not be expensive. **Drink** wine with the
meal; even the cheapest stuff is normally drinkable (which is
more than you can say for Italy). In bars, go for a *taberna* or
bodega, where the wine comes straight from the barrel, is
very cheap, and may be excellent. Alternatively, drink the
brandy – it is fashionable to be rude about Spanish brandy,
but I like it. Don't trust the water, and remember that the
chef may (or worse still, may not) have washed in water from
the same source. Most cases of 'gyppy tummy' are caused by
too much cheap wine – but not all. The blood alcohol level
is 80 mg/100 ml, but the police can still do you for drunken
driving even if you are under the limit.

Accommodation Half-way decent hotels start at around 1000 ptas for a double room, and go up without limit, but at the time of writing 1500 or 2000 ptas should see a decent double, with bath. *Pensiones* start as low as 300–400 ptas, but this is for a real flophouse; expect to pay 500+ ptas if you don't want too many cockroaches. For relatively inexpensive luxury, try the *paradores* (state-run, like the Portuguese *pousadas*, but not usually as welcoming). The state also runs *albergues*, which are like simplified and cheaper *paradores*, meant for overnight stops in more remote areas, and *refugios*, which are way off the beaten track and meant for hikers and mountaineers. Youth hostels are administered by the *Red Espanola de Albergues Juveniles*, Jose Ortega de Gasset 17, Madrid 6 (telephone 401 1300); they are not particularly cheap when compared with hotels, and you would have to be on a pretty low budget to worry about the difference. Camp sites are cheap, usually under £1, or $1.25 for two people, tent, and parking, and apparently good; contact the *Agrupacion Nacional de Campings de España*, Medinaceli 2, Madrid 14. Wild camping is permitted, but you must get the landowner's permission for private land, or approach the Town Hall for public land. You must not camp in dry river beds (arroyos), areas liable to flood, urban areas, or close to roads, military bases, or sources of drinking water, or within 1 km (1100 yards) of an official camp site. Sleeping rough is legal, but unless you are out of the way, the police may well wake you up to see if you have any money (they'll bust you for vagrancy if you haven't). Sleeping rough in town parks is illegal, and attracts police and muggers.

South-Eastern Europe

Introduction

It is easier to list the disadvantages of visiting these countries than the advantages, but advantages there undoubtedly are. Once you venture off the beaten track to the popular resorts you will be a true traveller, not a tourist, and you will not only discover some amazingly beautiful countryside, forgotten antiquities, and mediaeval villages: you will also be able to live very cheaply indeed. Unless you are unlucky, you will meet with old-fashioned hospitality of the kind that you normally only read about in books, and the food and drink will be a revelation.

Most of the disadvantages depend more on the sort of person that you are than on any external circumstances. You may well have to use sign language, and the ten-word vocabularies in this book, a great deal of the time. You may well find that accommodation is primitive in the extreme. You will often be riding on truly appalling roads, some of them unsurfaced. If all this merely makes you more interested, rather than less, you are likely to have a holiday that you will never forget.

It is important, though, to prepare thoroughly for this sort of trip. Take your first aid kit, and your water-purifying tablets. Take a few basic spares, because you are not going to be able to get them when you arrive. Make sure that the bike is in good condition before you go, and take out all the insurance that you can afford, especially insurance to pay for bringing the bike back; at the very worst, you can hire a truck to get it to the nearest railway station. . . .

Because the roads are so bad, spoked wheels (lace-on, not cast), soft suspension, and a good saddle are a boon. Petrol stations are few and far between, so a good range (at least 200 miles) is virtually essential unless you want to be forever topping up. Even when you do find a petrol station, it may sell only 80-octane muck, so a low-compression engine is a must. All this adds up to a low-tech bike, preferably with some trail-bike characteristics. On the other hand, a 'pure' trail bike is no use, because you must have carrying capacity and a decent- sized gas tank. My ideal would be either an old British single or twin, or a BMW R80G/S.

Remember that Greece and Turkey are permanently either at war, or on the verge of war. This can make border crossings between the two rather interesting, and if it comes to shooting, you would do best to be out of the way. It is also a good idea to be tactful. On the other hand, I have never actually met anyone who was inconvenienced any more than being delayed for a while, even in the middle of a war, so don't let that put you off. Remember, too, that you can always enter Turkey via Rumania rather than through Greece. Once you are inside either country, you can forget about the war.

Finally, these are old-fashioned countries with old-fashioned ways. Men are men, women keep out of the way, and men do not pursue women unless they want to marry them. Whether Orthodox Christian or Muslim, this rule holds good. By the same token, dress modestly: keep swimming gear for the beaches. Women should not wear shorts, or even short skirts, and jeans are only barely tolerated. My wife finds that it is best in Islamic countries never to look a man in the eye: always avoid his direct look. This may seem rather sick, and in a way it is, but you are not going to change things single-handed.

Apart from this – which sounds much worse than it is – you really will be missing something if you don't go to these countries – especially Turkey, where you will literally be able to ride from one continent to another.

Cyprus

Cyprus, the 'last island in Europe', is one of those places that offers something for everyone. If you want the standard sun, sea, and booze holiday, there are coastal resorts which offer that. If you want to relax in a haven of peace and quiet, there are inland resorts where you can do just that. Or if you want to explore a surprisingly unspoiled island, thick with history, that is also perfectly possible.

There is, however, a worm in Aphrodite's Golden Apple. In 1974, the Turks invaded northern Cyprus and split the island in two. They had slender but just about plausible excuses for doing so, because Cyprus had been a part of the Turkish empire from 1571–1878, when the island became a British protectorate, and the Turkish Cypriots were rather second-class citizens in predominantly Greek Cyprus. The Turks, however, have behaved far worse than the Greeks ever did, and a measure of the success of the so-called Turkish Federated State of Cyprus is that while Cypriot currency is acceptable in the Turkish-occupied north, Turkish lire are just so much waste paper in the south. The 'green line' between the two parts of Cyprus is patrolled by United Nations troops, and it is as well not to get too close. If you stick to the south, however, you will find a delightful country, very cheap, very hospitable, with classic Greek food and drink, and a tremendous range of scenery from the 6400 foot Mount Olympus to sandy, sunny beaches.

Climate The best time to go depends on where you want to stay, what you want to do, and how much you like hot weather. On the coast, the most delightful times are probably May/June and October, when temperatures in the high seventies and low eighties are commonplace; September is also a good choice, though it may be a little warm for some people. In July and August, coastal temperatures often exceed 100°F, and temperatures a few miles inland can be even higher. In the mountains, though, temperatures can be as much as 20° cooler, so the high summer can be perfect there. Even March, April, and November should not be excluded; there will be days in the

70s, and the temperature at night will rarely fall below 50°.
December, January, and February are mild on the coast (50–
60° on average, with the coldest days touching 40° and the
warmest 70°), but you can always ski in the mountains ...
there really is no closed season.

Papers No visas are needed for most countries, but bike
documents are another matter. To bring in your own bike,
you will need an international driving licence, registration
document or log book, and specially arranged insurance –
Cyprus is not a signatory to the Green Card convention. In
fact, it may be a better idea to hire a bike in Cyprus. There
are several 'rent-a-wreck' places, at least one of which bears
the delightful sign, 'FOR HIRE: Scooters, Motorcycles, and
Hondas'. If you do this, formalities are negligible; they don't
even bother to look at your licence most of the time, or issue
you with a **helmet**, which is not compulsory in any case.
Renting a bike is all the more a good idea because of the
difficulty of getting your own bike to Cyprus; the usual routes
would be the long ride to Athens, and then a day or more
on the ferry, or a slightly shorter ride to Italy and a rather
longer ferry ride, depending on which Italian port you
left from.

Customs regulations are a little tight on booze and
cigarettes – 200 cigarettes plus one bottle of spirits *or* two
bottles of wine – but apart from this, it is all 'reasonable
qualities', and the customs officials are not harsh. Once you
are inside, riding is old-fashioned fun on the often **bad
roads**; as the tourist office puts it, 'be prepared to use your
horn and your patience'. Cypriots drive on the **left**, as in
England, and the rules of the road are identical to those in
England. **Speed limits** are 30 mph in town, 50 mph outside
(yes, they use miles per hour), and given the state of the
roads and the size of the island, there is no point in going
much faster. **Petrol** roughly equivalent to British 3-star (96
octane) is readily available; anything better is not. Petrol
prices are high (but bike hire rates are very low). **Police** are
amiable, and trying to telephone them will take longer than
waiting for someone to fetch a policeman. The number
varies from village to village, but in any case you only have to
call the police where someone is injured or there is serious
damage, or where the two parties cannot come to an
amicable arrangement about the damage. Local mechanics
are usually excellent, spares are next to impossible.

Currency is the Cypriot pound, worth about 20–25%
more than the £ sterling, or close to $2. It is divided into
1000 mils, with coins for 1, 5, 25, 50, 100, and 500m. So
strong is the English influence that 50 mils is known as a
shilling! There are notes for 250 and 500m, and £1, £5, and
£10. Declare large sums on entry, or you may not be able to
re-export more than C£10 and £50 sterling. **Plastic money**
is virtually worthless outside the most expensive hotels. **Bank
hours** are 8.30 am to noon, Monday to Saturday, and shops
are open from roughly 7 am to 7 pm on weekdays, with a
long siesta (say 1 pm to 4 pm) and half-day closing on
Thursday and Saturday. Tips are the international standards
(10–15%) in the more expensive places, but only a few coins
– say 5% – in the cheaper places. And Cyprus can be *cheap*;
even first-class hotels and restaurants are affordable, and
good middle-range ones are very cheap indeed. Picnic **food**
is practically given away, but you have to get used to the odd
Cypriot measures: 44 okes (about 1 ounce each) to the
kantar (close to 3 lb), and a 'litre' that is about 3 pints. Good
wine and **brandy**, to say nothing of *ouzo*, are very cheap,
and the laws against drunken driving are simple: if you're
drunk, you're not allowed to drive, but there's no official
definition of drunk. The water is perfectly drinkable, it is said,
but most people stick to the wine, so I don't know how true
this is! Camping is legal anywhere – get permission first – or
you can even stay in a monastery, for a modest donation (try
£1–2 a night). It is a remarkably laid back place.

Greece

The traditional traveller, making the Grand Tour, went to Greece to marvel at the ancient ruins. The modern package tourist goes because it is hot, cheap, and vastly more pleasant than Spain. The motorcyclist adds another reason: the chance to explore a large, hospitable, unspoiled, and laid back country.

There is much more to Greece than most people realise. The average tourist goes to the islands (the trendy place to go), to Athens, or to the new resorts at Khalkidiki. The most enjoyable islands, though, are too small for motorcycling (and besides, you have the hassles of the ferries), and driving in Athens is a bit like riding round Hyde Park Corner in the rush hour, one-handed, whilst playing Russian roulette with the other hand. Khalkidiki is really aimed at the family package tourist, so the motorcycle tourer will do best to stay away from the usual tourist attractions on the mainland and the islands.

The rewards of doing this are tremendous. Greece is littered with magnificent classical ruins (no, not Triumphs, BMWs, and Harley-Davidsons), and the scenery is, for the most part, stunning. The Peloponnese, in the south-west, is a joy; but the central mountains, and the north, where hardly any tourists go, can be unequalled for small-village hospitality. If you stay in some villages for even a couple of days, you will rapidly become well-known and your bike will be safer than it would be at home, because everyone will keep an eye on it.

You will, however, have to make some adjustments. Outside the tourist areas, attitudes are very old-fashioned. Clothes should be decent, even swimming costumes, and women are expected to defer to men. If you can make these adjustments, you should have a wonderful time. If you cannot, you might as well not go. And if you want to try to change things single-handed, you are asking for trouble. Men who make passes at Greek girls can expect nasty retribution from brothers and uncles, and women who do not behave modestly will have endless trouble with Greek men.

Motorcyclists are welcome; in Greece, as in many other cultures, the wildly overloaded moped, light motorcycle, or scooter has to some extent taken over from the donkey. Bigger bikes (anything over 125cc!) are admired by all, though Greek roads and Greek taxes make them impractical for most Greeks. The only places you may run into trouble are in the extreme north-east, on the Bulgarian and Turkish borders, where there is some tradition of banditry.

Climate The best time of year to go will depend on where you are going, and what you want to do. High summer is July and August, and temperatures in the south *average* over 80°F; over 100° is not unusual, even at night, and even the sea temperature in the afternoon can be in the 80s. In the north, summer temperatures are only two or three degrees colder, but the winter climate changes dramatically: from late November to mid-March, the south can be 10° warmer than the north, so (for example) Athens in March averages 58°, whereas Thessaloniki averages 50°. A further consideration is the *meltemia*, a warm wind that blows in August, which most people find very uncomfortable. As a rule, then, August is a month to be avoided, except in the mountains, and in the south, July and even June may be too warm for some tastes. In the winter, the north will be uncomfortably cool, but the south will still be pleasant.

Papers Visas are not required for most Western European nationals, Americans, Canadians, or Australians (though New Zealanders do need them), for stays of up to 3 months. For the bike, carry the registration document or log book and either an IDP or an Austrian, Belgian, British, Dutch, or West German licence. At the time of writing, a Green Card was required even though Greece had joined the EEC. Even if this is changed, a Green Card would still be a good idea: passenger insurance is limited, and overall limits are 600,000 drachmas for injury and 200,000 drachmas for property damage, per accident. Very roughly, 600,000 drachmas is £4000 – not a realistic limit. You can buy insurance in Greece; talk to the Motor Insurance Bureau, 10 Xenofondos Street, Athens, tel. 3236 733. Unless you have a *carnet* for the bike, you will be given a temporary importation form and the fact that you have brought a bike in will be entered in your passport. Sell the bike to a Greek, and you are in deep trouble, though you are allowed to sell it to a non-Greek in the presence of a notary. As far as I was able to discover, you can ride in Greece at any age, provided you have a full licence from your home country.

Helmets are compulsory, and although the law is somewhat patchily enforced, Greek driving means that the penalty for non-compliance is more likely to be a coffin than a ticket. You are also supposed to carry a first-aid kit, though I have never heard of a tourist being prosecuted for not carrying one on a motorcycle. Daylight riding lights are not compulsory, but you must use headlights (not parking lights alone) from half an hour after sunset to half an hour before dawn, or in poor visibility. It gets dark very quickly in Greece. so you are unlikely to forget to put the lights on!

Actually getting to Greece is something of a problem, partly because of the sheer distance (Athens is about 2000 miles from London), and partly because of the poor roads of Yugoslavia and Greece itself; the *autoput* through Yugoslavia is notorious. No doubt there are those who ride it in four or even three days, but any reasonable person would allow more like a week. The quickest route is via München–Salzburg–Belgrade–Skopje–Athens, but a more attractive (and slower) route through Yugoslavia could be along the coast; if you decide to do this, you might also go through Switzerland and Italy instead of Germany and Austria. Ferries from the UK are irregular, expensive, and no quicker than riding, but a good option might be to ride right down through Italy and take a ferry from Brindisi. It will not save much time, and it will probably cost slightly more than the straight ride, but at least you don't have to thrash through Yugoslavia. Using the train is possible, but expensive, and you may have some difficulty in keeping track of the bike.

On arrival, **customs** allowances are the EEC standards, plus an 'other goods' limit of 11,000 drachmas for EEC visitors over 15 (3100 for those 15 and under); for non-EEC visitors the over-15 limit is 2850 drs and the under-15 limit is 1450 drs. The age limit for booze and cigarettes is 17. Greek customs have been known to get funny about prescription drugs, so carry a letter from your doctor if necessary.

Currency control places a limit of 1500 drs per person in banknotes only, entering or leaving Greece, and although there is no limit on importation of foreign currency, it is a good idea to declare it if you are likely to be taking out more than $500 US when you leave. Travellers' cheques are exempt from this, provided they are in the traveller's name.

When leaving, you may be searched again by Greek customs looking for antiques and works of art. Even if the stuff was legitimately obtained, penalties are heavy; if the bargain ikon you bought turns out to be stolen, they lock you up and throw away the key.

Currency The Greek drachma (plural *drachmae* or *drachmas*, abbreviation Drs. or drs) was, at the time of writing, worth about 150 to the £ sterling or 120 to the $ US. The drachma is divided into 100 lepta, but the smallest coin is 50 lepta, and in any case, there is a chronic shortage of change: chewing gum, etc., may well be used to make up small change. In Athens and Thessaloniki, you may find some use for **credit cards**; otherwise, Greece is strictly a cash economy. **Bank hours** vary slightly, opening at 8 or 9 am and closing for the day at 1 or 2 pm, Monday to Friday, and a few big banks in a few big towns may also open on Saturday mornings. Changing money other than at banks and accredited *bureaux de change* (which stay open longer, but give a worse rate) is theoretically illegal, and not worth doing anyway, because the black market premium is negligible. Shopping hours are basically 8 am to 8 pm, with a long, late siesta (maybe 2.30 to 5.30 pm), but there can be considerable variations. A 15% tip is usually included in hotel, restaurant, and bar bills; hotels expect nothing more, but because the tip in a restaurant or bar is regarded as a part of the proprietor's profits, not a waiter's perk, give an extra 10% unless it is a one-man show, in which case simply rounding up is enough. This massive level of tipping is one of the less attractive things about Greece, but fortunately the very low prices mean that it doesn't matter much anyway.

As already intimated, Greek **driving** is pretty horrifying. The main roads are full of terrible Greek drivers, and the back roads are marked by smaller numbers of even worse drivers plus pedestrians, animals, and dogs sleeping in the road. Road surfaces vary from indifferent to awful, so Greek roads are best for slow exploring, rather than high-speed riding. The **limits** are 100 kph (62 mph) on the motorways – which are often not even divided with a central reservation, and which charge tolls to boot – and 80 kph (49 mph) on other open roads, with 50 kph (31 mph) the limit in town. In all cases, lower limits may be posted. Greeks treat speed limits with disdain, but visitors are advised to devote their concentration to staying alive, rather than to going quickly.

The same goes for **right of way** – priority to the right, *including* traffic entering roundabouts, except on main roads outside town, where minor roads give way. **Overtaking** is theoretically signalled and undertaken cautiously; remember this when you come around a corner and find three vehicles abreast coming straight at you, on a road wide enough for two push-bikes!

Outside Athens and Thessaloniki, **parking** is unlikely to be a problem – there will always be somewhere you can pull off the roads – but in Athens in particular, it can be murder. One particularly cunning trick is for the police to remove the numberplates of illegally parked vehicles, which makes them easy to spot, and then charging the owner both for the return of the plates and with not displaying them! The main restrictions, anywhere, are the usual ones: curves, brows of hills, tunnels, railway lines, tramlines, pedestrian crossings, within 3 metres (10 feet) of fire hydrants, 5 metres (16 feet) of inter-sections, stop signs, traffic lights, 15 metres (49 feet) of level crossings or bus or tram stops, or anywhere causing an obstruction (especially across entrances, haulingways, etc). It is also illegal to park where there is a continuous white line in the middle of the road, unless there are two lanes in both directions. Parking on the pavement is theoretically illegal, though some Greek motorcyclists seem to get away with it.

Fortunately, Greeks use mostly international road signs; few people can learn to read Greek fast enough to interpret the others, so I will quote just one written sign:

ΠΡΟΣΟΧΙ
προσοχι   Caution
PROSODI

If you do fall foul of the Greek **police**, you can expect a fairly unpleasant time, but if you are not breaking the law, they are charming – asking the way, and so forth, will be met with beaming smiles and great helpfulness. The police emergency number is 100 or 109, and 105 will get you the Red Cross. To get a list of local hospitals, ring 166. In case of accident, the police need only be called if there is personal injury, or if there is vehicle or property damage which cannot be settled amicably by the parties involved.

For **breakdowns,** the Greek Automobile Touring Club (ELPA, 2-4 Messogion Street, Athens, tel 779 1615) offers a breakdown service within a 60 km (37 mile) radius of both Athens and Thessaloniki, and a 25km (15½ mile) radius of the following towns: Agrimion Larissa, Patras, Volos, Lamia, Heraklion, Ioannina, Kaval, Kalamata. If you do not belong to an affiliated organization (such as the AA or RAC), you can join the ELPA at the time of the breakdown for 1200 drachmae. Dial 104 for assistance.

Otherwise, Greek mechanics tend to belong to the ingenious bodger school: high-tech and light alloy tend to suffer at their hands. Really basic machinery is best, and big Japanese machines can pose real spares-and-repairs problems.

By the same token, 90 octane regular **petrol** is all that will be obtainable in many places, and even the 96-octane 'super' is not all that good. Petrol prices are high – about 25% higher than the European average – and filling stations are thin on the ground outside the cities or away from the tourist routes.

The ten-word vocabulary is:

please	*parakolo*
thank you	*efharisto* (eff-harry-stow)
yes	*ne* (the *e* is short, as in *yes*)
no	*ochi* (ockey)
where is?	*pou ine* (poo ee-neh)
room	*thomatio*
toilet	*toualeta* (too-a-leh-ta)
more	*perisotero*
how much?	*posso kani?*
food	*faghito* (fa-hhee-tow)

Of course, life is made more difficult by the Greek alphabet, and by the way that the Greeks shake their heads for 'yes' and nod for 'no'. If you make any attempt at the language, though, it will be very well received.

Opinions vary about Greek **food**. Its critics call it oily and monotonous. Oily it is, but I do not find it monotonous. In any case, with the ever-increasing number of Greek restaurants outside Greece, the chances are that most people will have had a chance to form their own opinions before going to Greece. The Greeks tend to concentrate on meat (especially lamb) and bread, though sea food also plays a major part; the usual warnings about Mediterranean bivalves

apply. If you are prepared to rely on good will and poor
translations, eat very cheaply at village *tavernas* or *kaffenia* –
but watch out for tourist-trap *tavernas*, where you can pay
through the nose for an indifferent meal. Picnic food,
especially goat's milk *fetta* cheese, salads, and bread, are a
bargain – but wash salads in water to which you have added
a little potassium permanganate, or use water purifying
tablets.

Greeks drink **wine**, of all sorts; the famous *retsina* is
matured in pine barrels, which gives it a taste not unlike
cheap white wine mixed with disinfectant, but many people
(including me) love it. The national spirit is *ouzo*, which goes
cloudy when you add water; alternatively, Greek brandy is
very palatable. The same cannot be said for the tap water
(use purifying tablets), or the rather dull beer. The blood
alcohol limit is an astonishingly low 50 mg/100 ml, as
against the usual 80 mg/100 ml; this, combined with no
licencing hours, places the thirsty motorcyclist in a terrible
dilemma.

The range of **accommodation** is very wide, with
government fixed rates for the hotels. All but the most
expensive places are excellent value for money, with the
pensions going for as little as 100 drs. a night in Athens, or
50 drs. or less in the villages. An unusual option in Athens is
sleeping on a hotel roof, for as little as 50 drs a night; fair
security, and accesss to bathrooms, etc, make this worth
considering. Not all hotels offer this, obviously.

There are also youth hostels (Greek YHA, 4
Dragatsaniou Street, Athens TT 122, tel. 3237 590), and
both a YMCA and YWCA in Athens. There are under 100
official camping sites in the whole country, but 'wild' camping
is permitted anywhere except close to major archaeological
sites or any digs in progress. You must have the landowner's
permission, though. Sleeping rough is theoretically illegal,
though there are designated 'simple camping sites' where it
is very cheap, and legal. In any case, Greek prices are very
low, and if you do sleep rough, the odds are that no one will
catch you outside the major cities or tourist beaches.

Turkey

Strictly speaking, the majority of Turkey is in Asia, and not in Europe at all, but there are several good reasons for including it in this book. First, a small part *is* in Europe; second, the Turks pride themselves on their European outlook and modernization plans; and third, it is a fascinating country which represents one of the last reasonably accessible unexplored areas for the independent rider. By 'unexplored', I do not mean literally; but from the point of view of tourism, much of it might as well be.

The meeting point of many major cultures, an Islamic country dragged into the twentieth century by Kemal Ataturk, formerly the head of a great empire; Turkey has accumulated a great deal, and the centuries can be seen side by side in many of the streets.

Having said this, it has to be admitted that away from the big cities (and indeed in the poorer parts of those), you are pretty much on your own. You will usually be able to find someone who speaks a few words of English, and understands more than he speaks, or an *ex-Gastarbeiter* who picked up a little German, but, in many places, unless you speak Turkish you are going to have to rely on dumb-show, mime, and pointing at what you want. Accommodation is likely to be rock-bottom basic, especially in the sanitary department, and you are not going to be able to find quite a lot of the things which you may regard as normal – such as toilet paper. All in all, you will be on a bit of an expedition. In the vast majority of places you will, however, be made very welcome, *so long as you are male*. A combination of history and Islam means that women walk the unhappy knife-edge between being ignored completely and being treated like whores. This may be unfair to some Turks, but it is more than true of many others, so unaccompanied women should avoid Turkey more than any other country in this book. There is also a tradition of banditry and worse, in some of the more remote parts, although at least you are unlikely to suffer the fate of a Dutch couple who drove through Afghanistan – where they were *both* raped.

So: if you are feeling *macho* and adventurous, and have
a strong, simple, reliable machine which you can fix yourself,
you have a choice of mountains, sea-shores to both the
Mediterranean and Black seas, and an inland plateau
characterized by extremes of temperature. Unless you are in
the mountains, the high summer can be *very* hot ($100° +$),
especially inland, so the spring and autumn are the times to
go. On the other hand, the winters in the mountains,
especially to the east, can be very cold indeed; do not
assume that the **climate** is as mild everywhere as it is at the
shores. The same goes for rainfall (or snowfall, in the East):
the Mediterranean autumn can be very wet, but in the
interior, rainfall is extremely low.

Papers Visas are not necessary for nationals of most
countries for a stay of up to three months, but you do need
an IDP. The minimum driving age for Turkish nationals is
18, but foreigners can ride at whatever age their own
countries permit, if they have a full licence, according to the
Tourist Office in London. Carry the registration document or
log book, too, and a Green Card: be particularly careful here,
as some companies will only endorse the Green Card for
European Turkey and require a separate entry (and
sometimes an additional premium) for Asian Turkey. You
can buy insurance at the border, but compulsory minimum
limits are low: about £500/$700 per person for death or
bodily injury, with a limit of £1000/$1400 per accident, and
about £25 for property damage. You need more than this!
Helmets are compulsory (but patchily enforced) and first aid
kit and spare bulbs are advised, but not compulsory.

It is a long ride to Turkey: Istanbul is nearly 1900 miles
from London, and there is still plenty more of Turkey after
Istanbul. Moreover, the roads you will be using – through
Yugoslavia and Bulgaria or Greece – are not good. *Fodor*
reckons 4–5 days, but a week would be more realistic, and
two weeks would not be out of the way. Once you get there,
customs are fairly relaxed (except for dope – remember
Midnight Express): the limits of 200 cigarettes or 20 cigars or
50 gm of tobacco, and 1 litre of alcoholic drinks (any kind –
Islam strikes again), plus 200 gm of tea, will be enforced, but
the stated limits of 'two different kinds of cameras, plus ten
films' are unlikely to be enforced, as are the other limits on
personal goods. Be careful with drugs of any kind: if you
need any, make sure that you have a letter from your doctor,

and preferably contact the Turkish Consulate nearest you before you go. There is an import and export limit of 1000 Turkish Lire (TL), about £2, in Turkish currency; other currencies should be declared on entry if you want to take them out again. On the way out, you must have exchange certificates for all goods exported, but their combined value must not exceed $1000 US, except for modern carpets, where the limit is $3000. Antiques require a permit.

Currency There is a minimum exchange requirement of TL 1000 a day – hardly worth worrying about – but even this is normally only enforced when it comes to re-exchanging money: carry all your exchange slips with you, so that you can (a) change the money back at all and (b) prove that you spent your TL 1000 a day. The TL is a very weak currency; at the time of writing, it was about 500/£, 350/$, with over 20% annual inflation. **Bank hours** are 8.30 to 5 pm, with a lunch hour from 12 noon to 1.30 pm, Mondays to Fridays (despite Islam), and a few banks will also open on Saturday mornings. Shop hours are about 9 am to about 7 pm, with a 1–2 pm closing, Monday to Saturday; there are also wide variations, with longer hours in the big cities, and shorter in the villages, as a rule. Outside the biggest hotels, and the most expensive shops, **credit cards** are going to be completely useless. Tips will normally be added into the bill at the bigger places (where they go the the management, so give another 10% or so to the waiter), but in the kind of places the independent traveller is likely to patronize, 10–15% is reasonable and will be well appreciated; it will not be added into the bill.

Once you are in and riding, you will be faced with truly awful **roads** and appalling **driving**. The roads themselves are not always surfaced at all; there were at the time of writing under 20,000 miles of asphalted road, about the same again of 'macadam' (not tarmacadam – just packed stone) roads, and plenty of earth tracks, ridged bike-smashers in summer and gooey mud-puddles when it rains. Road maintenance is casual in the extreme, so be prepared for huge pot-holes, or tar *everywhere* if the road is being resurfaced. A trail bike is a good idea.

In the cities, traffic lights are regarded mainly as ornaments, and what little order there is will be imposed by whistle-blowing policemen. Traffic theoretically drives on the **right**, but it is very much a matter of theory rather than practice; everything is strictly catch-as-can. People **park** everywhere (including on the pavement), except in the very centre of Istanbul and Ankara, and people **overtake** merrily on both sides. Outside the towns, the rule of the road is Might Makes Right, and motorcyclists come pretty low in the pecking order. For what it is worth, the **speed limits** are 50 kph (31 mph) in town, and 90 kph (56 mph) outside; there are places where everyone ignores this, and places where you could never get within 20 mph of it, so it is mainly of academic interest. As long as you are not involved in an accident, the **police** are likely to leave you alone – which is just as well, because they are not the nicest people in the world. You must, however, call the traffic police in the event of all but the most minor accident: the number varies, but a patrol will probably find you soon enough.

The whole motoring scene is pretty primitive, and most of the time you will be lucky if you can get 'super' **petrol** at all – which is only 92 octane!. Instead, you will be forced to use 80 octane 'regular' or 'normal', which requires a bike with a low compression ratio and a strong digestion. Spares are virtually impossible to come by, and Turkish **mechanics** are for the most part out of their depth when it comes to a truck or tractor engine, never mind a motorcycle. There are occasional honourable exceptions, and the Turkish Automobile club (whose address I was unfortunately unable to get, though I was told that there were branches everywhere) may be able to recommend one. They will also normally aid members of related organizations, even to the extent of helping them to ship damaged bikes home; check with your own club, or when you arrive in Turkey. If the bike is totalled, get confirmation of this from the Traffic Police and have the entry in your passport cancelled, or they will try to charge you duty on it as you leave.

You would be well advised to get a good phrase book, and a pocket dictionary (buy it in Turkey), because the ten word vocabulary is going to be stretched to the limit when you get out of town. Fortunately, the Turks use the Roman alphabet, and the pronunciation is straightforward, except for the 'c', which is 'ch' as in 'check'.

For the determined:

please	*lutfen*
thank you	*tesekkur*

yes	*evet*
no	*hayir*
where?	*nerede?*
room	*oda*
toilet	*tuvalet*
more	*daha*
how much?	*ne kadar?*
food	*yiyecek*

Attempts to speak Turkish are usually well received, though you may have to repeat yourself a few times to be understood – the Turks have regional accents, too.

Turkish **food** is justly famous, but it should be even better known. For the most part, it is like the very best Greek food, with a strong Middle Eastern influence governing the use of butter, spices, and rice. If all else fails, just point to what you want: they will usually let you into the kitchens in the smaller places, which makes this even easier. Incidentally, in the course of researching this book, I found out that the 'doner' in 'doner kebab' means 'turning' – just that, so obvious! A good cheap meal should cost £2–4 per person, plus another £1 or so for wine or beer ($3–5 + $1.50, say). Neither the **beer** nor the **wine** is particularly exciting, but they are both drinkable; the hard booze is *raki*, an aniseed-flavoured firewater a bit like ouzo or anisette. There is also locally-made brandy, whisky, gin, and vodka, which have to be worth trying at least once, as well as some very sweet but rather good liqueurs. There are no licencing hours, and no age limits, but the blood alcohol limit for driving is very low; the nice lady at the office was not sure, but thought that it was a positively Scandinavian 50 mg/100 ml. Not that such details worry the police: if they think you're drunk, especially if you've been in an accident, they will throw you in the clink anyway.

Outside the jails, **accommodation** is still cheap – but you get what you pay for. Plumbing, electrics, and door locks may or may not work: keep asking to see another room until you are satisfied, or go to the next place. A one-star hotel should cost TL 2400–7000 (say £5–12, $7–15) in Istanbul at the time of writing, appreciably less elsewhere. *Pensions* are even cheaper, starting as low as TL 1000, though that is likely to be pretty rough, and the one youth hostel (Cerrahpasa Cad. 63 Aksaray) in Istanbul is apparently reliable. During the school holidays, July 1st to August 30th, boarding schools and universities may also provide accommodation; contact your nearest tourist office for information, or write to TMGT, Tunel, Istiklal 471/2, Istanbul.

Camping is legal everywhere, subject to common sense (get permission from land-owners; stay away from military bases, or anywhere else with NO ENTRY or KEEP OUT signs), or there are apparently fairly basic, but cheap and well-maintained, organized sites.

Yugoslavia

To most people, Yugoslavia means one of two things: either the highly commercialized package-tour resorts of the Adriatic coast, or the appalling *autoput* which has to be transversed as fast as possible on the way to Greece.

Because of this, much of Yugoslavia is amazingly unspoiled; in fact, 'primitive' would not be too strong a word. But it is a fascinating country, from whatever direction you approach it. The landscape is incredible, with something like three-quarters of the country at over 3000 feet; the political structure, freedom within Communism, is remarkable; and the diversity of peoples and cultures which make the country up is extraordinary. There are Montenegrins, Croats, Macedonians, Moslems, Slovenes, Serbs, Albanians, Hungarians, Turks, Slovaks (not the same as Slovenes!), and Ruthenians. No wonder the Victorians were so concerned with what they called the Balkan Question!

This extraordinary alliance of Balkan states, who spent most of their history warring with each other and with anyone else who was handy (especially the Ottoman Empire), results in tremendous diversity of every aspect of life: religion, food, architecture, clothing, customs, everything. There is not even an official language for the country, though Serbo-Croatian is about the most widespread. It is a truly fascinating country, and for the rider who is prepared to meet the odd inconvenience and discomfort on the way, it is tremendously rewarding. Just one warning: in really remote areas, the fine old Balkan tradition of banditry has not been entirely abandoned, so if you see a villainous-looking gentleman trying to wave you down, it may be best to ride on.

Climate The usual tourist season is April to mid-October, and there will be snow in the mountains from December to the end of March; as usual, the climate varies with altitude, and in July and August the heat in places may be too much for some people, with temperatures sometimes exceeding 100°F. Rainfall is fairly constant throughout the year, and not excessive; the driest month in the tourist season is September, and the wettest is June, but the variation is only about 50%.

Papers British passport holders do not need visas, but most non-Europeans do. These can be issued at a consulate, or you can get a 30-day Tourist Pass at the border, and apply for a visa once you are inside if you want to stay longer.There is a nominal charge for the Pass. For the bike, you will need log book or registration book and letter of permission, national driving licence, and a Green Card. Insurance can be bought at the border, and minimum cover is not at all bad – 5,000,000 dinars – but check what other cover you are getting. You must carry a spare set of light bulbs and a first aid kit; anyone arriving at an accident is required by law to render first aid. **Helmets** are compulsory, and so are daylight riding lights *outside built-up areas*.

Most people will ride to Yugoslavia, usually through West Germany and Austria. From Calais to Zagreb is 936 miles, and it is another 242 miles to Belgrade (Beograd), so allow at least three days for the journey. On arrival, the **customs** allowances are 200 cigarettes or 50 cigars or 250 gm of tobacco, or a mixture of tobacco products not exceeding 250 gm; a bottle (750 ml) of wine; a quarter litre (!) of spirits; a quarter litre of eau-de-cologne; a 'small amount' of perfume; and the usual other goodies, except that there is a limit of one camera and 5 rolls of film per person – though a modest excess is unlikely to cause trouble. Import and export of Yugoslav currency is limited to 1500 dinars per person in denominations of less than 100 dinar notes, but there are no restrictions on other currencies or travellers' cheques. If you make more than one visit per year, the dinar limit drops to 200 on subsequent visits.

You should also make sure that any damage visible on the bike as you enter the country is recorded on a special form. Otherwise, when you try to leave, you may be detained until the cause of the damage has been ascertained.

On the way out, the only export difficulties arise with antiques, works of art, and other items of 'archaeological, historical, sociological, artistic, or other cultural or scientific value'.

Once you are actually inside, the **roads** are mostly awful. A few of the major ones are not too bad, though the state of the *autoput* that most people use in traversing the country is legendary for its awfulness, and back roads are tracks. So-called motorways (*autoput*) are not always divided by a central reservation, and a toll is charged on most of them – though it does not amount to much. The **speed limit** on a motorway is 120 kph (75 mph); on other main roads it is 100 kph (62 mph); on secondary roads it is 80 kph (50 mph); and in town it is 60 kph (36 mph). The distinction between 'main' and 'secondary' roads will normally be clear: main roads are bad, but secondary ones are unbelievably bad. **Priority** is to the right, as usual, but in towns and cities the traffic on the major road has precedence unless otherwise indicated, and in the country the international priority sign is used if appropriate.

Overtaking is prohibited at bends, or anywhere else that visibility is reduced, as well as at pedestrian and level crossings. Trams in motion may be overtaken on the left only if the position of the rails makes overtaking on the right impossible; stationary trams may be overtaken on the right only if there is a pedestrian island at the tram stop.

The horn must not be used at all in built-up areas at night, or in built-up areas during the day except in case of emergency, but on the open road it is used with gusto.

It is illegal to **park** on bridges, bends, cycle tracks, on or near pedestrian crossings, crossroads, or public transport stops, in tunnels, or in front of public buildings or garages, and parking on the pavement is illegal except in marked bays. In practice, parking is rarely a problem, even in big cities. Road signs (including NO PARKING signs) are the international standards.

The Yugoslav **police**, like all communist police, can be a bit heavy; dial 92 only if you have to. If anyone is hurt, you *must* call them, and they may throw you in jail if they decide that it was your fault. Knowing this, blackmail is something of a cottage industry among accident victims: 'You pay me, I don't call the police'. This is where belonging to a motoring organization can be useful, or try the *Auto-Moto Association* (AMSJ), Ruzveltova 18, Beograd (tel. 440 185). The police can also impose on-the-spot fines, which you can either pay on the spot or contest and appeal in court. Unlike some countries, you cannot use this means of delay as a way of getting time to do a bunk without paying: you may well be arrested at the border.

In case of **breakdown**, the AMSJ runs a motoring help and information service called SPI; dial 987 in most places.

They will also order spares for you, if you belong to an associated club. Yugoslav mechanics are at their best with truck and tractor engines; faced with subtleties such as overhead cams, light alloy, and torque wrench settings, they tend to fade out. Spares are, of course, a perennial problem. So, for that matter, is **petrol**: 86 octane *normal* is widely available, but 98 octane *super* is normally only obtainable near major roads and tourist areas.

Although there is no minimum **currency** exchange, there are a few interesting moments when it comes to dealing with dinars (divided into 100 paras). At banks and other places where you can change money (including post offices!), you can change your money either for cash or for 'dinar cheques'. The dinar cheque has two major advantages: it gets you a 10% discount when you use it instead of cash, and it is the *only* way to get reconvertible currency. The receipt for the dinar cheque allows automatic reconversion of any surplus currency (so keep the receipts!), whereas cash will not be reconverted unless you can show these receipts. It also has the disadvantage that it can only be used in those hotels, shops, etc., showing the dinar cheque sign – but there are plenty of these, and in any case, you can exchange dinar cheques for cash by buying something (anything) from such a shop and taking your change in cash. Dinar cheques are available in denominations of 100, 200, 300 and 1000 dinars. Another source of discounts is petrol vouchers, available in 400 dinar reconvertible blocks, which bring the price of petrol down to about the European average. These are only available abroad, or at the border. **Plastic money** is virtually useless.

Bank hours are among the longest in the world, from 7 or 8 am to 7 or 8 pm, Monday to Saturday, though some small-town branches may take a siesta from 1 to 3 pm. Shop hours are even longer, with many opening until noon on Sunday, and some staying open very late indeed. In hotels and restaurants, tipping is a vexed question: some people seem to regard the whole business as condescending, whereas others are very grateful. As a general rule, tip only when you think it is really deserved, and make it a decent-sized tip of 10% or more.

Because of the linguistic mish-mash in Yugoslavia, there is not much point in giving a vocabulary. English and German are probably the most useful, with English and the

English-speaking peoples much more popular, unless you speak Serbo-Croat. Both the English (Roman) and Cyrillic (Russian) alphabets are used, so SARAJEVO can appear as CAPAJEBO, for example – watch out for this one.

Food is best described as a cross between Italian and Greek, filling rather than elegant (especially in the villages), but hearty and satisfying. On the other hand, the tremendous variety of cultures which coexist in Yugoslavia means that there are all kinds of local and regional specialities, most of which are well worth trying. Prices are very low indeed, and you can eat handsomely for very little, but picnic food is also delicious and very cheap.

Yugoslav **wines** are mostly the sort you swill rather than sip, but again they are very palatable – especially with Yugoslav food – and if you want spirits, try *slivovitza* (plum brandy) and *vinjak* (grape brandy). Some of the cheaper ones can bring tears to your eyes, but the better varieties are very drinkable. Watch out when riding, though, as the blood alcohol level permitted is only 50 mg/100 ml. If you want to drink water, stick to the bottled variety or carry water purifying tablets, especially in remote areas.

As for **accommodation**, the official gradings are De Luxe, A, B, C and D hotels, 1st. 2nd., and 3rd class *pensions*, and inns. These can be surprisingly expensive in the tourist areas: a double room, high season, on the coast could easily cost well over £20 ($30) *plus breakfast*; an inn might cost £15 ($20). Out in the sticks, however, the prices would be dramatically lower, and out of season you should be able to pick up some real bargains in full board accommodation. An alternative is to look for private houses which let out rooms, where prices should be rather lower and where some food may be included.

There are cheap youth hostels, administered by NAROMTRAVEL, Mose Pijade 12, 11000 Beograd, tel 011-339-030, and you can camp either at authorized sites, which are inexpensive, or 'wild' if you have a letter of authority from the local area tourist office or the local municipal authority. No matter where you stay, you will still be subject to the visitors' tax, which at the time of writing varied from about 10–30 dinars per day; this applies even if you are camping.

Scandinavia

Introduction

This section breaks with alphabetical order, and for good
reason. Although there are plenty of good reasons for going
to Scandinavia, the countries which make up this group are
a long way north. This means that the riding season is short
– many Scandinavian motorcyclists lay up their machines for
the winter, because it is simply too cold to ride – and that
the distances involved are such that many people will never
bother to try exploring this northernmost part of Europe.

Consequently, the section begins with Denmark, the
most accessible of all the Scandinavian countries to most
people, and then goes on to Greenland, which is effectively a
part of Denmark, despite 'home rule', and where a great deal
of the practical information for Denmark still applies. Next
comes Sweden, as the second most likely country to attract
visitors, and then Norway, which concludes Scandinavia as
far as most people are concerned. In the interests of
completeness, Finland follows, and then Iceland. Quite
honestly, it is fairly unlikely that most motorcyclists will visit
Finland, very unlikely that they will visit Iceland, and a virtual
certainty that they will not visit Greenland – but if you do
want to go, then here is the basic information.

Although each country has its own national character, it
is not unreasonable to make several generalizations about
the three main countries (Denmark, Sweden and Norway),
and to say that a lot of what is said applies to Finland too.
Most people immediately associate Scandinavia and sex –

especially the beautiful Swedish girls. In fact, Denmark is probably the home of the hardest-core pornography, with virtually no restrictions, and for actual sleeping around, it is probably a tie (if that is the right word!) between Denmark and Sweden. Both the Norwegians and the Finns are much more restrained by comparison. If you want to sample this lifestyle, though, it is no use just hanging around and waiting for something to happen: you will have to get to know people, and you will then find out about the odd combination of freedom and formality which makes up the Scandinavian character. The older people in Scandinavia are almost all relentlessly formal, and even cold, and it is unkindly said that the reason why so many Scandinavian girls are free with their favours is that the alternative is trying to talk to Scandinavian men.

Another generalization is that the Scandinavian countries are expensive. Admittedly, if you have come straight from England the prices may not look too bad, but compared with the rest of Europe, accommodation is rather steep and food and (especially) drink can be horrendous.

Third, the Scandinavian countries all seem to have a liquor problem. Unbridled drinking is the order of the day, and because this does not mix with motoring, the usual blood alcohol maximum is 50 mg/100 ml – and if you're over the limit, you're in the slammer for two or three weeks before you have to worry about paying the fine, losing your licence, and so forth. You do not even need to be over the limit to have a hard time, nor do you need to break any other law if you are over the limit; you go to jail anyway. If you do not pay your on-the-spot fines in some countries, the police can impound your bike – or just make you walk into the next village to pick up the keys, as I have heard of happening in Sweden. The 'nanny state', in which the government tells you what is best for you, and you do as you are told, is very highly developed in Scandinavia. The police, as Chief Nannies, are polite, and friendly, and expect you to behave like a good little boy and do exactly as you are told – or 'this hurts me more than it hurts you'.

Although there are some fine roads in the southern parts of some Scandinavian coutries, or near major towns, as you go north the traffic density diminishes and the frost damage increases, so gravel-surfaced roads are regarded as perfectly normal. These are not much fun – or rather, they are altogether too exciting – for motorcyclists.

The most useful generalization, however, is a legal one. The Scandinavian countries are all treated as one area for passport purposes, and you can spend up to three months without a visa, in any nine months, if you have any of the usual passports (British, European, US, Canadian, Australian, New Zealand). Furthermore, the Green Card is only required in Iceland; otherwise, the minimum cover is as given in the individual sections.

All in all, there are two main reasons for visiting Scandinavia. One is to try the modern life, with plenty of pornography and sex, and the other is to explore the wide open spaces. For the first, you will be confined to the big cities for the most part, and you need not even take the bike unless you think it may be useful for posing. For the second, it is worth remembering that those vast empty spaces really are vast and empty: a reliable bike and (better still) a travelling companion on a second machine will greatly improve your peace of mind.

Denmark

As the introduction to this section has already made clear, Scandinavia is not to everyone's liking. But if you are undecided, a visit to Denmark is an excellent idea. It has many of the attractions of Scandinavia, and rather fewer of the drawbacks; and, of course, it is easier to get to and (because of its relatively small size) easier to get around in. Rather surprisingly, it is nothing like as flat as you might expect, though the scenery is better described as pretty than as dramatic.

The Danes themselves are comparatively easygoing, with the most liberal pornography laws (and laws governing other forms of sexual activity) in the world. Their booze laws are also a lot easier than others in Scandinavia, though going over the 50 mg/100 ml blood alcohol limit still lands you in deep trouble. In general, the Danes seem to be a lot less repressed than their neighbours, but you can still expect the odd mixture of puritanism and sexual freedom which characterizes that part of the world. Denmark was also the home of that unique Scandinavian motorcycle, the Nimbus in-line four, which changed surprisingly little from its inception in 1920 to its final demise in 1957. You still see these rather improbable shaft-drive machines, with their pressed-steel frames, being ridden on the streets.

Climate The best time to go is undoubtedly high summer; July is the only month when average daily maximum temperatures regularly exceed 70°F, though August is very nearly as warm and June and September rarely see average daily temperatures below 50°, with highs in the 60s and even the low 70s. August is rather wetter than average, so July is your best bet – though many swear that May and June are the most beautiful months. The winter, autumn, and early spring are pretty cold and wet or snowy.

Papers Danes need to be 18 to ride a full-size motorcycle (15 for mopeds), but as far as I was able to discover, you can ride on a full British licence (no IDP needed) at 17. The minimum insurance limits per accident are 10,000,000 Kr *per accident* for personal injury, and

1,000,000 Kr per accident for property damage; passenger insurance is compulsory. **Helmets** are compulsory, and so are daylight riding lights. You should also be careful that you mask your headlamp to dip to the right: you can be prosecuted for left-dipping lights, and although you are unlikely to be run in unless someone complains (or you dazzle a policeman), Danes are unusually sensitive to bright lights because their lamps are, for some obscure reason, legally restricted in output. There are no other unusual requirements.

To get there, you can either ride through Holland and Germany, or take a ferry to Esbjerg from Harwich, Hull, or Newcastle. The ferries are quite expensive, but they do save a dull day's ride through flat northern Europe so you might consider riding one way, and taking a ferry the other.

Customs rules are slightly confusing, because of inter-Scandinavian treaties. There are three groups of allowances, depending on your nationality and where you are coming from. In the table, Group 1 is for residents of Europe, entering from an EEC country; Group 2 is for residents of Europe entering from a non-EEC country; and Group 3 is for non-EEC residents.

Goods	Group 1	Group 2	Group 3
Spirits *or*	1.5 l.	1 l.	Note (a)
Fortified or sparkling wine	3 l.	2 l.	Note (a)
Still wine	3 l.	2 l.	Note (a)
Cigarettes *or*	300	200	400
Cigarillos *or*	150	100	200
Cigars *or*	75	50	100
Tobacco (smoking)	400 gm	275 gm	500 gm
Perfume	75 gm	50 gm	Note (a)
Eau-de-cologne	375 cc	250 cc	Note (a)
Coffee *or*	750 gm	500 gm	Note (a)
Coffee extract/essence	300 gm	200 gm	Note (a)
Tea *or*	150 gm	100 gm	Note (a)
Tea extract/essence	60 gm	40 gm	Note (a)
Other Articles, *including beer*	1500 Kr	375 Kr	Note (a)

Note (a): *Allowances are determined by where you are coming from, as in columns 1 and 2.*

The age limit for booze and tobacco is 17, and for coffee 15. Tax-free import is permitted only once every 24 hours, and if you are staying less than 24 hours you may not be given the full allowance. If you want to import any more than the smallest quantities of food, ask at Customs: the Danes themselves admit that the regulations are too complicated to explain briefly.

There are no restrictions on the import and export of any kind of currency, except that:

1   You must be able to show on entry that you can afford to get yourself home again, and

2   If you want to export more than 50,000 Kr in any currency, you must prove that it is not more than you brought in. In other words, if you are carrying over £4000 in cash (say $5000) when you enter, tell them!

The Danish **currency** is the Krone and is worth about 11 to the £ sterling, 8 to the $ US, as a very rough guide. **Credit cards** are less use than in England, but should be acceptable in the bigger petrol stations, in many hotels and restaurants, etc. **Bank hours** vary widely, especially in small towns, but are basically 9.30 am to 4.30 pm, Monday to Friday (6 pm on Thursday), often with lunch from 1 to 2 pm. Shopping hours are mostly 8 or 9 am to 5 or 5.30 from Monday to Thursday, 7 or 8 pm on Friday, and noon or a little later on Saturday. In the big towns, hours tend to be longer, and smaller shops may take a lunch-hour.

At the time of writing, VAT was a hard-to-calculate 22%, with exemptions on single expensive items for export. Tips are normally written into the bill, even on taxi meters. Hotels and restaurants are usually content with the 15% they stick you for, but taxis expect another 10% on top of the 10% they have already added on. So forget being flash – stick to the bike!

As in the rest of Scandinavia, Danish **drivers** tend to be law-abiding and very, very sober. There is a fair-to-good motorway system, roughly cross-shaped, centred on Kolding; the **speed limit** is a miserly and strictly enforced 100 kph (62 mph), but since the whole country is only 250 miles north-to-south, this is no great hardship. The speed limit on other roads – probably the best-surfaced in Scandinavia – is 80 kph (50 mph) on the open road, 60 kph (37 mph) in town. Danes drive on the right, and **priority** is to the right, *including roundabouts*, unless otherwise marked.

It is illegal to **overtake** at bends, intersections, pedestrian crossings, or the brows of hills – the usual common-sense restrictions – and horns are not widely used; they must, by law, be 'low toned', so multi-tones, Klaxons, and anything unusually piercing are illegal. **Parking** is 'parkering' in Danish; parkering on the pavement is *forbudt* (forbidden) except in marked bays, but otherwise the restrictions are common-sense. You must use parkering lights at night unless you are under a street lamp, or in a marked parking bay. Danish street signs are not fully internationalized, so watch out for:

Ensrettet kørsel	One way street
Fare	Danger
Farligt sving	Dangerous bend
Gennemkørsel forbudt	No through road
Holdt	Halt
Hold til højre	Keep right
Hold til venstre	Keep left
Indkørsel forbudt	No entry
Korsvej	Crossroads
Omkørsel	Diversion
Parkering forbudt	Parking forbidden
Vejarbejde	Road works
Vejen er spaerret	Road closed

As already indicated in the introduction, any offences are likely to result in prosecution. The **police** are a bit like the Germans, generally very friendly as long as you do not break the law, but firm to the point of merciless if you do. On-the-spot fines really have to be paid on the spot, and they can impound the bike if you don't. In the event of an accident, you are not obliged to call them if there is no personal injury. The emergency number (all services) is a very logical 000.

Breakdowns will normally be efficiently but expensively dealt with: labour costs are steep, and 22% sales tax makes parts dear too. British bikes are well catered for, as are BMWs (inevitably), and Nimbus owners are better served than anywhere else in the world. There is no free breakdown patrol, least of all from the *Forenede Dansk Motorejere* (Danish Motor Club) of Blegdamsvej 124, 2100 København Ø, but there are several commercial organizations.

Petrol comes in three grades, 92, 96, and 98 octane, which correspond to British two-, three-, and four-star; all three are widely available. There are no petrol stations on the motorways, but on other roads you will often find that apparently closed gas stations have one automatic pump, accepting 20 Kr notes. Petrol prices are rather higher than the European average, perhaps by 25%.

The basic vocabulary is:

please	*vaer sa venlig* (vayr saw venlee)
thank you	*tak*
yes	*ja* (yah)
no	*nej* (nay)
where is?	*hvor er der?* (vohr ayr der)
room	*vaerelse* (vay-rul-suh)
toilet	*toilettet (almost as good as parkering)*
more	*mere* (me-rah)
how much?	*hvor meget?* (vohr mayud)
food	*mald* (mahld)

Danish **food** is justly famous, and anyone who has eaten at a *kolde bord* will know what to expect: innumerable kinds of pickled and smoked fish, roast pork (hot or cold), and rich, creamy stews. The **beer** that accompanies it is equally famous, and you can get legless for free in København on the free tours of the Carlsberg and Tuborg breweries – but don't try riding afterwards, or it's the nick for you. Unfortunately, restaurants are expensive, and will charge three times as much for a bottle of beer as a supermarket will, so picnics are a good idea. Spirits are frighteningly expensive anywhere, and mostly firewater; with a blood alcohol level of 50 mg/100 ml, walk if you're going to drink. Tap water is safe.

Accommodation is probably the least expensive of any major Scandinavian country; even in København, prices are no worse than England, and outside the capital they are usually cheaper. Breakfast may or may not be included, and can vary from a roll and a cup of coffee to something quite substantial, so it pays to check this out before you check yourself in. You can also stay at inns, rather like the traditional English inns; at the end of 1984, a single room without bath might cost 160 krone (just over £12, say $17), and a double with bath about twice that, including a large breakfast in both cases. Farmhouse accommodation is cheaper again, and gives you an excellent chance to try real Danish home cooking at quite reasonable prices.

Youth hostels cost 30–40 Kr per person per night at the time of writing; they also provide relatively cheap fixed-price meals which will keep you alive, but neither fill you nor excite you. Camping costs about half as much as a youth hostel, but you will need an International Camping Carnet, which costs about the same as one night's stay. Some camp sites rent out tents, which can be useful. 'Wild' camping is permitted only with the landowner's permission, and there is no right of overnight stay as there is in other Scandinavian countries. Write to *Det Danske Lejrpladsudvalg*, Skjoldsgade 10, København Ø, for a full list of camping sites (35 Kr including postage). Sleeping out is actually illegal, and so is camping on beaches, which can bring an on-the-spot fine.

Greenland

Greenland is huge (840,000 square miles), thinly populated (50,000 people), and mostly covered in ice. Roads are virtually non-existent, except near a few settlements. The vast majority of it is inside the Arctic circle, and most communications are by air. Some idea of the terrain may be gained from the fact that it is possible to hire dog sleds, and that all treks into the interior have to be approved by the Ministry for Greenland, Hausergade 3, 1128 København K.

To get there, fly or take a ship from Denmark; contact KGH, Strandgade 100, København K. Accommodation is very limited once you arrive, but not expensive; there are a few hotels, seamen's hostels, and hikers' huts. For the last, contact *Udvalget for Vandreturisme*, Kultorvet 7, 1175 København K, and book well in advance. Alternatively, camp.

In all fairness, I don't think anyone has ever been motorcycle touring in Greenland, and I am not sure that anything except a specially-prepared trail bike (preferably with studded tyres) would be much use – and even then, you would need to fly it out if it broke down. If anyone tries it, perhaps they would let me know!

Sweden

Mention Scandinavia to most people, and they will think of Sweden first; probably Swedish girls, and then Swedish blue movies. In fact, Sweden offers a greater variety of Scandinavian experience than any of the other countries in the group, but the scenery is not *quite* the wildest, and the pornography is not *quite* the hardest, and so forth. On the other hand, the police are possibly the strictest, taxation and 'nanny state' welfare is probably most comprehensive, and there always seems to me to be something in the average Swede of a poseur's pride at living in the showcase of Scandinavia.

What you get out of Sweden depends very much on where you go. The extreme south is very much like Denmark, with a European rather than a Scandinavian flavour, whereas the extreme north is very much like Norway, all bleak and empty and sweeping and grand. The summer can be surprisingly warm (well into the 80s on a good day) but it is also very changeable; skies can cloud over, and you can be soaked, in a matter of minutes. The winter is, quite simply, harsh. As in much of Scandinavia, many motorcyclists only tax their bikes for the summer months – but when you do meet fellow-motorcyclists, they are usually very friendly, if a little intense. Even the manic ones seem to be manic seriously. Their rules allow them to ride mopeds at 15, 125cc bikes at 17, and bigger bikes at 18, but you can ride at 17 on a full British licence – though if you hire a Swedish bike, Swedish laws apply.

The standard Scandinavian formalities apply for entry; log book, UK or other national licence, and insurance. The Swedish legal minimum is 50 million kronor per accident, undivided as to personal and property damages, and includes passenger liability. As this is around £5 million, there is not much to worry about. Daylight riding lights are compulsory for cars as well as for motorcycles! Otherwise, there are no special requirements, apart from the inevitable helmet.

You can drive to Sweden via Denmark, or take a ferry to Göteborg (or any other Scandinavian port); allow 16–30 hours for the ferry, depending on route, or 2–3 days riding. Once you arrive, the **customs** rules vary according to your country of residence. Everyone over the age of 20 is allowed 2 litres of beer, 1 litre of wine, and 1 litre of spirits, or two litres of beer and two litres of wine if no spirits are carried. Otherwise, European residents over 15 are allowed 200 cigarettes or 100 cigarillos or 50 cigars or 9 oz (250 g) of tobacco *and 200 cigarette papers* (which are apparently heavily taxed!), whilst non-European residents of the same age are allowed double these tobacco allowances (though I am not sure about the cigarette paper allowance). There is also a limit of 15 kg of food per person (over the age of 12), with a maximum of 5 kg of fats including $2\frac{1}{2}$ kg of butter, but fruit, coffee, tea, spices, and vegetables are not included, and with an absolute ban on fresh, frozen, or smoked (but not canned) meat. Is that clear? If you are not confused enough yet, the 'other goods' limit is 600 Skr, but the value of the food will be set against this. You will also have fun with medicines; carry a doctor's note if you have anything that could be classed as 'narcotics', and note that they will not allow more than a 5-days' supply into the country. After all that, currency control is comparatively simple: import and export limits of up to 6000 Skr, but only in notes of 100 Skr or less.

Currency As a rough guess for the value of the krona, say 10/£ and 7/$. **Plastic money** is useful in towns, especially in hotels and restaurants, but should not be relied upon for petrol, or out of town. Change your money at the **banks** from 9.30 am to 4 pm, Monday to Friday, but expect shorter hours out of town and possibly longer ones (like re-opening from 4.30 to 6 pm) in the bigger towns. Most shops open from about 9 am to 6 or 7 pm, Monday to Friday, with early closing (anything from one o'clock onwards) on Saturdays – though Saturday closing is getting more common, and there are even a few places in Stockholm which open on Sundays. The weirdest hours are kept by restaurants – only the expensive places are likely to stay open after 9 pm – and bars, where it is illegal to sell spirits before noon.

Tips are almost always added into the bill (*service inkludert*) and no more is expected, except perhaps rounding it up a bit. Sales tax was, at the time of writing, a massive 25% or so, and applied to almost everything; single expensive items were eligible for a refund at the border, if you got an export certificate.

The general standard of **riding and driving** is high, as you might expect in a country where drivers are always stone cold sober, and where the police enforce the law to the letter, every time – even exceeding a speed limit by 5 kph (3 mph) can land you with a stiff fine, but as it is not payable on the spot, you might do best to forget about it until you leave the country. The **speed limits** are 110 kph (69 mph) on motorways and a few other fast roads, 90 or 70 kph (56 or 43 mph) as signposted on most other roads, and 50 kph (31 mph) in built-up areas. Watch out for schools, where a 30 kph (19 mph) limit may be posted *and enforced*, and if you are misguided enough to use a trailer, remember that you will *always* be subject to a 40 kph (25 mph) limit for an unbraked trailer, or 70 kph (43 mph) if it has brakes – unless even lower limits are posted. In the south, the roads are good, and you have the choice of motorways; in the north, because of frost problems, many are gravel-surfaced.

The Swedes **drive** on the right (they changed over comparatively recently, in the 1950s or 1960s), and the usual **priority**-to-the-right applies unless otherwise indicated. The only major 'funny' on right of way is that buses always have right of way when pulling away from stops in built-up (50 kph) areas. **Overtake** only on the left, and carefully: the police don't like 'carvers', and gravel surfaces mean that you have to plan ahead. **Parking** restrictions are simple: commonsense in most places, but *never* on main roads (except in rest stops), and only in marked bays in town. Never on the pavement! One restriction that is worth knowing about, though, is that there are a few areas on the Baltic coast which are not open to tourists, and where only designated roads may be used. Bear in mind that Sweden's nearest neighbours include Russia and East Germany, and you will understand why. These roads are clearly signposted in several languages, including English.

The unpleasantness of the **police** has already been mentioned, but you only have to call them in the event of personal injury or severe property damage. The emergency number (all services) is 90 000. For **breakdowns**, Larmjanst AB is a private organization which covers almost all of the

country; their number will be in the telephone directory.
Alternatively, many garages offer a 24-hour accident and
breakdown service. Either way, it is likely to prove expensive,
and holiday insurance is particularly worthwhile. This is
especially true in the vast empty north, where recovery can
cost a fortune. Petrol stations will be rare in the north, too,
though self-service automatic pumps accepting 10 kr notes
are quite common. Petrol prices are surprisingly reasonable,
whether for 93 octane regular or 99 octane super.

The basic vocabulary is:

please	*var sa god*
thank you	*takk*
yes	*ja* (ya)
no	*nej* (nay)
where?	*var?*
room	*rum*
toilet	*toalett*
more	*mer*
how much?	*vad kostar?*
food	*matsäck* (mat seck)

Food is expensive, with cafeterias the best bet for most
people's budgets, but apparently station buffets have huge
all-you-can-eat breakfasts at very reasonable prices. Look out,
too, for the set 3-course *menu* if you want to save money.
Remember that the *smörgasbord* is delicious, but expensive,
and that you will need plenty of beer to help down all that
salty fish. The usual **drink** is weak beer (2.8% alcohol), with
extremely weak beer as the alternative (*lättöl*, 1.8%). *Starköl*,
or 'strong' beer, which is over 2.8% alcohol, can only be sold
in the state-owned *Systembolaget* liquor stores, as can wines
and spirits. The minimum age for buying alcoholic drinks is
20, the maximum permitted blood alcohol level is 50 mg/
100 ml, and the standard sentence for being over the limit is
3 weeks inside, unless you hurt anyone....

Accommodation costs can also be terrifying. Hotels are
worse than England, bed-and-breakfast in private homes or
on farms are about the same as England (starting at under
100 Skr per person, including breakfast), and youth hostels
cost under 30 Skr a night at the time of writing, provided
you were a member of your national YHA; otherwise, there

is a 10 Skr surcharge. Camping is cheaper still, and if you want to camp 'wild', the 'all-man's-right' allows you one night (and one night only) in any reasonable location, even without permission. Like other Scandinavian countries, there are strong laws governing pollution and damage to the environment, so camp carefully.

Norway

The different Scandinavian countries each emphasize a
different aspect of Scandinavia. Norway, a curiously long,
thin country which stretches well into the Arctic Circle and
has land borders with most of Sweden, northern Finland,
and even with Russia, typifies the huge empty spaces – four
million people in 125,000 square miles, with 10% of the
population in Oslo and over 50% in towns – the bleak,
brooding beauty, and the great dark forests. The coastline is
famous for its fjords, and for its thousands of islands, most of
which are uninhabited.

You will really need to be something of an addict of
Scandinavia to venture this far north, but you will be
rewarded with surprisingly friendly people, who are often less
given to extremes than other Scandinavians. (Except when it
comes to drinking – as a Norwegian girl I was trying to pick
up years ago said, 'If you find a crowd of drunks, you vill
almost always find a Norwegian in the middle'; thank you,
Synøve.) The Norwegians, although reserved, are not usually
actively gloomy. You will, however, find it expensive; North
Sea oil has been used rather more intelligently than in
Britain, and so both the standard and the cost of living are
high.

Climate Although the winters are bitterly cold and
snowy, and many passes will be closed by snow from as early
as October to as late as June, summer can be surprisingly
warm. Well over 80° is by no means unusual in Oslo in July
and August, and June can be delightful. Obviously, the
further north (or the further up) you go, the colder it gets.
You can actually see the midnight sun from the middle of
May to the end of July in the north, and even in Oslo, a
midsummer's 'night' is more like twilight; it never gets really
dark.

Papers Formalities are minor, like the rest of
Scandinavia, and you can ride your own bike at 17 – but
you need to be 18 to ride a Norwegian-registered vehicle.
Norwegian minimum insurance provides unlimited cover for
personal injury (including passengers), and 150,000 kr. for

property damage – a good deal better than English third party insurance! **Helmets** are compulsory, and so is a spare set of light bulbs; as far as I was able to discover, so are daylight riding lights.

In order to get there from the UK, you can either take a ferry (roughly 16–30 hours, depending on departure and arrival points) or ride via Sweden; Oslo is about 1000 miles from the usual channel ferry ports, but you will need to allow plenty of time for the journey because of the borders, other ferries, and slow roads that you will encounter *en route*. Once again, taking the ferry one way, and riding the other, may be a good idea.

Liquor allowances at **customs** are mean – 2 litres of wine, or 1 litre of wine and 1 litre of spirits – and you can also have 200 cigarettes or 250 gm of other tobacco products, a kilo of candy (!), and 'other goods' to a value of 350 kr, or 700 kr for European residents in transit or 3500 kr for non-European residents in transit. Otherwise, 'personal effects' is reasonably widely interpreted. **Currency** control is a little eccentric: you can import any amount of Norwegian currency, *but only in denominations of up to 100 kr notes*! Export is limited to 800 kr, and you may not export any more foreign currency than was imported; as usual, declare large amounts at the border. The *krone*, divided into 100 *øre*, is worth about 11 to the £, 8 to the $US.

Bank hours are different from summer to winter: 8.15 am to 3.45 pm Monday to Friday (6 pm Thursday) in winter, and 8.15 am to 3.15 pm Monday to Friday (5 pm Thursday) in summer. They may also open on Saturday mornings, and small branches may keep shorter hours. Shops mostly open 9 am to 5 pm, Monday to Friday, half-day closing Saturday (about 1 pm). **Credit cards** are very little use anywhere, so carry cash. As far as I was able to discover, there is no scheme for the refund of sales tax. Tips are normally figured into the bill, with no need to give any more (unless you want to round the bill up); if it doesn't say *service inkludert*, give the usual 10–15%.

Driving is deadly slow and somewhat primitive. Only in the south are the roads regularly well-surfaced; in the north, gravel and macadam (stone) are quite usual, often with very soft verges. The general **speed limit** out of town is only 80 kph (50 mph), though a few motorways allow you to scorch along at 90 kph (56 mph); in town, you are restricted to 50

kph (31 mph). Driving is on the right, with **priority** to the
right unless otherwise posted, and trams always have right of
way. Stationary trams may be **overtaken** only on the right,
unless there is no room; moving trams may be overtaken on
the left where there is no room on the right, or in one way
streets. You are expected to use your lights, indicators, and
horn 'as necessary', but no more than that. With the
rigorously enforced speed limit, and the poor roads in the
country, anyone who can cover 200 miles in a day is doing
very well indeed. **Parking** is simple: subject to the usual
commonsense rules about obstruction, bends, junctions, and
other dangerous places, you can usually park anywhere that
it does not say ALL STANS FORBUDT – which also means no
stopping, even for map-reading and the like. Other signs
worth reading include:

Arbeide pa Vegen	Road works
Bakketop	Hill top
Envegskjøring	One-way traffic
Ferist	Cattle grid
Gammel Veg	Old road
Grøfterens	Ditch-clearing
Ikke Møte	No overtaking, single file
Kjør Sakte	Drive slowly
Løs Grus	Loose gravel
Møteplass	Passing place
Omkjøring	Diversion
Rasteplass	Rest-place (lay-by)
Svake Kanter	Soft verges
Veg under Anlegg	Road under construction

Norwegian **police** are about the same as any others in
Scandinavia, but red-hot on drunken driving. The normal
penalty, if you haven't hurt anyone or caused any damage, is
3 weeks in jail and confiscation of the licence for a year.
Emergency numbers vary from place to place; it is only
compulsory to call the police if someone is hurt. For
breakdowns, the Norwegian Motoring Club (engagingly
abbreviated to NAF), Oslo 1, 2–4 Storgaten, offers a limited
service during the summer (late June, July, and August), and

will normally help members of affiliated foreign clubs as a matter of courtesy. Usually, though, you will need to use *Viking Redningstjeneste*, a profit-making organization who will make a profit out of you. Spares and repairs will be expensive, but efficient. **Petrol** is only slightly more expensive than the European average, but the Super is a delightful 99 octane; regular is 92. In the north, petrol stations are rare, and you will need a big tank.

English is usefully widespread, and you may never need Norwegian, but to be on the safe side:

please	*vaersågod*
thank you	*takk*
yes	*ja* (yah)
no	*nei* (nay)
where is?	*hvor er?* (vohr er)
room	*rom*
toilet	*toilett*
more	*mer*
how much?	*hvor coster?*
food	*niste*

As already mentioned Norway is an expensive place to visit. The **food** is very much like the rest of Scandinavia – fish, in many forms, and pork dishes. To save money, eat in a place labelled 'bar' (where they don't sell alcohol), which can be half the price of a full-scale restaurant; or in a cafeteria or pizzeria. Some hotels serve breakfast, included in the price – check this, and check what the breakfast consists of, as it may be either hearty or negligible. **Drinking** is usually done with the intention of getting drunk. Because of the prices, and the drunk-driving laws, you may have to stick to non-alcoholic refreshment with your meals. Fortunately, the water is very pure and pleasant; if you want to try booze, the locals drink beer, firewater, and imported whisky. If you are drinking with a Norwegian, one little piece of etiquette worth knowing is that as long as the bottle is open and on the table, it is taken as an invitation to help yourself. The blood alcohol limit for driving or riding is 50 mg/100 ml.

Accommodation is similarly expensive, even worse than England, unless you go for the more primitive end of the market. The classification (and price) ranking is *hotel*, *pensjonat* (large guesthouse), *gjestgiveri* (small guesthouse, or inn), *høyfellstue* (mountain lodge), *seter* (farm with accommodation), and private houses. Youth hostels are a good bet – there are over 100, and they are open to all – and if you really want to rough it, consider a *rorbu*, a hut used by fishermen in the winter but let out in the summer. There are innumerable camping sites, some of which will rent you a hut or a tent as well as a site, and a law translated as the 'all-man's-right' allows you to camp for up to two nights on any private or public property, without even notifying the owner, provided you leave no mess and cause no damage, and are more than 150 metres (165 yards – say 500 feet) from a house or chalet.

Finland

Although Finland is a more practicable destination than
Iceland or Greenland, it is still a country that few people will
think of visiting. It is a fascinating place: there are tens of
thousands of lakes – estimates vary from 60,000 to 200,000
– and very nearly as many islands offshore. Helsinki, the
capital, is very nearly at the southernmost tip, but still has 21
hours of daylight in the summer; in the far north, nomadic
Lapps follow the reindeer herds, and snow lies on the
ground for well over half the year.

Everything is an intriguing mixture of old and new;
Finland is another Nanny State on the standard
Scandinavian pattern, but its comparative remoteness means
that some of the changes seem more superficial, even
'pasted on', than in the rest of Scandinavia. On the other
hand, one thing which does not change is the prices: that
same remoteness means that imports are expensive, and
high taxation finishes the job.

Climate If you decide to go, the best time to go is
June-July-August, when long days will be combined with
surprisingly high temperatures – usually in the 70s, but still
subject to sudden showers. In the winter, you can expect
snow on the ground for three to four months! To get there,
a ferry from Stockholm is probably easiest; riding involves
going way up into the north, within 60 miles of the Arctic
Circle, and then heading south again if you want to see the
lake country. You might, however, decide that getting inside
the Arctic Circle is an experience you want for its own sake.

Papers Formalities are the same as anywhere else in
Scandinavia: most people do not need a visa, your own
licence will do (though as I understand it you cannot ride
until you are 18 – Finns certainly cannot), and your policy
should cover you to the minimum requirement of Finnish
law, which is unlimited personal injury cover and 1.8 million
Finnmarks for property damage. Crash **helmets** and daylight
riding lights are compulsory, but not spare bulbs, first aid kits,
etc. On arrival, the booze and cigarette allowances are the
same as for Norway, with a 400 Finnmark 'other goods'

allowance; Finnish **customs** are reasonably relaxed apart from the liquor and tobacco allowance. You can import any amount of money, in Finnish or foreign **currency**, but you can only export 5000 FIM in notes of up to 100 FIM; declare large sums on entry, for ease of export. Allow 10 FIM to the £ sterling, 7 FIM to the $ US, as a rough guide.

Bank hours are 9.15 to 4.15, Monday to Friday, and shopping hours are basically 8.30 or 9 am to 5 pm, though late opening (to 8 pm) is common on Mondays and Fridays and early closing is usual on Saturdays, especially in winter. Sales tax, at various rates up to 20%, can only be recovered if the goods are shipped directly out of Finland by the shop itself, to your home address (or to anywhere else you want to send a present). Tipping is the usual 10–15%, but additional tips are unnecessary if service has already been added in, as is usually the case. **Plastic money** is only any use in big towns, and then only in expensive places.

Driving and riding standards are high, but road surfaces are very variable – especially in the north, where gravel is usually the best you will find. Driving law is much like the rest of Scandinavia, except that it is flatly illegal to drive immediately after a drink. After you have had plenty of time to sober up, the blood alcohol limit is 50 mg/100 ml, with ferocious penalties for exceeding it. **Speed limits** are 120 kph (75 mph) on the few motorways; 100 kph (62 mph) on good, wide roads; 80 kph on most others (50 mph); 60 kph (37 mph) on lesser country roads; and 50 kph (31 mph) in town. All speeds are posted. As for road signs, look for:

Tietyö	Road works
Aja Hitaasti	Drive slowly
Kelirikko	Frost Damage
Paane	Slippery surface
Irtokiviä	Loose gravel
Lossi	Ferry

and a particularly entertaining one for Goldwing riders:

Räjäytystyö, sulje radiolähetin	Danger: Explosives. Switch off radio.

There are also clearly posted restrictions on travelling near the Soviet border; contact the Ministry of the Interior for information.

The **police** are averagely authoritarian, but need not be called to minor accidents: the general emergency services number is 000. There is no general **breakdown** service (certainly not from *Autoliito*, the Finnish motoring club, Fabianinkatu 14, Helsinki 10), so call a local garage. It will cost you an arm and a leg, and spares may take several days to order, but the work should be reasonably well done – the same as any other well-off western European country. **Petrol** is reasonably priced, but gets more expensive as you go north, and the petrol stations get rarer. Regular is about 93 octane, Super about 98/99.

The Finnish language is weird, and related to Hungarian, Mongolian, and possibly Tibetan. Swedish is an official second language, and English is also widely spoken, but the actual Finnish 10-word vocabulary is:

please	*olkaa hivä* (ollka heevay)
thank you	*kiitos* (keeto)
yes	*kyllä* (kulla – almost kurlla)
no	*ei* (ey)
where is?	*missä on?*
room	*hurne* (hoornah)
toilet	*WC* (vay-say)
more	*lisää*
how much?	*kuinka paljon* (koo-inka pally-on)
food	*ruoka* (rooaka)

Food is the usual Scandinavian variety, good and expensive, and beer is the usual **drink**. Ordinary beer (up to 3.6° – about 2.8° alcohol) is freely available from 9 o'clock onwards in restaurants (the minimum drinking age is 18), but anything stronger must come from licenced bars, restaurants, or state liquor stores (*Alkoholiliike*) which keep short hours, close early on Saturdays, and close all day on Sundays and holidays. Spirits may not be sold before noon; Finland really does have a drink problem. Drinking is known as 'the poor man's opera', and there are said to be a thousand words in Finnish to describe drunkenness! Furthermore, a drunk Finn is usually a fighting Finn, so steer clear of rough bars.

Accommodation is averagely expensive, though not as bad as some parts of Scandinavia. The Finncheque system, which allows pre-booking and pre-payment, saves a little money and a fair amount of time, but locks you into a fixed schedule: you have to book the first night's accommodation for each place you want to visit. Farms and private houses are another reasonable choice – comparable with English prices again – or there are 130 youth hostels (contact *Suomen Retkeilymajajärjestö*, Yrjönkatu 38B, 00100 Helsinki 10), 320 camping sites, and 200 'holiday villages' for self-catering accommodation. 'Wild' camping is legal, but Finnish environmental protection laws are the strictest in Scandinavia.

Iceland

Iceland is, undoubtedly, one of the less likely destinations for the motorcycle tourist. Just getting there is difficult: the usual ferry route is from Aberdeen, via Lerwick and Torshaven, and at the time of writing the fare for the $1\frac{1}{2}$ day journey was over £200 per person return, plus about £90 for the bike. Once you are there, the main attraction is the unbelievably bleak landscape, and some really demanding riding on roads which have to be seen to be believed – the road network was extended all around the island only in 1974, and the usual means of private transport outside Reykjavik is a sturdy four-wheel-drive vehicle, often a Land Rover, because anything else falls to pieces after a few months.

Nor is it cheap once you are there. Camping is permitted anywhere, subject to the landowner's permission and rather stringent conservation laws, and some hotels run cheap dormitories rather like youth hostels, in addition to the six youth hostels themselves; otherwise, even rooms in private houses and on farms are expensive. **Petrol** is roughly twice the price of any other European country, and the only grade available is 92 octane. The people are reserved to the point of gloom; perhaps it is the realization that 25% of children are born to unmarried parents, so that they are bound to get caught sometime.

In short, it is a love-it-or-loathe it country for well-off masochists, or those to whom isolation, even desolation, is so important that they will pay handsomely for it. The food is unusually limited, and a sales tax approaching 25% does nothing to make the place more attractive. It is, however, one of the last wildernesses, and if you want to say that you have been somewhere really unusual, Iceland is one of the better bets in Europe.

Climate Contrary to the name, it is not covered in ice, but nor is it warm: the only month where the average temperature range is in the 50–60°F average range is July, with maximum temperatures typically below 40°F from October to April. The driest month is May, the wettest (or snowiest!) is January, and the increase or decrease in rainfall per month follows a fairly smooth curve.

Papers To get in, you will need a passport (but no visa), the bike registration book or log book, your national driving licence, and a Green Card. Once you are in, you must wear a **crash helmet** and ride with the headlight on. **Speed limits** are 45 kph (28 mph) in built-up areas, 70 kph (44 mph) elsewhere. If you plan on going out along some of the more remote roads, you would do well to travel with a friend: with only 2.3 million Icelanders spread across nearly 40,000 square miles, you can get a long way from help and other people. The general rule of the road is the same as for other Scandinavian countries, allowing for the fact that there is only one large town (the population of Reykjavik is about 85,000, or 37% of the population) and the state of the roads elsewhere.

Currency is the Icelandic Krona, divided into 100 aura; it was revalued in 1981, so that 100 old kronur = 1 new krona, which can lead to some confusion when you ask older people about prices. Allow 8 kr to the £, 5 kr to the $ US. The coins are 5, 10, and 50 aura, and 1 and 5 kr, with notes for 10, 50, 100, and 500 kr. **Plastic money** is little use. **Bank** hours are 9.15 am to 4 pm, with some banks offering an exchange service from 10 am to noon on Saturdays, and shops are mostly open from 9 am to 6 pm from Monday to Thursday, with late shopping (10 pm) on Fridays. The few shops that do open on Saturdays close at midday.

Because of the extremely limited appeal of Iceland, there is little point in giving details, vocabulary, etc. The **food** as already mentioned, is limited, and the attitude to **booze** can be summed up by pointing out that the beer is non-alcoholic, a relic of partly-abolished prohibition. The blood alcohol level is 50 mg/100 ml, but that is academic; if they can't have you for drunken driving, they will try to pin dangerous driving on you. The **customs** limits are 200 cigarettes or 200 grammes of other tobacco products; one bottle (750 ml) of spirits; one litre of wine; and 12 bottles of beer. There is even a limit on the strength of the spirit permitted, namely 47°. Carry prescriptions for medicines, or they may not let them in. You may not import or export more than 500 kr in Icelandic notes, and that must be in denominations of 50 kr and below.

The Communist Bloc

Introduction

In the Great Hereafter, three generals are watching a military parade in Red Square. They are Alexander the Great, Caesar, and Napoleon. First, the MiG fighters scream overhead. Alexander the Great turns to the other two, and says, 'With weapons like those, I would never have lacked for worlds to conquer!' Caesar shakes his head in amazement, but Napoleon does not even look up. He is reading *Pravda*, the official Russian newpaper. Next, as the endless columns of soldiers and tanks and missiles roll past, Caesar says, 'With this sort of manpower, I could have controlled the greatest Empire in the world!' Alexander the Great agrees with him, but Napoleon stays buried in *Pravda*. 'What's up with you?' say the other two. 'Don't you admire this tremendous display?' Napoleon looks up. 'Oh, sure,' he says, 'but this newpaper is pretty amazing, too. If I had had this, no one would ever have heard of Waterloo!'

This kind of bitter joke is common in Eastern Europe; they can be told indefinitely. A great Czech athlete, denied the chance to compete in the Olympics, goes to East Germany and throws the hammer to a new world record distance – nearly twice as far as the old record. When he is interviewed afterwards, he says, 'Oh, it was nothing. Give me a sickle and I'll throw the fucking thing even further!'

Bulgaria, Czechoslovakia, East Germany, Hungary, Poland, and Romania are all occupied countries: if their governments step too far out of line, the Russian armies are

ready to step in and 'restore order for the people'. The kind of control that they exercise is such that anyone trying to take this book into a communist country is likely to have it confiscated – not just for telling anti-Russian jokes, but for saying that the Russians 'occupy' anywhere: everyone knows that they are peace-loving ... er ... soldiers, defending their comrades from the filthy capitalists. That's why they built the Berlin Wall to keep the capitalists from escaping to East Germany. . . .

As long as you bear in mind that the dead hand of communism and military occupation tries to stifle the list of countries at the beginning of the last paragraph; that communist agriculture and industry are so inefficient, and so geared to the war machine, that standards of living are unbelievably low; that bureaucracy is a way of life; and that breaking the rules can land you and anyone you are associating with in serious trouble, you can enjoy a visit to Iron Curtain countries. If this sounds a bit like, 'Apart from that, Mrs. Lincoln, how did you enjoy the play?', there is a good reason for that. But I would be the last to knock the people in those occupied countries. Among my close friends, I number or have numbered Czechs, Hungarians, and Poles, and the few Bulgarians I have met have been charming. The Bulgarian Tourist Office in London was one of the most helpful, knowledgeable, and friendly of all the ones I visited; I would hate to say anything against their country. But their governments – well, the two jokes given above are both current in Eastern Europe, so the man in the street feels the same way I do.

Of course, there are two countries in the group which I have not mentioned yet. One is Russia itself, where motorcycle touring is forbidden to Western visitors (though they will admit cars, provided they keep to an agreed itinerary and report to Intourist good and often), and the other is Albania, where the chances of any sort of independent travel are negligible. But the six countries in the list are independently-minded, have their own traditions, their own scenery, their own great cities, their own food and drink, and their own attractions. Everyone I know who has been to Eastern Europe agrees that it is fascinating, that prices are agreeably low (especially if you stay out of the places set aside for Western tourists, and sleep and eat in the same places that visitors from other communist countries do), and

that it is an experience they would not want to have missed.
The bureaucracy is appalling, it is true, but there are far
fewer restrictions than you might imagine: as long as you are
careful about what you photograph, and do not break the
law, you can do pretty much as you please. This even
includes travelling: there are no restrictions on the roads you
may use, nor do you have to describe your route in detail
beforehand (though motorists in Russia do). One of the few
benefits of the truly repressive police state is that petty crime
is negligible, and because the people get so few opportunities
to mix with other Europeans, you will find that they are often
tremendously friendly and eager to talk to you. If you ride a
big Japanese or Italian motorcycle, you will be a demi-god;
Iron Curtain motorcyclists are keen, but mostly confined to
CZs, Jawas, and MZs, though they do see the occasional
BMW.

Your bike will need to be in good condition, however,
because the chances of getting spares are negligible. In
theory, they can be ordered across the border, but in
practice, the bureaucracy would probably hold them up for a
month, so it is quicker and probably cheaper to put the bike
on a train and get back to the Decadent West. It should also
run on low-octane petrol, which is often all that will be
available (and it may be as low as 80 octane), have a large
petrol tank (gas stations can be few and far between), and be
strongly built, with good suspension: because private vehicles
are a capitalist luxury, road maintenance is negligible in many
places, and a sports bike will shake you or itself to bits.

In all six of the countries which you can visit, tourism is
tolerated rather than encouraged. To begin with, you will
need a visa for each country, which will cost money and take
anything from a day or two to a couple of weeks or more, so
you need to plan well in advance. Sometimes, there are two
(or more) different kinds of visa, such as a tourist visa and a
transit visa, which may only be good for a maximum of three
days, or even less. When you are ordering your visas, find
out which sort you want. For the rest of the paperwork, you
will need the registration document or log book, a letter from
the owner if applicable (which, in Czechoslovakia, *must* be
countersigned and stamped by your national automobile
club), a driver's licence, and insurance. National licences are
OK in most places, and (as far as I could discover) you can
ride at whatever age your national licence permits (17 for

Britons). In Hungary, though, you must be 18 and must have an IDP, and Poland asks for an IDP if uou want to stay more than a month. You need a Green Card for Bulgaria, Poland, and Romania, but not in Czechoslovakia, East Germany, or Hungary if your bike is European-registered. You can buy insurance at the border, too, but it is expensive. Helmets are compulsory in all countries, and in Czechoslovakia, you must wear eye protection (goggles or visor) when riding outside built-up areas. First-aid kits are compulsory only in Poland, and spare bulbs (as far as I could discover) are not compulsory anywhere, but since riding with defective lamps is an offence, and you can't get spares, you would be well advised to carry them.

'As far as I could discover' is something which I will not say again, but which is particularly relevant in Eastern Europe. Obviously, I am not going to take legal responsibility for anything I say in this book, but most of the time, I am pretty confident that what I have said is true. In the communist bloc, however, the majority of the tourist offices were absolutely hopeless, and no one was prepared to put anything in writing. As a result, the information in this last section is a little less reliable than the rest – but it should still provide a practical working guide, and I do not think that there are any major holes.

Customs regulations are surprisingly varied but currency control is another matter. With the exception of Hungary, where the limit is 400 forints, the import and export of national currencies is forbidden in all the communist countries; if you want to import or export travellers' cheques or foreign currencies, it is a good idea to declare large sums on entry, so that you can get them out again. All communist countries have 'soft' currencies, where the exchange rate is government controlled and has nothing to do with free market forces. As a result, there may be three effective rates of exchange: the base rate, the tourist rate (better than the base rate), to which you will be entitled, and the black market rate, which may be twice as good again. If they catch you, though, the least you can expect is to lose all the money you were changing, and probably some more besides, as well as being thrown out of the country.

Nevertheless, the temptation to change on the black market is so great, and the communist governments' need of hard currencies so desperate, that several impose a compulsory minimum exchange *per day*, at the official rate. Never change more than you have to, because changing it back will be very difficult (or even impossible), and you will in any case need both to prove that you have exchanged and spent the compulsory minimum amount, and that the money was legally exchanged – so keep all exchange slips.

There are also several other currency tricks that you may encounter. Some countries issue petrol coupons, but read the small print: unless they are completely used up, they may be non-refundable, which makes 'cheap' petrol very dear. A similar swindle may be worked on pre-paid accommodation, even for camping. If you need to reconvert currency, you may find that it will not be done immediately, but that a cheque will be sent to you – perhaps months later. Credit cards, incidentally, are only useful in the most expensive shops and restaurants, and in the special 'hard currency' shops which exist to take money off tourists. Tipping is a vexed question: officially a relic of the past, some people really will take it as an insult, but others will be very grateful – but **don't** tip in hard currency, welcome though it may be, because it is very, very illegal.

On the other hand, the 'black market' in some Western goods is (comparatively) tolerated, so things like genuine Levi's, training shoes, and electronic gadgets like pocket calculators or watches, can be sold or (better still) swapped for all kinds of things. Even plastic carrier bags are prized, especially if they have a well-known brand name on them, and advertising-slogan garments (T-shirts, sweatshirts, windcheaters, etc) were *the* in thing at the time of writing. Be careful, though – this is all technically illegal.

Actually riding inside Iron Curtain countries is surprisingly similar from country to country, because of the low traffic densities; only in the very centre of the biggest cities is there any form of parking control, and then you are unlikely to have difficulty in finding a marked bay. There are just two things to remember. The first is that lack of traffic makes everyone – you and the other guy – less alert and careful. The other is that the Police really will have you if you break the law. You may be lucky, and get away with a caution, but nine times out of ten it is an on-the-spot fine, payable then and there. The fines are fortunately not too high, but they are still worth avoiding. Central and Eastern Europeans do not break the law – they have learned what happens to them if they do. On this topic, if you are involved in an accident, the 'victim' (I use inverted commas because he may or may not be genuine) may well offer an out-of-court settlement for cash, in used notes, in return for not calling the police – which could land you in jail, if you really were to blame, or even if you cannot actually prove your innocence. I do not personally know anyone who has been caught on this one – it may be just a travellers' tale – but I pass it on for what it is worth. Of course, the general rule is that the police must *always* be called – if they don't get there before you call them! Oh, yes – and **never** drink and drive, at all.

All the rest of the information about the Iron Curtain countries belongs in the country-by-country guides, but this introduction should be taken as applying to all of them unless specifically stated otherwise.

Albania

Albania is, according to the few who have been there, a beautiful country. The countryside is apparently magnificent: there are mountains, there are lakes, and the coast is said to be particularly attractive. Many of the picturesque old towns and cities are completely unspoiled; new developments are carried out at a decent distance from old town centres. Prices are low, and crime is almost unheard of.

Despite its innumerable natural advantages, Albania has one major man-made disadvantage: the government. Their form of communism can only decently be described as rabid. They used to have links with Stalin's Russia, but after Stalin died the post-Stalinist regime was too revisionist and decadent for their tastes. Next, they fell in with Mao's China; then Mao died, and China wasn't left-wing enough any more. They now have no real friends or allies; as far as I know, they do not even speak to the GLC.

Not surprisingly, they restrict admission. If you hold a US passport, you will not be allowed in. If you are a journalist, you will not be allowed in. If you have a beard, you may not be allowed in unless you let them trim it or shave it at the border. Men with long hair will also be refused admission, unless they agree to the attentions of an Albanian barber.

If you are short-haired, clean-shaven, non-American non-journalist, they may let you in, provided you travel in a group supervised by an Albanian courier. You will not be allowed outside the limits of the city you stay in, except on an organized tour with all the other members of the group. Because everyone (with the exception of a very few hardy business visitors) travels on a group visa, everyone in the group has to travel together.

In theory, it might be possible to organize a motorcycling group. In practice, it is not. As far as I could discover, there is only one travel agent in the English-speaking world that deals with the People's Socialist Republic of Albania, and they were sure that a motorcycling group would not be feasible: even they admitted that the Albanians liked everyone to stay inside the mini-bus, so that they knew where they were: motorcyclists were simply too hard to trace.

Most things which are not compulsory are banned. Given the present Albanian regime, I cannot imagine that any sane, freedom-loving person would want to go there, except possibly out of curiosity. I for one am not that curious. If, however, there are any signs of relaxation (and there are already some – short beards *may* be permitted), and you want to try organizing a motorcycling group, speak to: Regent Holidays, 13 Small Street, Bristol (0272) 211711.

Bulgaria

With the exception of the Black Sea resorts, Bulgaria is little known to most people; but anyone who knows anything of Bulgarian history will know both why this is, and why it should be better known. The Thracians of Greek antiquity left many traces, and after the Bulgarian state was created in 681 AD the next major influence was the Orthodox Church; the country was converted in 865, and Rila monastery dates back to the 10th century. The Ottoman empire occupied Bulgaria from about 1400, and the Turks were not thrown out until the Russians intervened in 1877, despite a massive but unsuccessful uprising in 1876; even then Bulgaria remained under Turkish suzerainty until 1908. In this century, the fascist movement was strong in Bulgaria, and the country fought on the side of Germany in both World Wars. Since 1944, when the Russians invaded, it has been a Communist satellite state.

This troubled and often oppressed history has, however, led to both an enormous number of influences on Bulgaria, and a backwardness from which the country has only recently begun to emerge. Folk ways were preserved in Bulgaria for far longer than in other countries, and now they stand side by side with the achievements of the modern country. It is all very well to dismiss Bulgaria as a Soviet puppet, but the Bulgarians are still people; they like to enjoy themselves; and it is not difficult to make Bulgarian friends. If you do visit Bulgaria, you will find all the usual controls and regulations of a Communist country, but you will also find countryside that ranges literally from the mountains to the sea (and sometimes very quickly!), all kinds of reminders of the distant and not-so-distant past, good food and wine, and remarkably few hassles, because Bulgaria has taken to tourism in a big way. The **best time** to go is generally agreed to be the late spring or early autumn for inland Bulgaria, where the summer (except in the mountains) can be too hot for some, whilst the mountains and the Black Sea are also delightful in the summer. May is particularly attractive, because of the spring flowers, and if you want something off-beat, try the Black Sea in winter, when it is all but deserted and very tranquil. The coastal winters are mild, but you may have some difficulty on the ride there!

Papers If you have pre-paid your accommodation (including camping vouchers, which are incidentally non-refundable), you do not need a visa for up to two months. Otherwise, you will need to allow about 7 days and £10 (at the time of writing) for a regular visa, or get a 30-hour transit visa for £7, issued on the spot at an embassy – **not** at the border. Your national driving licence is sufficient, and you will need a Green Card, or to insure at the border. **Helmets** are compulsory.

Customs allowances are a lean 200 cigarettes or 25 cigars or 250 gm tobacco, plus 1 litre of wine and $\frac{1}{4}$ litre of eau-de-cologne, plus 100 leva worth (say £70, or $100) of 'other goods', including food. You are required to declare all that you are carrying, including duty free allowances, on entry; you are also required to declare any oil you are carrying (!) and you may be charged duty on it. Tough on two-stroke owners! At the time of writing, there was no compulsory minimum daily exchange, but re-exchange was complex: only 25 leva could be re-exchanged easily, and any more had to be deposited with customs, who would give you a slip to send to the National Bank, who would send the money to the bank of your choice.

Currency The exchange rate is also extremely complicated, as anyone changing more than a certain amount, or who had pre-paid services, could get a 50% better rate. Also, uncharacteristically, tipping someone in hard currency is legal, but black marketeering is as illegal as anywhere else. There are also hard currency shops, which do not accept leva at all, but will take **credit cards** as well as hard currency. The leva, incidentally, is divided into 100 *stotinka*! For a rough guide, allow 1.3 leva/£, 1 leva/$ US.

Petrol is best bought with (non-refundable) petrol coupons, which can be bought abroad, at the border, or even at *Shipka* (Motorists' Tourist Office) branches in major towns. These give a 25% discount, bringing prices down to around the European average – gas is very expensive otherwise, but at least you are allowed to buy it with leva if you don't mind paying the price. The grades are usually 78 and 86 octane, though 96 octane super can be found, but only if you look for it.

Bank hours are variable, but biased towards the morning: typically 8 am to noon Monday to Friday, 8 am to 11 am Saturday. Shop hours are also variable, with food shops opening as early as 7 am and most others being open by 9 am, with closing hours some twelve hours later – minus a long siesta, typically from 1 pm to 4 pm or so. Tipping is a national custom, with 12% often being added into the bill. If this is done, round up a bit if the service has been good, but nothing more is expected ordinarily. If it is not done, give 10–15%.

Roads are very varied, but the standard **speed limits** (which may be varied by sign) are 80 kph (50 mph) on the open road and 60 kph (37 mph) in town. The very thin traffic means that speeders are easily seen, but then, so are police. Vehicles on the right have **right of way**, unless you are on a 'priority road', marked by the international symbol *or used by public transport*. All vehicles with sirens and/or flashing lights (police, fire, etc) automatically have right of way: you must pull over *and stop*. Road signs are standard, with Cyrillic and Roman alphabets used in parallel. **Parking** in the city is in marked bays (which may be on the pavement), or higgledy-piggledy in the country; the only restrictions, other than those posted, are those dictated by common sense. Both 'obstruction' and 'obscuring visibility' will, however, be interpreted widely. The **police** can be officious, but they are not vicious: the number for calling them is 877 777 or 870 441 in Sofia, or look in the phone booth elsewhere. In case of **breakdown**,the 'Yellow Angels' of the Union of Bulgarian Motorists (UBM, 6 Sveta Sofia Street, Sofia) will provide a free assistance service, charging only for parts used, or arrange to transport you to the nearest garage if they cannot fix it on the spot. This service is free for all. Otherwise, expect cheap (but variable quality) labour, and expensive parts.

Because Bulgarian is written with the Cyrillic alphabet (like Russian), an English rendition is more use.

The ten-word vocabulary is:

please	*molya*
thank you	*blagodarya*
yes	*da*
no	*ne*

where is?	*kuhde e?*
room	*staya*
toilet	*klozet*
more	*oshte*
how much?	*kolko struva?*
food	*hrana*

Bulgarian **food** is Balkan in style, similar to that of Yugoslavia, or northern Greece; hearty, spicy, and based mostly on lamb. Watch out for heavy use of salt, though, and drink plenty of water with the meal. Tap water is said to be safe 'almost' everywhere; I'll stick to mineral water, or wine – some superb reds, and very drinkable whites. The main spirits are *mastica*, a bit like Greek *ouzo*, and *slivova*, a plum brandy which varies from the delightful to the almost undrinkable – pure paintstripper.

Accommodation is weighted towards the pre-paid, pre-packaged tour, but there is plenty for the independent traveller too. A few hotels are expensive tourist traps, but most are very good value, and the smaller, cheaper ones can be very cheap indeed; there is no official distinction between small hotels and *pensions*, just ever-decreasing prices. If you want to stay in one place, you can hire holiday villas on the Black Coast at very low rates – often well under 5 leva per person. Alternatively, bed-and-breakfast deals are nearly as common in parts of Bulgaria as in England, and admirably cheap. Camping sites are well organized and supplied with excellent facilities, and are consequently relatively expensive – though still very cheap in absolute terms. Camping away from sites is (predictably) illegal.

Czechoslovakia

Few people have any very clear image of Czechoslovakia, which is perhaps not surprising, because it has only existed as an independent country from 1918, when it was created out of the ruins of the Austro-Hungarian Empire, to 1938 when it was invaded by Hitler – who, of course, was replaced by the Russians.

The historical importance of Bohemia, however, means that the country is packed with towns and villages like something out of a Victorian story book – though Slovakia is more like a movie set for a horror film – and the scenery, especially among the Tatra mountains, is superb. Prague is one of the great cities of Europe, and was once the capital of the Holy Roman Empire; Czech food is designed for those who like both quality and quantity; Czech beer gave the world a taste for *pilsener*, from Plzn; and the country is one of the great wildlife reserves (and hunting grounds) of Europe.

Motorcyclists are welcome; the ordinary 'cooking' Jawas and CZs are pretty dire, but the competition models are very successful, and many Czechs follow motorcycle sport enthusiastically. Big bikes, especially Japanese big bikes, will attract attention everywhere. Unfortunately, the Czechs are no longer quite as open as they were before 1968, but they are still very friendly people.

Climate Despite the country being entirely landlocked, the climate is surprisingly mild, but May–September represents the real season; spring and autumn may not be too warm, but they will be very beautiful, and June, July, and August will be delightful. In the high Tatras, on the other hand, June–August are the only practical time unless you actually like riding in snow.

Papers Everyone except citizens of other communist countries needs a visa, which *must* be obtained beforehand – you cannot get them at the border. Transit visas are only issued if you already have a visa for your destination country, *and* if the normal route to that country lies through Czechoslovakia: they only allow you to pass through, non-stop except for petrol, etc. 'Real' visas can take anything up to two weeks. As with Bulgaria, there is no need to get a visa if you are on a pre-paid package tour, but that is not going to affect motorcyclists.

Europeans need only their national licences (Americans and some others need an IDP); the minimum riding age is that of the country issuing the licence. Although the Green Card is not in theory compulsory, it may be difficult to persuade border officials of this. The minimum insurance cover is unlimited, except in respect of damage to jewellery, works of art, and similar objects owned by an individual (!). The need to have a letter of authorisation stamped by your local motoring club, if you are not riding your own bike, has already been mentioned, as has the need for **helmets** *and eye protection*. Daylight riding lights are not compulsory.

Customs on the way in holds no great surprises, apart from the astonishingly low limit of 3 rolls of film per person (in practice, a few more do not matter). You are allowed 250 cigarettes or 'a corresponding quantity of other tobacco products', 2 litres of wine, 1 litre spirits, $\frac{1}{2}$ litre eau-de-cologne, 1000 shotgun cartridges and 50 rifle cartridges (!), 3 kilos of foodstuffs, and gifts up to 600 crowns (about £25, or $35). On the way out, you may be charged duty on any gifts worth over 300 crowns total, and some kinds of food, clothing, and footwear are prohibited exports! Goods bought at Tuzex hard-currency shops are exempt from duty, and *only* those antiques bought from Tuzex shops will be allowed out – so keep your receipts.

Currency There are about 10–20 koruna (crowns, abbreviated Kcs) to the £ sterling, 8–15 to the $ US; the reason for the range of conversion values is that the tourist rate is about 75% better than the base rate. In order to get the best rate, buy currency vouchers from Cedok (the Czech tourist office) before you go. If you do this, it also exempts you from the minimum exchange requirement, which was £7 a day at the time of writing. Petrol coupons are another way to get a good deal, with about a 25% saving, but there are a couple of drawbacks. The first is that they are good for *super* 96 octane only, which may not always be available (*normal* is 80, *special* is 90, and these may be all that you can get away from tourist centres), and the second is that they are sold only in *non-refundable* 100-litre (over 22-gallon) blocks. That is about 900–1200 miles on my bike!

Bank hours are 8 am to 2 pm, Monday to Friday, and shopping hours are 9 am to 6 pm, Monday to Friday, with late shopping (to 8 pm) on Thursday in some places, and a half-day on Saturday in all but the biggest shops. Some shops close for lunch, at any time between noon and 2 pm. Only the big hotels, and hard-currency stores, accept credit cards. Tipping is not customary, but a tip of 5–10 Kcs for particularly good service will be well received.

The main **roads** in Czechoslovakia are very good, but the lesser ones vary from fair to bad. The motorway network is limited, but toll free, and **speed limits** are hellishly confusing, varying both with the type of vehicle and the time of day. Motorcyclists come off badly, with what amounts to a blanket limit of 80 kph (50 mph) on motorways, other roads, and in town between eleven at night and five in the morning (!); the daytime limit in town is 60 kph (37 mph), and the limit across railway crossings is 50 kph (31 mph) for everyone. The limits for cars are the same, except on motorways, where they are allowed to go at 110 kph (68 mph), or in towns at night, where they are allowed 90 kph (56 mph). Until a few years ago, there were no limits at all, except in towns during the day, but 'progress' comes to us all.

Right of way, **overtaking**, etc are matter of common sense; priority-to-the-right is the rule, unless clearly signposted otherwise. Czechs do not use the horn much, and the police will not like it if you do. Except in central Prague, where **parking** is only in marked bays, there is normally ample roadside parking. Do not park on the pavement, and use your discretion when it comes to parking near junctions, bus stops, railway crossings, etc. Road signs are international, and the Roman alphabet is used. The **police** are averagely merciless, but very formal and correct – not overbearing. The number for calling them varies, so look in the phone booth. In Prague, the accident number is 242424, and the ambulance number is 155.

The *Central Automotoclub* (Prague 1, Opletalova 21) will assist at **breakdowns**; call 224 906 in Prague, or look in the phone book. From April to September, 10 am to 6 pm on weekdays and noon to 8 pm on weekends, they operate a breakdown service on main roads in yellow Skodas – the 'Yellow angels'. If this rather limited service is not enough, call a local garage; most Czech mechanics are excellent.

The ten-word vocabulary is:

please	*prosím* (proseem)
thank you	*děkuji* (dyekuyi)
yes	*ano*
no	*ne*
where is?	*kde je?* (ke ye?)
room	*pokoj* (pokoy)
toilet	*toaleta*
more	*víc* (veets)
how much?	*kolik to stojí?* (kolik to stoyee?)
food	*potraviny*

Czech **food** has already been mentioned; it is influenced by the solid German tradition, the rather Eastern cuisine of Slovakia, and of course Hungary, so it tends to be both varied and filling. There is a great tradition of eating game – Czechoslovakia has practised game conservation, along with hunting, for centuries – and there is a fine tradition of heavy soups, usually with dumplings made of dough, bread, or potatoes. Even the tourist restaurants are not usually expensive, but others are astonishingly good value. Choice of **drink** varies: Bohemians drink beer, Slovaks drink wine, and *slivovice* is the ubiquitous plum brandy; the water is always drinkable, too.

Accommodation *Interhotels*, a subsidiary of Cedok, owns most of the hotels; if you can, it is easiest to pre-book before you leave, or you may have difficulty in finding a room, especially in Prague. Alternatively, use the local Cedok offices inside Czechoslovakia, or just keep your eyes open. All but the most expensive hotels are good value, and bed-and-breakfast is even more so – maybe as little as one third of UK prices, but bank on half. Camping is legal only at authorized sites, and camping in a wood (where fires are forbidden) can bring heavy fines. There are no youth hostels as such, but during the summer it may be possible for members of youth organizations to find cheap, basic accommodation: check through Cedok for the area you are going to.

East Germany

It is all very well to blame Adolf Hitler for what happened in
Germany, including partition; but it is now more than a third
of a century since he died, and nations must surely be
allowed to absolve their mistakes. The boundary between the
Federal Republic of Germany and the German Democratic
Republic (to give West and East Germany their official titles)
divides families, and shows achingly clearly the differences
between the two political philosophies. Imagine a road, well
surfaced, with houses either side ... which suddenly is
divided by a barbed wire fence, overlooked by machine gun
posts, and which on the other side of the fence is cracked
and weed-grown, with the tumbledown houses on either side
of it looking like ghosts of those that they mirror. That is
Germany.

Because of the contrast with West Germany, the 'time
capsule' effect of East Germany is all the more marked.
Clothes are shabby and old fashioned, cars are few and
mostly crude, the MZ is a work of genius as 1950s bikes go
but does not cut much ice in the 1980s, shop windows have
little to show; it reminds me of my early childhood in the
1950s, when there was still bomb damage everywhere and
we were recovering from the twin disasters of the Second
World War and a socialist government. And East Germany is
one of the more prosperous Iron Curtain states: another joke
is irresistible. The Russians and the Chinese are negotiating,
and the Chinese have the Russians over a barrel. Their
demands become more and more outrageous, and the
Russians keep giving in. The Chinese say, 'And we insist that
you provide a pair of shoes for all the people in our beloved
country!' The Russians agree. The Chinese wonder what to
ask for next. 'You must also provide a bicycle for all the
heads of families in our beloved country!' To their
amazement, the Russians agree. Then they say, 'And our
final demand is, a kilo of rice for every family in our beloved
country!' The Russians do not even confer among
themselves. 'No!' they say. 'Zis cannot be done!' The Chinese
are amazed. 'But what is rice, next to all these shoes and

bicycles?' 'Comrade,' says the Russian negotiator, 'do you not realize? You cannot grow rice in Germany!'

Actually, this 'time capsule' effect is fascinating, and because East Germany is comparatively prosperous, it may be the best Iron Curtain country to visit first – although as the favoured route for defectors, the police are unusually suspicious.

Papers You can get two types of visa: visitors' and transit. A transit visa is cheaper than a visitors' visa, but allows only a short stay in pre-arranged places. Regular visas can be bought before you leave, or at the border (in hard currency) if you are prepared to wait – and wait – and wait. Transit visas are available only at the border, for hard currency. If you do not have a Green Card, your British or other European insurance will cover you for unlimited personal injury and property damage insurance, or you can buy insurance at the border. Your booze and tobacco **customs** allowances are one litre of wine and one of spirits, or two of wine, plus 200 cigarettes or 250 gm of tobacco or tobacco products. You may also import gifts worth up to 100 marks for a stay of less than 5 days, 500 marks for longer stays. There is a minimum exchange requirement, which is apparently different for Berlin, of M 13 per day at the time of writing. When you come to leave, you will have to pay duty on gifts worth over M 100.

Accommodation must be booked in advance, and may be pre-paid (but you can change your mind once you are inside), and there are two ways of buying **petrol**: either go to a hard-currency gas station (*intertank* – their *Superblau* is the highest-octane petrol in East Germany), or buy non-refundable petrol vouchers at the border or before you go (they cannot be bought inside the country), and use *Minol* stations which will give you a 35% discount on regular prices. *Minol* grades are 79, 88, and 94 octane, so you may prefer *Superblau*. Trying to buy petrol in the ordinary way, with ordinary currency, is theoretically possible, but such hard work that I have never met anyone who has done it.

Currency is the Mark, at about 4/£, 3/$ US, and **bank hours** are basically 8 am to 11.30 am and 2.30 to 5 pm, Monday to Friday, but with wide local variations. Shopping hours outside Berlin are roughly 9 am to 6 pm, Monday to Friday, and 10 am to 7 pm in Berlin; Saturday opening is optional, and normally only larger shops take up the option.

Speed limits are 100 kph (62 mph) on the *autobahns*, which look as if they have not been touched since Hitler built them, 90 kph (56 mph) on other open roads, and 50 kph (31 mph) in town. *All* roads are subject to a toll, based on total distance travelled; this is true for motor cars, but I was unable to check if it was also true for bikes. The tolls are not crippling, but steep enough – just another way of screwing money out of the West. A few transit routes are exempt.

The vocabulary is as for the rest of Germany, and the general comments on food also apply, except that the Eastern influence can make for slightly spicier cooking, and prices can be delightfully low; one friend, who had no accommodation costs because he was staying with relatives of his girlfriend's, took several people out to dinner every night on his M13 compulsory exchange! The beer is excellent – but don't drink and drive – and you can live very well indeed if you go to the non-touristy places.

Accommodation, as already mentioned, is always pre-booked and usually pre-paid; but you get a voucher in return for your pre-payment which can (as far as I understand it) be used in another hotel, if you change your mind. Camping sites must also be booked and paid in advance, but it sounded (from the rather garbled explanation I got in London) as if you could change your mind there too – or just not use the camping vouchers, and stop at a hotel or *gasthof*. 'Wild' camping is, of course, illegal.

Hungary

When I was a student, one of my closest friends was a
Hungarian. I dropped into see him one day, and found him
mournfully drinking *szilva*, Hungarian plum brandy. 'What's
the matter?' I asked. He replied, 'This is my last bottle of
szilva.' By the end of the evening, we had finished the bottle;
we were smashing the glasses in the fireplace as we drained
them.

To me, this sums up a great deal about Hungarians;
their great style, their weakness for the throwaway line, and
the manic-depressive streak which means that every pleasure
conceals a twist of anguish, every misery a flash of humour.
Another view of Hungarians is that they are the only people
who can walk into a revolving door behind you, and come
out in front: 'resourceful' is too mild a word. Then again, all
the Hungarians I have known well have lived in exile. Many
left after the War, and another 200,000 or so left after the
1956 Hungarian Uprising against the Russian occupation.
The modern Hungary has managed to create close ties with
Western Europe, which offsets the enforced linkage with the
Soviet Union; an old Hungarian joke says that the chief
cause of death among Russians living in Hungary is ...
Hungarians.

There is a lot to see in Hungary, too, whether your
tastes run to mediaeval castles and villages or to beach
resorts. Although Hungary is totally landlocked, it has the
huge Lake Balaton, the biggest lake in Central Europe, about
50 miles long, for swimming and water-sports of all kinds.
And Hungarian food, influenced by almost all the major
culinary traditions of Europe, is superb.

Climate The best time to go is generally agreed to be
autumn or spring; in May and September you can expect
reasonable temperatures (up to 75° or so, though 68–70°
would be more usual) and fairly dry conditions, because the
wettest months are rather surprisingly July and August –
though rainfall is never high. The main reason for avoiding
high summer is not, however, the temperatures (especially if
you are near Lake Balaton) but the crowds. Hungary is an

extremely popular resort with the other Communist countries. Winters – December to February – are cold and snowy.

Papers In order to get in, you will need a visa. You can get these at the border, but it may take some hours (especially in the summer, when traffic is heavy), so it is best to get it beforehand. It is not expensive and is usually issued quickly (inside 24 hours) by any Hungarian consular office.

For the bike, you need the usual things: log book or registration document, licence, insurance, but there are some catches. For a start, an IDP is compulsory: your national licence is not enough. Second, you need to be 18. Third, Hungarian minimum compulsory insurance does not apply if a foreign-registered vehicle damages or injures non-Hungarian property or people. This does not mean that you are not liable: merely that you are not insured. For this reason, a Green Card is essential.

The usual way to get to Hungary is through Germany and Austria; because of the old Austro-Hungarian Empire, the Vienna-Budapest route is one of the easier ones. The quickest possible time for the thousand miles or so between the French coast and Budapest might be two days, though three (to allow for border delays, and still averaging over 300 miles a day) is more realistic, and I would prefer to take four.

On arrival, **customs** will allow 1 litre of spirits and 2 litres of wine; 250 cigarettes or 50 cigars or 250 gm tobacco; a reasonable amount of goods intended for personal use; and (on the first visit in any calendar year), gifts up to a maximum of 5000 Forints (say £60/$85). On *leaving*, there is a rather curious restriction of food: you can only take 3 days' supply, with a maximum of 1 kg of meat, of which no more than 500 gm may be of one type! Import and export limits on Forints are 400 Ft, and it is a good idea to declare hard currency imports if you want to take any money out again at the end of your trip, even though this is not theoretically a problem.

Once inside the country, your only obligation is to wear a **helmet**; daylight riding lights, *etc*, are not compulsory. The **roads** are pretty fair, especially the major ones, though some country roads are real cart-tracks, and **petrol** stations are only a problem if you go well off the beaten track. At the major stations, you should always be able to get *super* (93 octane) and *extra-super* (98 octane), but in the country you may find that *normal* (86 octane) is all that is available, with *super* as often available as not.

Speed limits are a trifle complicated: for some insane reason, motorcycles are subject to the same limits as cars pulling trailers, and coaches: 80 kph (50 mph) on motorways (defined as having four lanes), 70 kph (43 mph) on other roads, 50 kph (31 mph) in towns. The comparable limits for cars are 120 kph/100 kph/60 kph (75 mph/62 mph/37 mph). This is bloody irritating and very dangerous. **Driving standards** in general are fair-to-indifferent, with rather more traffic than is normal in Eastern Europe, and more than averagely enthusiastic traffic cops. The usual **priority**-to-the-right rules apply, and it is worth noting that pedestrians have right of way between street-car stops and the pavement, so although it is not illegal to pass a tram on the inside, you had better watch out. **Parking** is in marked bays, or use a parking meter (the Hungarians really don't seem to like motorcyclists much!). Parking on the pavement, unless there is a marked bay, is illegal. Of course, outside the large towns, there is unlikely to be a problem. Road signs are mostly international, but watch out for KIVEVE CELFORGALOM (All Vehicles Prohibited). Sound your horn before overtaking, except in town, where what is compulsory out of town suddenly becomes illegal.

The **police**, who are firm but not unfair, are on 09. They must be called if there is injury or material damage, and especially if the bike is damaged – fresh damage, and no police report, will result in your not being allowed out of the country until everything has been sorted out to their satisfaction. For the same reason, it is worth having a note made by Customs as you enter the country, detailing any damage to the bike. A Polaroid picture may be useful, too. If you are involved in an accident which may result in an insurance claim, you must notify *Allami Biztosito*, Hamzsasbegi ut 60, Budapest XI (tel. 669 755) or any other Biztosito office – a sort of insurance clearing house – within 24 hours. For **breakdowns**, the *Magyar Auto Klub* (1024 Budapest II, Romer Floris utca 4–6, tel. 666 404) operates patrols on main roads and can be telephoned to other areas; their services are free to members of affiliated touring clubs, and you pay only for parts. For breakdowns which cannot be fixed on the spot, mechanics in Hungary are skilled and cheap, but underpaid; a tip will speed things wonderfully.

Spares for anything except BMWs (via Austria) can be deadly slow, though MZs and CZs are also in with a chance.

The Hungarian **currency** is the Forint (Ft), divided into 100 filler. For rough estimation, use 75 Ft/£, 50 Ft/$. **Plastic money** is acceptable at the hard currency stores (Intertourist, Konsumtourist, and Utastourist) and expensive hotels, but nowhere else much. **Bank hours** are 9 am to 1 pm, Monday to Friday, and shop hours are enormously variable. Food shops open earliest as a rule, perhaps at 6.30 am or earlier, but others may not open until 10 or 11 am, and closing hours may be similarly staggered from around 2 pm to 7 or 8 pm or later. Saturday is usually a half day, Thursday is 'late night shopping' (most shops stay open until at least 8 pm), and everything is closed on Sunday. In restaurants and hotels, tipping is regarded as quite normal, but the amount expected increases drastically as you go to the more touristy places. In the country, 5% may be plenty; in an expensive hotel in Budapest, they will expect 15%.

Hungarian is a fiendish language, related to Finnish, Lapp, Estonian, and (if you believe the mystical fringe) Tibetan. Russian, German, and English (in that order) are likely next bets, but if you want to try Hungarian:

please	*kerem* (keh-rem)
thank you	*köszönöm* (ku-sur-nurm)
yes	*igen*
no	*nem*
where is?	*hol van?* (hohl von?)
room	*szoba* (soh-bah)
toilet	*WC* (veh-tseh)
more	*jidlo* (yeed-lo)
how much?	*mennyibe kerül?* (menyibe ker-ewl)
food	*etel* (eat-el)

Prices for **food** are low, and quite memorable picnics (with a bottle of Egri Bikaver, or Bull's Blood) are a bargain. **Accommodation** in hotels is very reasonable, or you can look for bed-and-breakfast in private houses at very low rates indeed. A lot of this is, of course, due to the popularity of Hungary with other Eastern Bloc tourists, though if you go to hotels recommended for Western tourists you can find yourself paying almost London prices. It pays to shop around, and use the Hungarian vocabulary above! One warning about drinking – the rule is *zero* blood-alcohol, as in many other Communist countries, and they will throw a very large and heavy book at you if they catch you drinking and riding. Tap water is both non-intoxicating and safe.

Poland

Touring in Poland, in view of the tumultuous recent history of *Solidarnosc*, the independent trade union, may seem rash; but anyone who has lived through a time of civil unrest will tell you that the troubles are hardly ever visible to the man in the street, only to the man in front of the television set. Unless you deliberately hang around the shipyards of Gdansk, you are extremely unlikely ever to be aware that there is anything wrong.

It must be said, though, that Poland is a strange country, largely on account of the Poles. All of my close Polish friends have been exiles – Ekaterina Barbara Irena, where are you now? – and they all have terrible tales to tell. At a Communist rally when I was at university, Laurence stood up and said, 'I have two living relatives in the world – my mother and father. Half my family was killed by the Nazis, and the other half by the Communists. Don't tell me how bloody marvellous communism is!' His story is by no means unique: Barbara's parents were amazed when they met again after the war, in England. Each was sure that the other was dead.

And this is only recent history. Such tales can be carried back into history for a thousand years. The net result is that Poland's history is long and fascinating, but mostly tragic, and the tremendously varied Polish landscape is covered with reminders of the past – mediaeval churches, Renaissance piazzas, concentration camps. . . .

The welcome you receive will be mixed. Poles are friendly, and the young in particular are great admirers of the West; but they are tired, tired of oppression and the secret police and the endless shortages and queues. The face that you see will depend on luck, and on how well you get to know people.

Climate Go in spring or autumn, unless you like really warm weather, or snow; winter really is pretty disastrous.

Papers To get in, you will need either an entry visa or a transit visa; for transit visas, entry visas to the destination country must be shown. Visas *must* be bought in advance from a Polish consular office, and you must also show exchange vouchers for the minimum exchange per day *when you buy the visa*. These vouchers are bought at any Polish tourist office, and are exchangeable for *złoty* at the Polish border or any bank in Poland. You are exempt from the minimum exchange requirement if you have pre-paid your accommodation; if you have only a transit visa; or if you hold a Polish passport or are travelling with a Polish passport-holding wife, husband, father, or mother.

Your own driving licence will do for up to one month (after which you need an IDP), and you will need either a Green Card or insurance bought at the border. The minimum insurance requirement under Polish law is unlimited liability for personal injury and property damage, so you need not worry about the cover which border insurance gives. The log book or registration document is, of course, required, and so is a **helmet**; otherwise, there are no particular requirements.

Customs allowance on entry is 1 litre of wine and 1 litre of spirits; 250 cigarettes or 50 cigars or 250 gm tobacco; other goods to a value of 6000 zl. Customs allowance on exit is the same for tobacco, plus 2 litres of wine and 2 litres of spirits, plus other goods to a value of 5000 zl, except for items bought in special hard-currency shops or items purchased with złotys obtained by exchanging hard currency (so keep all receipts!). The export of some very odd items is restricted or prohibited: crystal glass, cotton products and children's clothes, books published before 1945 (!), works of art, and philatelic stamps. You are also forbidden to carry any more food than you might reasonably require on the journey.

Minimum exchange requirements have already been mentioned, and they go up fast. When I started the book, it was US $10 per day, and as I wrote this it was US $15. It is well worth buying your petrol coupons before you go, too: with Orbis (Polish Tourist Office) coupons, you get half-price petrol, whereas if you wait until you get to Poland, you still have to buy coupons, but they cost you twice as much. Be sure that you do not get more than you need, however: the exceptionally dull and uninformative Orbis office in London did not appear to be sure, but thought that they were not refundable. At least, that is what I thought they said, but they were so vague it was hard to be sure.

Currency The Polish złoty (the line through the 'l'
makes is into a 'w' sound, so it's 'zwoty') is a soft, not to say
soggy, currency; for a rough conversion, allow 70/£, 50/$
US, but remember that there is one rate for trading, one for
resident foreigners, and a third for tourists – which is, of
course, the best apart from the black market rate. **Plastic
money** is accepted in most hard currency shops and in
expensive hotels, but is useless elsewhere. Bank hours are 9
am to 1 pm, Monday to Saturday, and shopping hours are
mostly a sensible 11 am to 7 pm, except for food shops,
which open at 8 am.

Driving standards are the same as in most Iron
Curtain countries, except for an unusually high number of
Russian military vehicles, but here comes one of the big
drawbacks to visiting Poland: the **speed limit** for motorcycles
is 70 kph on the open road, a mere 43 mph, whereas for
cars it is 100 kph (62 mph). In town, everyone is limited to
50 kph. **Priority** is to the right, except on roundabouts,
where vehicles already on the roundabout take precedence
over those entering. With that speed limit, **overtaking** is
rarely possible, let alone a problem! The only **parking**
restrictions I could find, apart from commonsense ones
about obstruction and visibility, were within 100 metres (110
yards) of railway crossings and where prohibited by sign.

Polish **police** are not too bad at all; all accidents must
be reported to them and to the nearest Polish Insurance
Division. Dial 997 for cops, 999 for ambulance. In case of
breakdown, members of foreign touring clubs (AA, AAA,
RAC, etc) receive up to an hour's free attention from the
PZM breakdwn service – *Polski Zwiazek Motorowy*, Al.
Jerozolimskie 63, Warsaw – after which they have to pay;
non-members have to pay anyway, but can still use the
service. The PZM shop in Warsaw sells some foreign parts,
and will order others, provided you pay in hard currency.
Labour is cheap and mostly good (try to get a
recommendation if you can), but parts will be expensive.

The ten-word vocabulary is:

please	*prosze* (pro-she)
thank you	*dziekuje* (dgen-koo-je)
yes	*tak*
no	*nie* (nye)
where is?	*gdzie jest?* (gdge yest?)

room	*pokoj* (po-koo-y)
toilet	*toaleta* (to-a-le-ta)
more	*jeszcze* (yesh-che)
how much?	*ile to kosztuje?* (ee-le to kosh-too-ye?)
food	*zywnosc* (zeev-nosh)

Polish **food** is often heavy and filling, but is also very subtle and delicious; at least, this is true for tourists, though endless shortages bedevil ordinary people, and even ordinary restaurants, where you are more likely to find the hearty Polish soups than the game for which the country is well known. There are some very unusual dishes, such as cold summer soups made of *puréed* fruit thickened with sour cream; the only thing you can do is experiment. The national **liquor** is, of course, vodka, which comes in several varieties (plain; with 'buffalo grass'; sloe-flavoured; even with ground white pepper), and Poles drink vodka with meals, though you may prefer the excellent beer.

Accommodation follows the usual rules: the Orbis hotels for Western tourists (and visiting Soviet dignitaries) are surprisingly expensive, the rest are surprisingly cheap. In most towns there are 'reception centres', who will book you a room in the price range you want. If you are camping, you must have pre-paid camping vouchers; 'wild' camping is predictably illegal.

Romania

If you don't mind travelling very, very slowly, Romania is an interesting country. Despite its long Soviet border, it is one of the most independently-minded states in the Communist bloc, and (as the name implies) it is not a Slavic but a Latin nation. Unlike many other Central and Eastern European countries, which are made up of several countries which had spent centuries fighting with one another before being 'unified', Romania is made up mostly of Romanians – not half a dozen different groups, all going under different names.

It was originally a Greek province, in classical times, but then the Romans conquered it, and it was one of the most Roman of all their territories. The last major occupying empire, before the Russians, was the Ottoman Empire, of which it was just another backwater. Progress has never been rapid in Romania. Now, it is famous for its old buildings and castles (including Dracula's castle, in Transylvania – which was historically often a part of Hungary, so that there is an 8% minority population of Hungarians in Romania), for the health spas and 'alternative medicine' establishments which draw surprising numbers of tourists, and for the Black Sea holiday resorts.

Now for the drawbacks. To my mind, the largest single objection is the extraordinary system of speed limits, which depends on type of vehicle, cylinder capacity, and even the make of the vehicle! To show its complexity, it is reproduced in full on the following page.

Why on earth they should classify motorcycles with buses and minibuses, I am not sure; but the only reasoning I can imagine is that by imposing a 31 mph speed limit in the open country, they will utterly discourage motorcyclists. Another reason could be that Romanian roads are said to be the worst in the Communist bloc (and that is saying something).

Another drawback is the price of petrol, which is very high indeed (about twice as much as the European average for the natives, though only 30–40% more expensive for

Type of Vehicle	In built-up areas (kph/mph)	Outside built-up areas (kph/mph)
Over 1800cc (except Volga, Pobeda, Warsawa)	60/37	90/56
Between 1100cc and 1800cc	60/37	80/50
Under 1100cc, but including Volga, Pobeda, Warsawa	60/37	70/43
Cross-country car (Gasoline)	60/37	70/43
Cross-country car (Diesel)	60/37	60/37
Buses, minibuses, and motorcycles	40/25	50/31

tourists, with the compulsory petrol vouchers sold by the Romanian Automobile Club), and it is actually illegal to stay in private homes because there are too many hotel rooms, which the government is trying to fill. Delays due to Soviet-style bureaucracy are made worse by a southern European *mañana* attitude to speed and efficiency. Prices are not particularly low, because they are trying to soak you for every cent of hard currency they can get: single rooms start at about $16.50 (US – the currency they quote prices in), or about £12 including breakfast, and even a room in students' hostels is $5.57 (£4) sharing, $9.25 single. If you still want to go, here are the details:

Papers Visas are available at the border, or at consular offices abroad, 'against a tax in dollars or in any other freely convertible currency'. National licence OK for most Europeans; others may require IDP. Green Card. **Helmets** (I think) compulsory; no other special requirements. **Customs** on entry: 2 litres of hard liquor, 4 litres of wine, 200 cigarettes or 250 gm of tobacco, two cameras and '24 cassettes or 10 roll films', one 'small-format filming camera and 10 filming reels', and all the usual odd things like one typewriter, pair of binoculars, tape recorder, etc., which you are unlikely to carry on a motorcycle. You also need to declare any precious metals or stones, except (and I quote):
'– for men: one wedding-ring, two rings, a bracellet wrist watch or without bracellet, a chained medallion, one tie pin, a pair of cuff links, a fountain-pen-pencil kit, two pairs of glasses;
– for women: one wedding ring, two rings, a bracellet wrist watch or without bracellet, two chained medallions, two pairs

of ear-rings, two bracellets, a brooch, a necklace, two pairs of glasses;
– for children (under the age of 16): one ring, one bracellet wrist watch or without bracellet, one bracellet, one chained medallion, two pairs of glasses, one pair of ear-rings (for girls).'

And they'll charge you a deposit if they think you are carrying too much jewellery!

You can also carry goods to the value of 2000 lei as presents; there are about 10 lei to the £, 7 to the dollar. The **currency** is lei and each leu (singular of lei) is divided into 100 bani. On the way out, you will be charged tax on anything worth over 1000 lei in total, unless it was bought in a hard-currency shop. With few exceptions (the most important being people who have pre-paid their accommodation), everyone is required to change a minimum of $10 (US) per day.

Bank hours are variable, but 9 am to noon, and 1 to 3 pm are usual Monday to Friday, plus (in many places) 8 am to noon on Saturday. Shop hours are long, six or even six and a half days a week (early closing Sunday). **Plastic money** is avidly accepted by most hard-currency shops and similar organizations, and as the opportunities for spending money elsewhere are limited, this makes credit cards quite useful! Tipping is not usual.

It is not really worth saying much about riding conditions, because a 31 mph overall limit allows plenty of time to react to anything – and you aren't going to be doing much overtaking. Main roads are fair; back roads are awful. Road signs are apparently fully international, and parking is never a problem – just think in terms of avoiding obstruction, and you will be all right. Quite honestly, I find it hard to believe that anyone is going to bother to take a bike into Romania – I certainly have better places to go.

The vocabulary is:

please	*vă rog*
thank you	*mulţumesc* (multsumesk)
yes	*da*
no	*nu*
where is?	*unde est?* (un-day est)
room	*cameră*
toilet	*toaletă*

more	*mai mult*
how much?	*cît costă?* (chit kosta)
food	*alimente* (ali mentay)

The **food** is closely related to Greek or Yugoslavian, and is usually of very good quality – though service can be slow, and the food cold by the time you get it. Romanian **wines** are not great, but drinkable, and the local firewater is (as usual) a variety of plum brandy, *tuica* (tsweeka). Although it is an offence to drive with any alcohol in the blood stream, under 100 mg/100 ml is a much less serious offence than over 100 mg/100 ml! The water is said to be safe everywhere.

Accommodation, as already mentioned, is expensive by the standards of the area, but there are various kinds of camp site which reduce this considerably. A first-class camp site costs 55c per square metre per day (logical, but weird!); a tent with two beds costs $4 per night; a place in a 'bungalow' is $6.75; and car parking (they were not sure about bikes) is $1.20 a night. The possibility of getting accommodation in students' halls of residence have already been mentioned, and there are other kinds of rather basic youth accommodation at unjustifiably high prices, such as 'one bed in double room without bath or shower in second-class hotels, villas, and tourist inns ... $9'. Or, of course, you can always stay at one of those health spas. ...

Russia

Have you ever wanted to visit the second most powerful country in the world, a nation which spans almost two continents? Have you ever wanted to see for yourself whether Russia is as bad as it is painted? So have I – but if you want to go to Russia, you will have to leave your motorcycle behind. The same goes for the Russian-occupied countries of Latvia, Lithuania, Estonia, and Mongolia. After all, there are only 270,000,000 Russians, spread across 8,707,382 square miles (Russian figures!); think of the havoc a few motorcyclists could wreak. ...

Russia admits motor cars only grudgingly, because their disgracefully inefficient economy needs the hard currency in order to buy food from the United States. Motorcyclists, a hard-to-control minority group, are simply not admitted.

If they ever change their minds, and you want to go to a country which occupies half of Europe against the wishes of the whole of Europe, here is a capsule guide.

Papers Visas take at least ten days, and are expensive. Motorists are only allowed to use one of 8 border crossings (2 from Finland, 2 from Poland, 2 from Romania, and one each from Czechoslovakia and Hungary), which close from 8 pm to 8 am. Roads are appalling, petrol is hard to come by, and everything that is not illegal is compulsory; it is only the commonsense of the average Russian (which is not great) that enables the system to work at all.

Customs will itemize currency, valuables, and publications (including books, magazines, manuscripts, records, and tapes) as you enter; typewriters must be registered as dangerous weapons. **Currency** There are 100 kopecs to the rouble, which is arbitrarily maintained at a value slightly higher than that of the dollar, in a childish attempt at prestige. Once you are inside, you must stick to a pre-arranged route, and stay in pre-arranged accommodation. Often, there is a *compulsory* guided tour of the local attractions in the place where you are staying.

The whole place would be a joke if it were not a tragedy; so perhaps the best way to end is with a joke, from Russia itself:

A priest is sitting reading *Teach Yourself Hebrew*. Several people stop and stare; a state trooper comes by to break up the meeting, in case it is political. 'And what are you doing, old fool?' he says.

'I am an old man, and I shall not live long. When I die, I want to be able to speak to the Lord in his own language.'

The militiaman laughs. 'And what if you go to the other place?'

'Oh, I'm ready for that too. I already speak Russian.'

Appendix 1

NATIONAL ROAD SIGNS

France

Haute tension	Electrified line
Route barrée	Road closed
Attention travaux	Road works
Gravillons	Loose chippings
Allumez vos lanternes	Turn on your lights
Interdit aux pietons	Forbidden to pedestrians
Fin d'interdiction	
de stationner	End of prohibited parking
Chaussée deformé	Broken road surface
Nids des poules	Pot holes

A sign like castle battlements means you may park in laybys

Austria

Ausweiche	Detour
Fahrbahnschäden or	Damaged road
Frostschaden or	surface
Schadhafte	
Fahrbahndecke	
Lawinen Gefahr	Danger of avalanches
Strasse Gesperrt	Road closed
Steinschlag	Falling rocks
Beschränkung für Halten	(literally) Restricted
oder Parken	for Waiting or Parking
Halten Verboten	Waiting forbidden
Hupverbot	(literally) Horn-forbidden
Querstrasse	Crossroads
Schneeketten	Snow chains
Vorgeschrieben	compulsory

West Germany

Rollsplit	Loose grit
Frostschäden	Frost damage
Glatteisgefahr	Icy road
Radweg Kreutzt	Cycle track crossing
Strassenschäden	Road damage
Fahrbahnwechsel	change traffic lane (literally) drive-way-change
Baustofflagerung	Road works material store
Seitenstreifen	Use of road verge
nicht befahrbar	not advised

A picture of an eagle inside a green triangle means that you are inside a wildlife reserve, and may only park in marked bays.

Holland

Tegenliggers	Oncoming traffic
Pas Op: filevorming	Attention: lane control ahead
Langzaam rijden	Slow down
Werk in Uitvoering	Road Works in Progress
Wegomlegging	Detour
Doorgaand verkeer gestremd	No thoroughfare
Opspattend Grind	Loose gravel (upspitting grit?)
Rechtsaf toegeslaan	Right Turn Permitted.

Watch out especially for WOONERVEN, sleeping policemen, aka motorcyclist-killers.

Switzerland

See the tyre with snow chains (inside front cover) and the post horn (inside back cover).

Italy

Senso Vietato	No Entry
Vietato Ingresso Veicoli	No Entry for Vehicles
Sosta Autorizzata	Parking Permitted
Vietato Transito Autocarri	Closed to Heavy Vehicles
Sosta Vietata	No Parking
Pasaggio a Livello	Level Crossing
Rallentare	Slow Down
Entrata	Entrance
Uscita	Exit, Turn-Off
Svolta	Bend
Incrocio	Crossroads
Lavori in Corso	Road Works Ahead

Portugal

Pavimento Ondulato	Bumpy Road

Spain

Aduana	Customs
Cèda el Paso	Give Way
Cuidado or *Precaucion*	Caution
Despacio	Slow
Desvio	Diversion
Estacionamento de Automóviles	Car Park
Paso Prohibido	No Through Road
Curva Peligrosa	Dangerous Bend

Dirección Única	One-Way Street
Estacionamente Prohibido	No Parking
Obras	Road Works
Peligro	Danger
Llevar la Derecha	Keep Right
Llevar la Izquierda	Keep Left

Greece

ΠΡΟΣΟΧΙ	
προσοχι Caution	
PROSODI	

Denmark

Ensrettet kørsel	One way street
Fare	Danger
Farligt sving	Dangerous bend
Gennemkørsel forbudt	No through road
Holdt	Halt
Hold til højre	Keep right
Hold til venstre	Keep left
Indkørsel forbudt	No entry
Korsvej	Crossroads
Omkørsel	Diversion
Parkering forbudt	Parking forbidden
Vejarbejde	Road works
Vejen er spaerret	Road closed

Norway

Arbeide pa Vegen	Road works
Bakketop	Hill top
Envegskjøring	One-way traffic
Ferist	Cattle grid
Gammel Veg	Old road
Grøfterens	Ditch-clearing
Ikke Møte	No overtaking, single file

Kjør Sakte	Drive slowly
Løs Grus	Loose gravel
Møteplass	Passing place
Omkjøring	Diversion
Rasteplass	Rest-place (lay-by)
Svake Kanter	Soft verges
Veg under Anlegg	Road under construction

The sign ALL STANS FORBUDT means no stopping, for any reason whatsoever, even map reading.

Finland

Tietyö	Road works
Aja Hitaasti	Drive slowly
Kelirikko	Frost Damage
Paane	Slippery surface
Irtokiviä	Loose gravel
Lossi	Ferry
Räjäytystyö, sulje radiolähetin	Danger: Explosives. Switch off radio.

Hungary

Kiveve Celforgalom	All Vehicles Prohibited

Appendix II

VOCABULARY LISTS

France

please	*s'il vous plait* (seel voo play)
thank you	*merci* (mare see)
yes	*oui* (we –or 'ouais', way, for 'yeah')
no	*non* (surely you can remember this one: naw)
where is	*ou est?* (ooh eh?)
room	*chambre* (shombre)
toilet	WC (vay say)
more of	*plus de* (ploo duh)
how much?	*combien* (kom byen)
eat	*manger* (mon-jay)

Monaco

Use the French vocabulary above.

Austria

Use the German vocabulary below.

Belgium

In the south use French (above), in the north Dutch (p.312).

West Germany

please	*bitte* (bitt-uh)
thank you	*danke* (dan-kuh)

yes	*ja* (ya)
no	*nein* (nine)
where?	*wo?* (voe)
room	*zimmer*
toilet	*klosset* or *abort*
more	*mehr* (mayr)
how much?	*was kostiert?* (vass koss-tea-urt)
eat	*essen*

Luxembourg

Use the German vocabulary on p.311.

Holland

please	*alstublieft*
thank you	*dank je* (dank ee)
yes	*ja* (yah)
no	*nee*
where is?	*waar is?*
room	*kamer* (kammer)
toilet	*WC* (vay-say)
more	*meer*
how much?	*hoeveel?* (hoy feel?)
eat	*eten* (ay-teh)

Switzerland

Use French (p.311), or German (p.311) or Italian (below).

Liechtenstein

Use the German vocabulary (p.311).

Andorra

Use French (p.311) or Spanish (p.313).

Italy

please	*per favore* (pair fah-vaw-ray)
thank you	*grazie* (grat-zee)
yes	*si*
no	*no*
where is?	*dov'e* (doh-vay)
room	*stanza*
toilet	*gabinetto*
more	*piu* (pee-oo)
how much?	*quanto?*
eat	*mangiare* (manjee-ah-ray)

San Marino
Use the Italian vocabulary (p.312)

Malta
Use English.

Portugal

please	*por favor*
thank you	*obrigado* (for a man speaking)
	obrigada (for a woman speaking)
yes	*sim* (si)
no	*não* (nang; the 'ng' sound, which is represented in Portuguese by ão at the end of a word, is barely audible and not voiced)
where is	*onde?* (on-day)
room	*quarto*
toilet	*toilette*
more	*mais* (maysh)
how much?	*quanto?*
food	*alimento*

The 's' sound is 'sh', sho all Portugueshe shound ash if they're permanently shloshed (and shome of them are!).

Spain

please	*por favor* (por fah-bor)
thank you	*gracias* (grathy -ass)
yes	*si*
no	*no*
where is?	*donde esta?* (don-day esstah)
room	*habitación* (habby-tathyon)
toilet	*retrete* (ray-tray-tay)
more	*mas*
how much?	*cuando?* (kwandoh?)
food	*alimentación* (alley-men-tathion)

The *th* is always soft, like a lithp, not like *this* or *that*.

Cyprus

Use the Greek vocabulary below.

Greece

please	*parakolo*
thank you	*efharisto* (eff-harry-stow)
yes	*ne* (the *e* is short, as in *yes*)
no	*ochi* (ockey)
where is?	*pou ine* (poo ee-neh)
room	*thomatio*
toilet	*toualeta* (too-a-leh-ta)
more	*perisotero*
how much?	*posso kaní?*
food	*faghito* (fa-hhee-tow)

The Greeks shake their heads for 'yes' and nod their heads for 'no'.

Turkey

please	*lutfen*
thank you	*tesekkur*

yes	*evet*
no	*hayir*
where?	*nerede?*
room	*oda*
toilet	*tuvalet*
more	*daha*
how much?	*ne kadar?*
food	*yiyecek*

Yugoslavia

Use either English (preferably) or German (p.311).

Denmark

please	*vaer sa venlig* (vayr saw venlee)
thank you	*tak*
yes	*ja* (yah)
no	*nej* (nay)
where is?	*hvor er der?* (vohr ayr der)
room	*vaerelse* (vay-rul-suh)
toilet	*toilettet (almost as good as parkering)*
more	*mere* (me-rah)
how much?	*hvor meget?* (vohr mayud)
food	*mald* (mahld)

Greenland

Use Danish.

Sweden

please	*var sa god*
thank you	*takk*
yes	*ja* (ya)
no	*nej* (nay)
where?	*var?*
room	*rum*

toilet	*toalett*
more	*mer*
how much?	*vad kostar?*
food	*matsäck* (mat seck)

Norway

please	*vaersågod*
thank you	*takk*
yes	*ja* (yah)
no	*nei* (nay)
where is?	*hvor er?* (vohr er)
room	*rom*
toilet	*toilett*
more	*mer*
how much?	*hvor coster?*
food	*niste*

Finland

please	*olkaa hivä* (ollka heevay)
thank you	*kiitos* (keeto)
yes	*kyllä* (kulla – almost kurlla)
no	*ei* (ey)
where is?	*missä on?*
room	*hurne* (hoornah)
toilet	*WC* (vay-say)
more	*lisää*
how much?	*kuinka paljon* (koo-inka pally-on)
food	*ruoka* (rooaka)

Swedish is the official second language and English is also widely spoken.

Iceland

Icelandic is the official language but English is widely spoken.

Albania

Motorcyclists not encouraged.

Bulgaria

please	*molya*
thank you	*blagodarya*
yes	*da*
no	*ne*
where is?	*kuhde e?*
room	*staya*
toilet	*klozet*
more	*oshte*
how much?	*kolko struva?*
food	*hrana*

Czechoslovakia

please	*prosím* (proseem)
thank you	*děkuji* (dyekuyi)
yes	*ano*
no	*ne*
where is?	*kde je?* (ke ye?)
room	*pokoj* (pokoy)
toilet	*toaleta*
more	*víc* (veets)
how much?	*kolik to stojí?* (kolik to stoyee?)
food	*potraviny*

East Germany

Use the German Vocabulary on p.311.

Hungary

please	*kerem* (keh-rem)
thank you	*köszönöm* (ku-sur-nurm)
yes	*igen*

no	*nem*
where is?	*hol van?* (hohl von?)
room	*szoba* (soh-bah)
toilet	*WC* (veh-tseh)
more	*jidlo* (yeed-lo)
how much?	*mennyibe kerül?* (menyibe ker-ewl)
food	*etel* (eat-el)

Poland

please	*prosze* (pro-she)
thank you	*dziekuje* (dgen-koo-je)
yes	*tak*
no	*nie* (nye)
where is?	*gdzie jest?* (gdge yest?)
room	*pokoj* (po-koo-y)
toilet	*toaleta* (to-a-le-ta)
more	*jeszcze* (yesh-che)
how much?	*ile to kosztuje?* (ee-le to kosh-too-ye?)
food	*zywnosc* (zeev-nosh)

Romania

please	*vă rog*
thank you	*mulţumesc* (multsumesk)
yes	*da*
no	*nu*
where is?	*unde eşf?* (un-day est)
room	*camerǎ*
toilet	*toaletǎ*
more	*mai mult*
how much?	*cît costǎ?* (chit kosta)
food	*alimente* (ali mentay)

Russia

Motorcyclists not encouraged.